JANE AUSTEN

A STUDENTS' GUIDE
TO THE LATER MANUSCRIPT WORKS

JANE AUSTEN

A STUDENTS' GUIDE
TO THE LATER MANUSCRIPT WORKS

BRIAN SOUTHAM

CONCORD BOOKS
LONDON

First published in 2007
By Concord Books
3 West Heath Drive
London NW11 7QG, UK

Hardbound ISBN   978-0-86137-004-7
Paperback ISBN   978-0-86137-020-7

British Library Cataloguing in Publication Data
Data available from The British Library

Typeset and printed
by
Sarsen Press, Winchester

Contents

Preface

The use of the word 'Later' in the title of this book indicates that it does not include Jane Austen's *Juvenilia*, the collective term for her earliest childhood writing dating from about 1787 to 1793, when she was aged between eleven and seventeen or eighteen. This material has been expertly annotated by Peter Sabor in the *Juvenilia* volume in the current Cambridge edition. Instead, the focus of this *Guide* is on the writing of Jane Austen's later years. Much of this material has suffered from neglect or inattention, and I hope that the in-depth notes provided here will help readers to bridge the gulf that separates us from England in the early years of the nineteenth-century, the period of Georgian and Regency social culture in which Jane Austen was writing; and for much of this time Britain was at war, or emerging from it. This is the background – extending from about 1793 to 1817 – to *Lady Susan*, *The Watsons* and *Sanditon* as well as to Jane Austen's Prayers and her Poetry. In this present age of textual alertness and close reading, we are quite unable to share the sentiment of the great Austen editor, R.W.Chapman, when he declared in 1954 that 'These immature or fragmentary fictions call for hardly any comment'.[1] In truth, they call for a great deal.

I have included the full text of the three *Prayers* since all the versions presently in print are based upon the faulty Colt Press edition (1940) and this is the first text to follow the manuscript faithfully.

I should put on record that the Introduction and notes that follow were prepared for my *Later Manuscripts* volume in the Cambridge University Press edition of Jane Austen. However, in July 2006, the Press terminated my agreement.

1 *Minor Works*, [p.v.].

B.C.S.
October 2006

Acknowledgements

Thanks are due to the Morgan Library for permission to reproduce the pages from the manuscripts of *The Watsons* and *Plan of a Novel*; the pages from the manuscript of *Sanditon* are reproduced by kind permission of the Provost and Scholars of King's College, Cambridge; and thanks are due to Mills College, Oakland, California for permission to print the text of Jane Austen's three *Prayers* from the family manuscript in their Library. Despite my best endeavours, I have been unable to trace the copyright holders, the owners of The Colt Press, which first published a text of the *Prayers* in 1940.

I would like to thank all those who helped me in the preparation of this work and offer my sincere apologies to anyone I have inadvertently failed to mention. Mavis Batey; Professor Barbara Benedict, Trinity College, Hartford; Antje Blank, Janet Todd, Cambridge Edition of Jane Austen; Rachel Boak, Bath Museum; Dr Sally Brown and Michael Boggan of the British Library; Tom Carpenter, Jane Austen Memorial Trust; Professor Raymond Chapman; Professor Edward Copeland; Tony Corley; Geoffrey Day, Vicky Rutherford, James Sabben-Clare, Winchester College; David Crook, Richard Aldrich, University of London Institute of Education; Elizabeth Finn, Centre for Kentish Studies, Maidstone; Clare Fox, The Prayer Book Society; Professor Timothy Fulford; John Greenacombe, Survey of London; John Hardacre, Winchester Cathedral Library; Dr Isaac Gewirtz, Curator, The Berg Collection, New Yok Public Library; Olwan Hufton, Merton College, Oxford; Professor Kevin Hutchings, University of Northern British Columbia; A. Jackson, Masters of Foxhounds Association; Peter Jones, King's College, Cambridge; Deirdre Le Faye; Helen Lefroy; Brian Murphy, Anselm Nye, Queen Mary, University of London; John Naylor; Susan North, Victoria and Albert Museum; The Morgan Library: Robert Parks, Director of Library and

Museum Services; Christine Nelson, Curator of Literary & Historical manuscripts, Leslie Fields, formerly Associate Curator; Professor Claud Rawson, Yale University; Valerie Reilly, Paisley Museum; Professor Pat Rogers, University of South Florida; Penelope Ruddock; Professor Peter Sabor, McGill University; Helen Scott, Chawton House Library; David Selwyn; Eunice and Ron Shanahan; Patrick Stokes, Chairman, The Jane Austen Society; June Swann; Allison Thompson; Alan Thwaite; Gavin Turner; Robin Vick; Professor John Walton, University of Lancaster; Freydis Welland; Rev George Westhaver, Lincoln College, Oxford.

My deepest thanks go to Doris for suggesting how my own researches, and the generous and valuable contributions of so many scholars, might at least see the light of day in a usable form, for resuscitating Concord Books, and for seeing this book through from beginning to end.

How to use the *Guide*

The notes can be used alongside any edition or reading text of the manuscript works. The forthcoming Cambridge edition of the *Later Manuscripts* will include all the texts. However, it will be published initially in an expensive hardbound edition. The *Minor Works*, volume six in the Oxford edition of Jane Austen (rev edn 1969), now out-of-print, also contains the later manuscript texts.

The available paperback editions include

Lady Susan, The Watsons, Sanditon, ed Margaret Drabble (Penguin Books, 1974 etc).

Catharine and Other Writings, edd Margaret Anne Doody & Douglas Murray (Oxford UP, 1993): in addition to the Juvenilia, this volume contains the *Plan of a Novel,* Verses, Prayers.

Northanger Abbey, Lady Susan, The Watsons, Sanditon, edd James Kinsley & John Davie, Introduction & Notes by Claudia L. Johnson (Oxford World's Classics, 2003).

Jane Austen: Collected Poems and Verse of the Austen Family, ed David Selwyn (Carcanet, 1996).

The Index is to the words and phrases annotated in the manuscript works. It does not cover the main Introduction or the introductory sections to each work.

Abbreviations

JA   Jane Austen
JEAL   James Edward Austen-Leigh, son of her brother James

Manuscripts
In the description of manuscripts, ms *singular,* mss *plural,*
f is used for a folio, a single sheet of paper, ff *plural.*
f^r is folio recto, the top or first side of the sheet.
f^v is folio verso, the reverse or second side.

The works of Jane Austen
E   *Emma*
LS   *Lady Susan*
MP   *Mansfield Park*
MW   *Minor Works*
NA   *Northanger Abbey*
P   *Persuasion*
P&P   *Pride and Prejudice*
S   *Sanditon*
W   *The Watsons*

Other works

Brabourne	ed Edward, Lord Brabourne, *Letters of Jane Austen* (London: Bentley, 1884).
DNB	*Dictionary of National Biography* (Oxford: Oxford University Press, sec edn 2004).
Facts and Problems	*Jane Austen: Facts and Problems,* R.W.Chapman (Oxford: Clarendon Press, 1948).
FR	*Jane Austen: A Family Record,* Deirdre Le Faye (Cambridge: Cambridge University Press, 1989, sec edn 2004).

Gilson	*A Bibliography of Jane Austen*, David Gilson (Oxford: Clarendon Press, 1982, rev edn 1997).
James Austen	*The Complete Poems of James Austen*, ed David Selwyn (Chawton: Jane Austen Society, 2003).
Johnson	*Johnson's Dictionary of the English Language*, Samuel Johnson (London: J.Johnson, 1755, 8th edn, corrected and rev, 1799).
Lascelles	Mary Lascelles, *Jane Austen and Her Art* (Oxford: Clarendon Press, 1939).
L	*Jane Austen's Letters*, ed Deirdre Le Faye (Oxford: Oxford University Press, 1995, 1997).
Life and Letters	*Jane Austen, Her Life and Letters, A Family Record*, W. and R.A. Austen-Leigh, (London: Smith, 1913).
LM	*Jane Austen's Literary Manuscripts*, Brian Southam (Oxford: Clarendon Press, 1964, rev edn 2000).
M	*A Memoir of Jane Austen and Other Family Recollections*, ed Kathryn Sutherland (Oxford: Oxford University Press, 2002).
1870 M	*A Memoir of Jane Austen*, J.E. Austen-Leigh (London: Bentley, 1870).
M/*Memoir* (1871)	*A Memoir of Jane Austen to which is added Lady Susan and Fragments of Two Other Unfinished Tales by Miss Austen*, J.E. Austen-Leigh (London: Bentley, sec edn 1871).
Memoir (1926)	*Memoir of Jane Austen*, ed R.W.Chapman (Oxford: Clarendon, 1926, 1951).
Modert	Jo Modert, *Jane Austen's Letters in Facsimile* (Carbondale: Southern Illinois University Press, 1990).
OED	*Oxford English Dictionary* (Oxford: Oxford Uiversity Press, sec edn 1989, online 2004).
Sutherland	Kathryn Sutherland, *Jane Austen's Textual Lives: from Aeschylus to Bollywood* (Oxford: Oxford University Press, 2005).

Manuscript pages

Taken together, the four manuscript pages reproduced here convey a very good sense of the manuscript material as a whole. They enable us to get at least a glimpse into the sequence of alteration, correction and revision that the material underwent, giving us a valuable, if limited, insight on Jane Austen's writing procedures and processes of creation.

As the Juvenilia only come down to us as fair copies entered years later into the three manuscript notebooks, and the manuscript of *Lady Susan* is a fair copy made not earlier than 1805, the manuscript of *The Watsons* is earliest surviving of Jane Austen's working manuscripts. The first page given here, **(I)** reproduced just below full size (7½ x 4¾ in.), is page 11 in the manuscript (f.6ʳ). The relatively small page-size is engagingly explained in a family tradition, recounted in the *Memoir*: that as Jane Austen had 'no separate study to retire to', she had to use 'the general sitting-room'; and not wanting to be discovered 'by servants or visitors...She wrote upon small sheets of paper which could easily be put away, or covered with a piece of blotting paper.' These details were not in the original *Memoir* of 1870 and were added for the second edition, 1871, p. 96.

As to the variations in inking, the heavy crossings-out and the show-through from the verso of the sheet, metal nibs were not to arrive for another thirty years or so and it was quite difficult to manage the ink-flow of a quill pen. We can judge from the shaping of the letters and words in this and similar pages that Jane Austen was writing rapidly, with a clear picture in her mind of the characters, their dialogue and the lines of the story. Some changes, as we see in lines 11, 15-16, were alterations made at the very moment of writing, with the revised version coming immediately along the line. Other changes – corrections or revisions – were made later as insertions above the line, as in lines 3 and 4.

(II) is first page (f.1ʳ) of the *Plan of a Novel*, reduced from the original sheet size of 14¾ x 9⅛ in. The paper is watermarked 1813 and this fair copy, carrying a very few corrections and revisions, was probably made in the spring of 1816. The people named and numbered in the margin are linked to their suggestions in the text. Why Jane Austen replaced 'only child' with 'Daughter' is a matter for anyone's conjecture: could it be to tighten the sentence, giving it a slightly more emphatic ring? Similarly, a few lines later, why did she cancel 'doing infinite good in his Parish, a Blessing to every body connected with him, &': to avoid over-egging an already rich descriptive account of the father's perfections? On the other hand, Jane Austen's point in adding '& Harp' to the heroine's accomplishment in playing 'the Piano Forte' is clear: this is wholly in accordance with the fashion of the time, the harp carrying a high cultural cachet (see *Sanditon*, chapter 4, note 15).

From the manuscript of *Sanditon*, written between 27 January and 18 March 1817 come pages **(III)** and **(IV)**. These facsimiles are just below the ms size, which varies between 7½ x 4¾ in. and 6³/₈ x 4 in. **(III)** is the opening page (f.1ʳ), heavily corrected, as Jane Austen works to strengthen her account of the foundering of the coach and the injury suffered by Mr Parker. As I discuss later (see page 116), this burden of revision is not evidence of the writer's uncertainty but of her clarity of purpose as she re-works her material. This page also illustrates the difficulty that faces an editor in transcribing the cancellations, some of them near-obliterations.

(IV) is a few lines into Chapter 11, f.53ʳ ie page 105 in the 120 page manuscript. Although Jane Austen was only months away from death, and forced to abandon *Sanditon* out of bodily weakness, there is little here to betray this – unless we fasten on the looseness of the hand in the last three lines, with their hint of a sprawl; so great a contrast to the neat and compact hand that fills much of the page. There are few corrections and revisions: one, at least, a stroke of genius: at mid-page, 'to throw everything into confusion' becomes 'to make everything appear what it was not', a change which sustains the image of Sanditon's delusiveness, a speculative venture built, literally and metaphorically, on sand.

The manuscript changes to *Sanditon* can be followed clearly in the full transcription of the manuscript given in *Jane Austen Caught in the Act of Greatness* (1ˢᵗ Books Library, 2003) by Arthur M. Axelrad, with a valuable Introduction by David Gilson.

every little apology w.d be requisite to the
Edwardes, who must be more glad of your
company than of mine, & I shall more
readily return to my Father; & should not be
at all afraid to drive these quiet old creatures
home, your Cloathes I would undertake to find
means of sending to you—" "My dearest Emma
cried Eliz: warmly—do you think I would
do such a thing?—not for the Universe—
but I shall never forget your good nature
in proposing it. What a sweet temper indeed
you must have &—I never met with anything
like it!—And w.d you really give up the
Ball, that I might be able to go to it!—Believe me Emma, I shall never forget the
kindness of the proposal.—But I am not so
selfish as that comes to. No, tho' I am nine
years older than you are, I would not be
the means of keeping you from being
seen.—You are very pretty, & it would be
very hard that you should not have as fair
a chance as we have all had, to make
your fortune.—No Emma, whoever stays
at home this winter, it shan't be you.

I

The Watsons, page 11 of the manuscript (85% full-size).

II

Plan of a Novel, the first page of the manuscript (about half-size).

III
Sanditon, the first page of the manuscript (85% full-size).

Sanditon in those two Hack chaises.
The Mrs. G. who in her friend Mrs. Darling's
hands, had wavered as to coming & been
unequal to the Journey, was the very same
Mrs. G. whose plans were at the same
period (under another representation) perfectly
decided, & who was without fears or
difficulties. — All that had the appearance
of Inconsistency in the reports of the two,
might very fairly be placed to the account
of the Vanity, the Ignorance, or the blunders
of the many engaged in the cause
by the vigilance & caution of Miss Diana
P. — Her intimate friends must be officious
like herself, & the subject had supplied
letters & Extracts & Messages enough to
make everything appear what it was not.
Miss D. probably felt a little awkward
on being &c obliged to admit her mistake. A long Journey from Hampshire
taken for nothing — a Brother disappointed — an House on her hands for a
week, must have been some of her
immediate reflections — & much worse
than all the rest, must have been the
sort of sensation of being less clear-
sighted & infallible than she had
believed herself. — No part of it however
seemed to trouble her long. There
were so many to share in the shame

IV

Sanditon, page 105 of the manuscript (just below full-size).

Introduction

I

The history of the later manuscript works

In the early 1800's, Jane Austen collected her earliest writing – the pieces she composed between about 1787, when she was a girl of eleven or twelve, and 1793 – and transcribed them into three notebooks which she entitled *Volume the First, Volume the Second* and *Volume the Third.* Together, these constitute the *Juvenilia*, the collection of her childhood work which is not covered in this *Guide*. Beyond these three notebooks, a quantity of other literary manuscripts has survived and this material is introduced here. In effect, this is the residue of her writing career: the two unfinished novels, *The Watsons* (about 1804-05) and *Sanditon* (1817); *Lady Susan* (1793-94), a *novella* in letters, a form unpublishable for an unknown writer at this time; and the smaller pieces written for her family and friends, and largely depending for their effect upon a shared knowledge of people and books. Apart from the juvenilia, the only manuscript materials not included here are *Sir Charles Grandison*, which belongs to the same period as the juvenilia, and the original ending to *Persuasion*: chapter 10 of volume two, which Jane Austen cancelled and replaced with a chapter entirely new, together with chapter 11, which became, with some slight change, chapter 12 of the finished work. That manuscript is often included as an appendix in editions of *Persuasion*.

What gives the later manuscript material a particular importance is the fact that apart from the fragment of *Persuasion*, no manuscript of the six novels has survived. As for the fair copies that went to the publishers, we can suppose that they were regarded as waste paper once the printing of the books was completed. This was quite usual in the publishing-printing trade. And probably Jane Austen threw out her own working copies of the manuscripts in the same way, just as we can assume that she disposed of 'Elinor & Marianne' and 'First Impressions', once these early versions were rewritten as *Sense and Sensibility* and *Pride and Prejudice*;[1] and that Henry or Cassandra Austen similarly destroyed the working manuscripts of *Northanger Abbey* and *Persuasion*, when these two novels were published in December 1817, five months after their sister's death. So for an understanding of Jane Austen's methods of composition, correction and revision, we have to rely on the manuscripts of the unpublished material; and fortunately these were handled very differently. During her own lifetime Jane Austen kept them safely; and for their safety after her death, we have to thank Cassandra, who was both the executor and the chief beneficiary of her sister's will. Although in the 1840's Cassandra was prepared to censor or incinerate those of her sister's letters that she feared would be misunderstood or whose privacy she felt was too sacred to be intruded upon, she regarded her sister's literary remains differently: they were relics too precious to be tampered with. As relics of her sister, they were memorabilia to be treasured and she made certain that after her own death they were earmarked for those of the family 'to whom I think they will be mostly valuable'.[2] At Cassandra's death in March 1845, the responsibility for their distribution fell upon her brother Charles (1779-1852), named as her residuary legatee and executor. This duty he passed to his eldest child, Cassandra Esten Austen (1808-97), Cassandra's goddaughter, who acted as unofficial executrix. Cassy Esten cleared her aunt's possessions from Chawton Cottage, including the manuscript works, and arranged for their distribution within the family, retaining some items for herself, exactly as her aunt had intended. In this way, the manuscripts were handled with great care. Even the merest scraps of verse survive, and pages heavily corrected or cancelled, material that would seem to weigh as nothing when set against the published novels, and which could so easily have been disposed of as old rubbish; or, as in the case of *Sir Charles Grandison* and items in the juvenilia, could have fallen to Cassandra's censorship. For what was counted amusing in the 1790's could overstep the proprieties of the 1840's, when Cassandra was getting her affairs in order and settling the family inheritance of the manuscript material and other memorabilia.[3] But, blessedly, she regarded the literary manuscripts as inviolable and they survived intact.

And because successive generations of Austens inherited the spirit of Cassandra's guardianship along with the manuscripts themselves, these pieces have come down to us, dispersed but intact, as a substantial body of work; and their publication, together with knowledge of them, was for many years controlled by the family. In his 'Biographical Notice of the Author' (1818), other than referring to Jane's final poem, Henry Austen made no mention of this material, nor in his 1833 expanded version of the 'Notice',[4] preferring to give the limited space to his sister's character and her published works. The first real biography, A Memoir of Jane Austen by her nephew James Edward Austen-Leigh (1798-1874), was tantalising rather than revelatory. It provided the merest of glimpses: five of the poems in full; a version of the 'Plan of a novel', partly re-written and somewhat truncated, described as being 'amongst her papers'; and referred to as 'existing in manuscript', the first of the two chapters of Persuasion.[5] The Memoir also mentioned as 'extant an old copy-book containing several tales, some of which seem to have been composed while she was quite a girl...stories of a slight and flimsy texture...nonsense' with 'much spirit to it'. (The reference to 'an old copy-book' seems disingenuous on Austen-Leigh's part, perhaps an attempt to dampen the curiosity of readers. As Peter Sabor points out, he 'knew of the existence of all three' of the juvenilia notebooks – two with cousins and Volume the Third in his own possession).[6] Then came an intervening stage in Jane Austen's 'progress', 'between these childish effusions and the composition of her living works', 'during which she produced several tales, not without merit, but which she considered unworthy of publication' (probably referring to some of the more substantial pieces in the juvenilia and Lady Susan). The absence of this material from the Memoir Austen-Leigh explained as a family decision, one that he agreed with: 'The family have, rightly, I think, declined to let these early works be published', with the comment that 'it would be as unfair to expose this preliminary process to the world, as it would be to display all that goes on behind the curtain of the theatre before it is drawn up'.[7] By 'The family' Austen-Leigh meant himself and his two sisters, Anna (1793-1872) and Caroline (1805-1880), both of whom assisted their brother with the preparation of the Memoir, helping him to track down material and offering advice about what manuscript pieces might be included. For what she called the 'stuffing' of the book, Caroline envisaged possibly some of their Aunt's 'light nonsensical verses...& perhaps some few rimes or charades' and 'Evelyn' from

Volume the Third, a piece of 'clever nonsense'. Her objection was to making public 'the "betweenities" when the nonsense was passing away, and before her wonderful talent had found it's (*sic*) proper channel' and among the 'betweenities' she included 'a whole short story' (*Lady Susan*) that Jane Austen's niece, Fanny Knight (now Lady Knatchbull), and her family 'were wishing years ago to make public'. Caroline also judged it 'a difficult task to dig up the *materials*, so carefully have they been buried out of our sight by the past generat[ion]…'.[8]

So while the Knights – the children of Edward, George Austen's third son – were in favour of releasing *Lady Susan* to the world, Austen-Leigh and his sisters were not; and as the children of James, the first son, and thus the family's senior line, it was their views that prevailed. Their policy of caution and concealment arose out of a sense that they were protecting their Aunt's reputation, a position which found support, *The Times* judging that the family declined 'very properly' to publish Jane Austen's early papers and the *Quarterly Review* opining that such revelations were an 'indecorous practice' and that these writings 'ought to be sacred from being pored over and printed by posthumous busybodies'.[9] Nonetheless, however well-intentioned, it was a policy that backfired. While the *Memoir* was welcomed as a biography, there was also complaint. What Caroline termed as 'this vexed question between the Austens and the Public' was far from laid to rest.[10] Not content with Jane Austen's life, the 'Public', in its various guises, called for the disinterment of her literary remains. The *Athenaeum*, quoting Jane Austen's remark about working on her little bit of ivory to 'little effect after much labour', commented pointedly: 'But of this labour we hear scarcely anything.…Something further might surely be attained by referring to her papers'.[11] The same issue, now directed more specifically, was raised by Edith Simcox, an influential contributor to the *Academy*: lamenting the absence of the 'unpublished writing', she argued the value of being able to compare the cancelled chapter of *Persuasion* with its replacement, an 'opportunity' that should have been provided.[12] Then there were knowledgeable men of standing in private life, such as the fifth Earl Stanhope. Disappointed at finding the materials of the *Memoir* 'so meagre', he wrote to the publisher, Richard Bentley. Recalling Henry Austen's reference in the 'Biographical Notice' to Jane Austen's last poem, written on her death-bed, Stanhope queried its absence.[13] With the peer's permission, Bentley sent his letter on to Austen-Leigh, who, in turn, circulated it to his sisters. Indignant that 'L^d. S. should be raising a hue & cry', Caroline found her worst fears realised: 'see what it is to have a growing posthumous reputation! we cannot keep any thing to ourselves *now*, it seems'.[14] And we can be sure that Bentley added his commercial voice as well, a strong one. In 1832 he had bought the copyrights in five of the novels from Henry and Cassandra and it was certainly to his advantage to feed this growing interest in Jane Austen with a new and expanded edition of the *Memoir*.[15] At all events, whatever agreement was reached between Austen-Leigh and Bentley, and amongst the Austens, their policy of concealment was overcome. A second edition was rapidly agreed upon and when it appeared, in July 1871, the 'Public' was treated to virtually full disclosure. Impatient with what she regarded as Austen-Leigh's previous timidity, in her second *Academy* review Edith Simcox was outspoken. She pointed to the enlarged *Memoir* as the result of arm-twisting: 'In obedience to the unanimous demands of his critics...Mr.Austen Leigh has now produced from the family storehouse'.[16] What he 'produced', in one form or another, was the four major works: *Lady Susan*, the original manuscript made available to him late in 1870 by Lady Knatchbull; *The Watsons*, left untitled by Jane Austen and so-named by Austen-Leigh, from the autograph manuscript owned by Caroline; and two autograph manuscripts owned by Anna: the cancelled chapter of *Persuasion* – this last in response to 'wishes both publicly and privately expressed', Austen-Leigh explained in his Preface, a distinctly apologetic statement [17] – and 'The last work', the as yet untitled *Sanditon*, semi-revealed in a series of linked extracts. Austen-Leigh also indicated the existence of a larger body of juvenilia: the first edition's reference to an 'old copy-book' was now corrected to 'copy-books extant' and 'The Mystery' from *Volume the First* was given in full.[18] Just how conciliatory Austen-Leigh and his sisters were prepared to be in so expanding the *Memoir*, we can judge from the inclusion of *Lady Susan*, for this was by far the most important of the 'betweenities' and a work whose publication Caroline had previously been so set against. Its emergence in print represented a total *volte-face*.

With a view to increasing his market for the *Memoir*, Bentley reduced the page dimensions of the new edition, making it uniform in size and binding with his current edition of the Austen novels. The *Memoir* was listed alongside the Austen novels in Bentley's 'Favourite Novels' series, and *Lady Susan &c.*, judged to be a more saleable title, was put on the spine. This gimmick was against Austen-Leigh's wishes; he thought it 'somewhat ambiguous' and it was only used at Bentley's insistence;[19] although the other changes were made with Austen-Leigh's prior knowledge, possibly with his approval too. In November 1870 he was writing to an American correspondent, Susan Quincy, that the new edition of the *Memoir* would be 'smaller & less expensive than the former edition, being made to range with & form an additional Vol. to Bentley's last Edition of the novels'.[20] Three years later, however, his doubts about the wisdom of releasing the manuscripts still lingered. He told one correspondent that he would 'not be surprised or offended if some of her admirers should think that they had better not have been published. The works which she suppressed or abandoned cannot be expected to equal those which she voluntarily gave to the world'.[21] But Bentley was untroubled by such qualms. His final act was a full instatement of the manuscript works, locating them firmly in the canon. He placed the *Memoir* alongside the novels as volume six in the Steventon Edition of 1882 – and on its spine the *Memoir* now carried an enlarged title, *Lady Susan, The Watsons, &c.* .[22]

As the *Memoir* sold briskly, with regular reprints down the years, so *Lady Susan, The Watsons* and the cancelled chapter of *Persuasion* remained available in texts which were complete, reasonably accurate and perfectly satisfactory for the average reader. This left *Sanditon*, still in the summary form prepared by Austen-Leigh, as the only important later manuscript not yet fully in print. This deficiency was made good in 1925 in the publishing programme directed and inspired by the great Austen scholar R.W.Chapman. Having completed his monumental edition of the six novels in 1923 – the first scholarly edition of any English novelist – Chapman then turned to the manuscript works, treating them with the same attention, beginning with *Lady Susan* and *Fragment of a Novel* (*Sanditon*) in 1925, *Plan of a Novel* (including the 'Opinions' of *Mansfield Park* and *Emma*) and *Two Chapters of Persuasion* in 1926, *The Watsons* in 1927; and later, as these manuscripts came to his notice, *Volume the First* in 1933 and *Volume the Third* in 1951.[23] Chapman's position as Secretary to the Delegates of the Oxford University Press (in effect, Oxford's Publisher) played a decisive part in the production of these books, which came out in finely printed editions with extensive Notes recording the manuscript changes. Some of the volumes were also produced in limited editions for collectors and bibliophiles, printed on hand-made paper and with manuscript facsimiles. As one reviewer observed, such editions combined 'the devotion of a pious act with the luxury of a secret pleasure'.[24] In 1926, Oxford also published Chapman's edition of the 1871 *Memoir*. Chapman omitted *Lady Susan* and *The Watsons* but retained the summary account of *Sanditon* and added his own notes and index; and in the Introduction he included details of the surviving manuscripts – and it was for this feature that *The Times Literary Supplement* headed its review 'Manuscripts of Jane Austen' and announced the book as 'necessary to the complete Austenian'. As the reviewer remarked, Chapman was still on the look out for manuscripts as yet unlocated.[25]

Chapman followed this series of editions with a two-volume edition of the *Letters* in 1932 – 'monumental and definitive', E.M.Forster called it[26] – with four new letters added in the second edition, 1952. Finally, in 1954, Chapman added a *Volume VI: Minor Works* to the Oxford edition of the novels (1923 etc) – 'a fitting crown to a life's work on Jane Austen', as the reviewer in the *Times Literary Supplement* described the book.[27] In this volume, Chapman collected the manuscripts already published in the separate Oxford editions and added the three 'Prayers' and all the known 'Verses'. For these materials he provided Headnotes, brief explanatory notes, and (Chapman's special delight) an apparatus of indexes – indexes of characters, persons, places, authors and books. For details of the manuscript changes – none were included – Chapman refers his readers to the separate Oxford editions of the 1920's. Orginally, Chapman intended to accompany the standard edition of this volume with a limited edition on large paper to match the size and grandeur of the novels as they appeared in the original Oxford edition of 1923. However, according to Gilson, 'for practical reasons [unexplained] this intention was abandoned'.[28]

As to the explanatory annotation of the texts, Chapman was sparing. However, in the last forty or fifty years we have come to identify Jane Austen as an heir to the long eighteenth century, in touch with Enlightenment traditions of thought and concerned too with important current issues such as slavery, the rights, education and employment of women, the war-time and post-war economy and other areas of political and cultural resonance, all this involving a denser and wider body of knowledge and opinion than Chapman allowed for. And on the literary front, Jane Austen was unapologetic about belonging to a family of 'great Novel-readers',[29] a pointer to the fact, confirmed in these manuscript works, that Jane Austen read much further into the minor fiction of her day than Chapman observed. The consequence is that our annotation to-day needs to be far more extensive. There is also the passage of time. Present-day readers now stand at some distance from the social, religious and other customary *mores* that Chapman took for granted as the common stock of knowledge, the common understanding of his readers, and, as far as these texts are concerned, felt able to pass over in silence. Assumptions of such cultural familiarity can no longer be taken for granted. Fifty years on, it is no longer possible to hold the position Chapman declared so boldly in the Preface to the *Minor Works*: that 'These immature or fragmentary fictions call for hardly any comment'.[30]

Notes

1   The record of these versions is in Cassandra Austen's note, reproduced *MW*, facing p. 243 and discussed *LM*, pp. 52-54.
2   Letter to Charles Austen, written on the day on which she made her will, 9 May 1843; quoted in Deirdre Le Faye, '*Sanditon*: Jane Austen's Manuscript and her Niece's Continuation', *Review of English Studies* (new series vol. 38, 1987), p. 56.
3   See Anne Lefroy's letter to her brother JEAL, 20 May?1869: she is quoting from a letter from Cassandra Esten Austen to her sister Frances: ' "At Aunt Cassandra's death there were several scraps marked by her (of her Sister's compositions) to be given to different relations, & amongst others some to Lady Knatchbull [Fanny Knight] –" (of course Lady Susan is here referred to) "& some to my Uncle Frank…" ' (quoted in M, p.184).
4   The 'Biographical Notice' (1818) came at the head of the first edition of *NA&P*; this was expanded as 'Memoir of Miss Austen' and came at the head of *S&S* (1833), the first volume in Bentley's collected edition.

5 *1870 M*: 'To the Memory of Mrs.Lefroy', pp. 76-78; 'Mr.Gell to Miss Gill', p. 115 (ms facsimile, facing p. 122); 'On the Marriage of a Middle-Aged Flirt', p. 116; 'In Measured Verse', p. 117-18; 'This Little Bag', p. 124). On p. 115, ahead of the next three poems, Austen-Leigh mentions the amusement Jane Austen provided 'by relating in prose or verse some trifling anecdote coloured to her own fancy, or in writing a fictitious history of what they were supposed to have said or done, which could deceive nobody'. The 'Plan' is given on pp. 161-65; the cancelled chapter is referred to on p. 220.

6 Peter Sabor ed, Jane Austen, *Juvenilia* (Cambridge University Press, 2006), p. xxxviii.

7 *1870 M*: pp. 59-62;

8 Caroline Austen to J.E.Austen-Leigh, 1 April?1869 (M, pp. 185-87).

9 *Times*, 17 January 1870, p. 5; *Quarterly Review*, vol. 128, January & April 1870, p. 200.

10 Caroline Austen to J.E.Austen-Leigh, 1 April?1869 (M, p. 186).

11 *Athenaeum*, 8 January 1870, pp. 53-54.

12 *Academy*, 12 February 1870, pp. 118-20. Edith Simcox (1844-1901) has a considerable entry in the *Oxford Dictionary of National Biography*. Described there as 'anthropologist and political activist', she contributed to a wide range of the leading journals and papers and wrote a number of books, including one work of fiction. For her *Academy* reviews, she signed herself H.Lawrenny.

13 See Deirdre Le Faye, 'Jane Austen's Verses and Lord Stanhope's Disappointment', *The Book Collector* (1998), vol. 37, pp. 86-91. Le Faye points out that Lord Stanhope's interest in this matter was 'probably somewhat proprietary, as the rector of Chevening [Stanhope owned the Chevening estate] from 1813 onwards was a second cousin of Jane's, the Revd John Austen (1771-1851)', p. 86.

14 Caroline Austen to JAEL, undated letter (annotated July 1871), M, p. 190.

15 In December 1812, JA accepted an offer of £110 for the copyright of *P&P* from the publisher Thomas Egerton; and in 1832 Bentley purchased this copyright from Egerton's executors. Richard Bentley (1794-1871) was a shrewd publisher. Despite financial ups and downs, he combined a strong literary list with commercial success.

In 1867, he relinquished the management of the company to his son George (1828-95), who was succeeded by his son Richard Bentley jnr. For the sons, I have continued to use the company name of Bentley.

16 *Academy*, 1 August 1871, pp. 367-68.

17 *Memoir* (1871), p. [3].

18 Ibid., pp. 39-43.

19 From JEAL's letter of 16 September 1873 to Lady Laura Scott (JA Society *Annual Report*, 2004, p. 73. According to Austen-Leigh's son William and his nephew Richard, 'It was far from being his wish that *Lady Susan* should form the title of a separate volume'; and that it did was a 'mistake' (*Life and Letters of Jane Austen* , 1913, p. 80n). The reviewer in *The Athenæum* objected 'on behalf of some unsuspecting reader', pointing out how misleading the title was, and drawing this to the attention of 'either editor, publisher, or both, as a case of conscience for them to decide' (15 July 1871, p. 72).

20 JEAL's letter of 28 November 1870, in M.A. DeWolfe Howe, 'A Jane Austen Letter With Other "Janeana" From an Old Book of Autographs', *Yale Review* (1925-26), vol. 15, p. 333. Chapman suggests that Bentley 'lettered the binding' *Lady Susan &c.* 'by inadvertence or cunning' (*Memoir*, 1926, p. viii) – if 'inadvertence', it was a profitable mistake, repeated and compounded in Bentley's Steventon edition of 1882, where *The Watsons* is added to *Lady Susan* in the title.

21 From JEAL's letter of 16 September 1873 (JA Society *Annual Report*, 2004, p. 73).

22 By this time the Bentley connection with the Austen family had been further strengthened : Jane Austen's great-nephew Cholmeley Austen-Leigh (1829-99), eldest son of the author of the M, was a partner in the firm of Bentley's regular printers, Spottiswoode & Co., which passed into Austen-Leigh family ownership.

23 Chapman did not edit *Volume the Second*, deterred by the fact that it had already been published in 1922 by Chatto and Windus under the title *Love and Freindship* with a Preface by G.K.Chesterton.

24 Review of the Oxford editions of *Plan of a Novel* (1926) and *Two Chapters of Persuasion* (1926), *Times Literary Supplement*, 8 July 1926, p. 461.

25 *Times Literary Supplement*, 17 March 1927, p. 177.

26 *Listener* (1933), p. 799.

27 The *MW* volume was reprinted 1958, with revisions 1963, 1965 with further revisions by Brian Southam. The most significant changes are those made to the headnotes and to the text of *Volume the Second*, revised in the light of Southam's edition of *Volume the Second* (Oxford: Clarendon Press, 1963). *Times Literary Supplement*, 20 May 1955, p. 263.

28 Gilson, p. 387.

29 Letter to Cassandra, 18 December 1798 (*L*, p. 26).

30 *MW*, [p.v].

II

The history of criticism of the later manuscripts
Naturally, the focus of critical attention has always been on the novels. The principal manuscript works – *Lady Susan*, *The Watsons* and *Sanditon* (when the text became available in 1925) – have been regarded of secondary interest; and, until recently, their criticism has tended to be intermixed with biography. Much of the early comment came in reviews: initially, of the 1871 *Memoir*, and then, after a long interval, a small body of opinion in the 1920's, with the publication of the individual works. So there is almost no remnant of what we can identify as a critical tradition. Apart from the reviews by E.M.Forster and Virginia Woolf, for the most part the criticism has been of little substance and has passed with little trace. It is not until very much later, with the development of an Austen academic literature in the 1950's, that the discussion of the manuscript works begins to be sustained by any continuity and growth in ideas and debate; and since the 1980's, with new developments in textual scholarship and the study of print culture, there has been a further strengthening of interest in the manuscript works.

Austen-Leigh's Prefaces to *Lady Susan* and the *The Watsons* and his comments on *Sanditon* in the 1871 *Memoir* provided some of the points of departure for the earliest reviewers. In the 'Preface' to *Lady Susan*, he suggested that it might have been 'an experiment in conducting a story by means of letters', the form in which *Sense and Sensibility* was 'first written' and with which she was 'not quite satisfied'. It was, he wrote apologetically, a work 'too slight to stand alone'.[1] For *The Watsons*, Austen-Leigh raised a number of issues: that the work survived in an 'elementary...state'; that the watermarks 1803 and 1804 (1804 is an error) make it 'probable' that it was composed before Jane Austen left Bath in 1806 (mistakenly, he writes 1805); and he went on to speculate on the reasons why it was left unfinished, seeing that 'that there is much in it which promised well'– the 'vigour' and 'discrimination' of the character drawing, the power of the 'story' telling, and the effective characterisation conducted through dialogue. His 'own idea' why Jane Austen abandoned the piece is quoted here in full, since, down the years, it has been persistently drawn on by later critics and biographers as a convenient and ready-made explanation, despite Austen-Leigh's notion of ladylike 'refinement', which is both anachronistic and, as it relates to Jane Austen, mistaken:

> that the author became aware of the evil of having placed her heroine too low, in such a position of poverty and obscurity as, though not necessarily connected with vulgarity, has a sad tendency to degenerate into it; and therefore, like a singer who has begun on too low a note, she discontinued the strain. It was an error of which she was likely to become more sensible, as she grew older, and saw more of society; certainly she never repeated it by placing the heroine of any subsequent work under circumstances likely to be unfavourable to the refinement of a lady.[2]

As to *Sanditon*, Austen-Leigh felt that 'Such an unfinished fragment' could not be 'presented to the public'. He found no 'decline of power or industry' but confessed that 'It is more difficult to judge of the quality of a work so little advanced', with 'scarcely any indication' of 'the course of the story', nor 'any heroine yet perceptible'. Nonetheless, 'as some of the principal characters were already sketched in with a vigorous hand', he was ready 'to give an idea of them, illustrated by extracts from the work'.[3]

However, the immediate impact of the 1871 *Memoir* was not the influence of these remarks but the revelation of the manuscripts themselves. Although biography, now extended, remained the staple of the book, the life was regarded by the reviewers as somewhat *deja vu* and was overshadowed by this first sight of the manuscripts – a prioritising reflected in the headings to the reviews: in the *Spectator*, 'Miss Austen's Posthumous Pieces'; in the *Saturday Review*, 'Miss Austen's Lady Susan'; in the *Nation* (New York), 'The Early Writings of Jane Austen'.[4] For the *Athenæum* 'the unpublished fragments' provided the 'real interest' of the volume, giving it an 'interest' 'singular and varied', while in the *Spectator* R.H.Hutton welcomed the sight of works 'which the public have been so long and so eagerly expecting'.[5] According to the *Nation*, this was also true of Jane Austen's American 'admirers', 'eagerly curious' to see them. As for the individual works, *Lady Susan* proved to be a stumbling block for the *Athenæum*, which found the central figure 'simply odious' and the 'half rivalry between mother and daughter' 'disagreeable', while the *Nation* regarded *Lady Susan* as 'entirely unworthy of Miss Austen's hand...thoroughly unpleasant in its characters and its details'. On the other hand, *The Watsons* was well received. The *Nation* found 'glimpses' of Jane Austen's 'talent' and the reviewer in the *Athenæum* judged it to have been written 'in a moment of gay and happy inspiration'. He was wholly dissatisfied with Austen-Leigh's suggestion as to why it was left unfinished; and wrote enthusiastically that 'The Watsons are at least as good as the Bennets, and Tom Musgrave is immeasurably superior to John Thorpe. As for the heroine herself, she is more charming that Elizabeth Bennet, or Fanny Price, or Catherine Morland, or any of Miss Austen's heroines, Anne Elliott alone excepted'. Anne Thackeray took the same line in the *Cornhill Magazine*. She found *The Watsons* 'a delightful fragment', something 'between' *Emma* and *Pride and Prejudice*, in which 'vague shadows of future friends seem to be passing and repassing', 'anteghosts...of a Mrs.Elton, of an Elizabeth Bennet, of a Darcy...'.[6]

The most striking review was by Edith Simcox in the *Academy*. She noted that her original complaint, voiced the year before in her review of the 1870 *Memoir*, had been attended to, at least in part, and she amused herself with a hint of triumphalism in announcing what Austen-Leigh had produced from 'the family storehouse'. Now she could compare the cancelled chapter of *Persuasion* with the published version and confirm that Jane Austen's success was the fruit of 'judgement...as well as inspiration', a judicious distinction. But she detected a remining lack of editorial 'courage': these extracts were not *Sanditon* 'in extenso'; and she rejected Austen-Leigh's explanation for the abandonment of *The*

Watsons: she found the fragment 'quite in Miss Austen's best manner', perceived in the Watson family 'the Bennets with a difference', and advised her readers that it was 'not easy to account for its having been laid aside'. Her own explanation was that Jane Austen 'could not get on comfortably without a leading idea of some sort or a moral to be enforced, and of this there was certainly so far no sign.' She judged *Lady Susan* a success, the portrait of 'a clever and attractive woman', and mercifully free from 'sensationalism',[7] the bane of the present-day novel. While she thought the 'device' of the letter form 'very well suited to a subject which turns more upon revelations of character than on incident', she saw a structural weakness: 'we have not time to feel at home with six or seven different correspondents'.[8] The other reviewer who treated *Lady Susan* with some perception was Hutton in the *Spectator*. He located the 'failure' of the piece in Jane Austen's 'double error of choosing a subject which required a bolder style than hers, and of fettering herself in its treatment by a method which robbed her style of its greatest grace as well as power'. *The Watsons* he found 'full of promise' and the passages from *Sanditon* suggested that 'the author's humour would probably have taken a broader and more farcical form' than ever before.

What was missing, however, from these accounts was a consolidating overview, a survey which would evaluate the manuscript works alongside and within the sequence of Jane Austen's development in the novels. There were two writers capable of providing this – Richard Simpson and Margaret Oliphant – as we can judge from their major essay-reviews of the 1870 *Memoir*:[9] Simpson's essay described by Lionel Trilling as 'perhaps the very first consideration of the subject undertaken in the spirit of serious criticism';[10] and Mrs Oliphant's Jane Austen, a writer armed with a 'fine vein of feminine cynicism', 'full of subtle power, keenness, finesse, and self-restraint', blessed with an 'exquisite sense' of the 'ridiculous', 'a fine stinging yet soft-voiced contempt'. But no reviewer of the 1871 *Memoir* followed in their steps and there followed a steep decline into a run of literary biographies, all of them based on the *Memoir* – there were seven up to 1913 – the year the *Memoir* was superceded by the next family biography, the *Life and Letters*. If these biographers touch upon the manuscript works at all, it is to provide plot summaries and descriptions of the characters. Only isolated comments are worth noting for the record.[11]

The first recognisable vestige of literary scholarship surfaces in A.C.Bradley's 'Jane Austen', a lecture first given at Newnham College, Cambridge in 1911.[12] Bradley pointed out to his audience 'two matters which seem to be unknown to many readers of Jane Austen....The first is the fact that the six novels fall into two distinct groups, separated by a considerable interval of time'; and the second, that the six novels 'are not quite all that remains to us of her writing: and this is the second fact which none of her readers should ignore'. He then went on to refer to manuscript material in the *Memoir*, still in print: 'the story she began in the last months of her life'; *The Watsons* 'begun and abandoned about 1803; i.e. in that long interval between the two groups'; and, before the first of the novels, *Lady Susan*, bearing 'the marks of immaturity'. It may seem curious to us that Bradley should describe these two facts as 'unknown to many readers'. However, forty years had elapsed since the arrival of *Lady Susan* and *The Watsons* had caused such a stir and there were other, more readable biographies than the *Memoir*, which remained the sole volume in which these texts were available. Accordingly, we can understand Bradley's emphatic tone in spelling out these points. Quite simply, he was addressing a generation to whom the chronology of composition and the minor works themselves were virtually unknown; and it is interesting to see that when he gave this lecture again, later the same year, to members of The English Association, he left the text unchanged.

From here, the line of scholarship take us directly to the first full-scale study, *Jane Austen and her Art* (1939), by Mary Lascelles, the 'art' being the narrative art of the novelist, and the connection with Bradley being Miss Lascelles' statement in her Preface that 'quotations from Bradley's essay might well head most parts of this book';[13] and a further nod to Bradley is in her meticulous placing of the manuscript works in 'Biography', the book's opening section, which provides what is emphatically a writer's life.

In the years between Bradley and Lascelles came the publication of Chapman's Oxford editions of the manuscript works, with the advance in textual scholarship that these volumes embodied. Strangely, however, the most valuable 'textual' review of this period discussed two editions of *The Watsons* that carried no textual apparatus whatsoever: an edition introduced by the theatre critic and journalist A.B.Walkley and *The Watsons* concluded by L Oulton, both books appearing in 1923, their publishers having taken advantage of the expiry of the fifty-year copyright period. In a review covering both books,[14] Virginia Woolf expressed her unconcern about Jane Austen's reasons for leaving the fragment unfinished – 'it does not very much matter'. But she showed a practitioner's interest in what the fragment revealed of the author's writing procedure:

> we…observe in the first place that Jane Austen was indisputably one of those writers who lay their facts out rather baldly in the first version, and then go back and back and back and cover them with flesh and atmosphere. How it would have been done we cannot say – by what suppressions and insertions and artful devices. But the miracle would have been accomplished; the dull history of fourteen years of family life would have been converted into another of the exquisite and apparently effortless introductions; and we should never have guessed what pages of preliminary drudgery Jane Austen forced her pen to go through. Then suddenly the story begins to live.

This was a passage that Virginia Woolf incorporated into the well-known 'Jane Austen' essay which appeared in *The Common Reader* (1925), with variations worth recording.[15] The passage opens

> The second-rate works of a great writer are worth reading because they offer the best criticism of his masterpieces. Here her difficulties are more apparent, and the method she took to overcome them less artfully concealed. To begin with, the stiffness and bareness of the first chapters prove that she was one of those writers…

and the original passage, in the review given above, continues with this addition:

> Here we perceive that she was no conjuror after all. Like other writers, she had to create the atmosphere in which her own particular genius could bear fruit. Here she fumbles; here she keeps us waiting. Suddenly she has done it; now things can happen as she likes things to happen.

The other important review from this period was E.M.Forster's notice of *Fragment of a Novel* (*Sanditon*) in the Oxford edition.[16] It is a curious piece. On the one side, Forster judged *Sanditon* to be of 'small literary merit', 'reminiscent from first to last', written when 'vitality was low' and 'the effort of creating was too much'. He judged that 'the numerous alterations in the MS. are never in the direction of vitality' (an observation we might mentally qualify with the information in Gilson's *Bibliography* that 'Forster clearly paid no attention to the variants, since the pages of notes' in his review copy 'are unopened'.)[17] Yet, at the same time, Forster was sensitive to new elements: 'topography comes to the front, and is screwed much deeper than usual into the story.' Of the investment that Mr.Parker and Lady Denham have made in the success of the resort, he asks, 'Isn't this new? Was there anything like it in the preceding novels which were purely social? And – now for the romantic flavour – is there not a new cadence in this prose?': 'this prose' being Charlotte's view 'over the miscellaneous foreground of unfinished Buildings, waving Linen, and tops of Houses, to the Sea, dancing and sparkling in Sunshine and Freshness'. Forster's response to the scene embraces the work as a whole: 'not only does the sea dance in freshness, but another configuration has been given to the earth, making it at once more poetic and more definite. Sanditon gives out an atmosphere, and also exists as a geographic and economic force'. It is hardly surprising to find that the later criticism of *Sanditon* is in step with the positive side of Forster's review whereas his enfeebled and reminiscent *Sanditon* has made little headway.

Mary Lascelles was the first critic to make full use of Chapman's texts and analyse the pattern and significance of Jane Austen's changes to the manuscript, which she referred to as 'those small but invaluable pieces of evidence'.[18] In 'Style', chapter 3 of *Jane Austen and her Art*, she drew upon the minutiæ of this evidence to illustrate the characteristic features and preferences evident in the sentence structures, diction and areas of description. Referring to the detailed changes in *The Watsons* and *Sanditon*, she illustrated the process by which Jane Austen achieved a 'discreet use of idiosyncrasy in speech'.[19] Miss Lascelles also laid the groundwork for the later interpretative and formal criticism of these works, describing *Sanditon*, for example, as 'a very surprising outcome' of the 'last six months of her life...a hilarious comedy of invalidism, and (what was even less to be expected) a bold venture in a new way of telling a story.'[20] And she was quite prepared to take issue with the great names of the past: with Virginia Woolf's analysis of the ball scene in *The Watsons* and with E.M.Forster's descriptive comments about the new prominence of 'Topography' in *Sanditon* and the presence of the resort 'as a geographic and economic force,' and the role of Charlotte Heywood and Clara Brereton in 'interpreting people and events to us'.[21]

The outcome of this close and detailed study was to disabuse the literary world of any lingering illusions about the nature of Jane Austen's art – it was not, as Caroline Spurgeon had told her audience at the Royal Society of Literature, 'of the nature of a miracle'.[22] However, the Cambridge critic Q.D.Leavis believed that by making use of the manuscript works much more could be said about Jane Austen's procedures and that the textual 'facts' made available by Chapman had not yet 'been translated into the language of literary criticism'. In 'A Critical Theory of Jane Austen's Writings' – a series of four essays published in *Scrutiny* between 1941 and 1944 – she set out to do just that: to demonstrate her belief that 'in Jane Austen literary criticism has...a uniquely documented case of the origin and development of artistic expression, and [that] an enquiry into the nature of her genius and the process by which it developed can go very far indeed on sure ground'.[23] It was, she claimed, a necessary enquiry, since without an examination of the way in which Jane Austen wrote, 'no criticism of her novels can be just or even safe'.[24] In this 'enquiry' the later manuscript works play a central part. According to Mrs Leavis, *Lady Susan* was first 'expanded into' an epistolary version of *Mansfield Park* in 1808-09 and this, in turn, was 'rewritten' in 1811-13 as the *Mansfield Park* we have to-day; and that in 1814-15 *Emma* was 'written up...from the earlier story of *The Watsons*'; futhermore, there was a 'prototype' *Persuasion* (now lost) which she places in what is described as 'the pre-1806 gap'.[25] The novels are a rich mix: elements of family history and friends and acquaintances entered during the course of these transformations, the principal assumption being that the figure of Lady Susan is in part based upon Jane Austen's cousin Eliza de Feuillide and in part on a society woman, 'The cruel Mrs Craven';[26] and that, in this literary embodiment, these figures were developed into Mary Crawford. The transpositions are mutitudinous – from life, from the juvenilia, and from other authors. Mrs Leavis is frank on this point: some of these figures, living or literary, 'altered almost out of recognition'.[27] Structural changes could occur. Accepting Austen-Leigh's explanation for the abandonment of *The Watsons*, Mrs Leavis has it that Jane Austen returned to the fragment 'to make a fresh start with the same materials by shaking the kaleidoscope to make a new pattern'.[28] The possibilities are wide, virtually endless; so wide and so endless that although Mrs Leavis has much of value to say on the literary front, the 'Critical Theory' has gained no hold in the field of textual scholarship. Its claims are beyond proof. By contrast, there is indisputable evidence – such as Cassandra's note providing the dates of composition for the novels and recording the existence of the early, epistolary versions of *Sense and Sensibility* and *Pride and Prejudice*.[29] Yet, nonetheless, as Marvin Mudrick remarked, the 'Critical Theory' constituted 'the most iconoclastic, the most confidently documented, and the most comprehensive effort to describe Jane Austen's method and development';[30] and, as such, it has won its supporters.[31]

These did not include Mudrick himself – see the even-handed critique in his Appendix: 'Mrs.Leavis's Jane Austen'.[32] Nonetheless, different as they were, the contributions of Lascelles and Leavis together gave an impetus and a direction to Jane Austen studies which was long-lasting. Issues of chronology and textual process were taken up by critics who primary interests might otherwise have lain elsewhere; and, increasingly, the three important manuscript works came to be discussed at length and in relation to the six novels. Although Mudrick's own book was primarily a study of Jane Austen's irony, he paid close attention to the questions of chronology around *Lady Susan* and *The Watsons*; and these works, together with *Sanditon*, enter fully into his critical discussion of the oeuvre. Chronology was also seen to be important to an understanding of Jane Austen's development as a novelist: 'crucial', Walton Litz declared in 1965, 'the dating of the works…. To a large extent' determining 'the critic's conclusions'.[33] This view was also reflected in Southam's 1964 study of the literary manuscripts, with its descriptive sub-title, 'A Study of the Novelist's Development through the Surviving Papers'.[34] These scholarly concerns were also registered in the Penguin edition of the three principal manuscript works, edited by the novelist Margaret Drabble in 1974.[35] As she explained, Drabble took her texts from Chapman's individual volumes of the 1920's and she recorded in her notes 'any interesting erasures or variations'. She explained her procedure in modernising the texts minimally, for the benefit of 'the general reader,' with the aim of presenting these works 'as interesting stories rather than literary curiosities'.[36] And Drabble used her Introduction to discuss the dating of the works as well as providing a critical introduction informed by her own experience as a novelist broadly in the Austen tradition.

Other approaches developed during this period. In the 1970's, *Sanditon* came to be seen as particularly open to historical interpretation, with studies by Duckworth and Southam, and a conservative placing by Marilyn Butler in the 'war of ideas'.[37] In 1979, Gilbert and Gubar set out the grounds of what they identified as 'a distinctively female literary tradition' in which Jane Austen stood as a primary figure and the minor works were discussed together with the novels.[38] Southam's edition of Austen's *Sir Charles Grandison* was published in 1980 and it soon entered the feminist historical perspective provided by Margaret Kirkham in *Jane Austen, Feminism and Fiction* (1983). Working within the terms of Leavis's 'Critical Theory', Kirkham also discussed Emma Watson's transformation in the refashioning of *The Watsons* as *Emma*, and considered *Sanditon* alongside *Persuasion*, a fruitful parallel from the standpoint of feminist interpretation. Tony Tanner's influential study, *Jane Austen* (1986), concludes with 'The Disease of Activity', a cultural-historical chapter on *Sanditon* which also attends to the detail of the manuscript text, to this conclusion – which we can take to be Tanner's riposte to E.M. Forster's 'reminiscent' *Sanditon*:

> It is often maintained that Jane Austen has reverted to the easy burlesque mode of her earliest writing, or that this is a crude first draft which she would have later written up in a more sophisticated way. This seems to me exactly wrong. The style is perfectly appropriate and adapted to the new world she is describing. There is a most uncharacteristic use not so much of dialogue as of actual unrefracted monologue. She lets the endless talkers talk endlessly, without the interposition of her own monitoring, adjudicating voice.[39]

In support of these advances in scholarship and criticism, a new generation of editions was made possible by the great expansion in student numbers on both sides of the Atlantic from the 1970's onwards. And in America, in particular, Jane Austen has emerged as a central figure in the range of intersecting debates: around the ideas of literary canonisation, historicist criticism, in its sub-sets of feminist and post-colonial criticism, her popular reception, Janeite or otherwise, and its reflection on the academy and on the state and concerns of the academic profession. In these respects, Jane Austen has come to be regarded as both a literary and a supra-literary figure, around whom a wide range of undergraduate and graduate courses can be constructed. This background helps us to understand how the Oxford University Press was able to publish scholarly editions of the manuscript works in paperback. In 1990, Oxford reissued in paperback an edition that included *Northanger Abbey* together with *Lady Susan*, *The Watsons* and *Sanditon*. This had originally been published hardbound in 1970 as a volume in the Oxford English Novels series and now appeared with the addition of a new Introduction by Terry Castle of Stanford.[40] With the growing demand for these texts, this volume was in turn replaced by a new edition in 2003. The original texts, dating back to 1971, were retained, but were now accompanied by an entirely new and extensive apparatus, with an Introduction and notes by Claudia Johnson of Princeton.[41] Moreover, in 1993 Oxford published yet another Austen paperback, *Catharine and Other Writings*, under the editorship of Margaret Anne Doody of Vanderbilt. This volume contained the three volumes of juvenilia, the *Plan of a Novel*, Verses and Prayers, and included 120 pages of textual and explanatory notes, an apparatus so far unequalled in Austen editions.[42] With these new editions, the study of the manuscript works has thrived, with particular attention to *Sanditon*, rich in historical and cultural material and with its promise in opening a new phase in the development of Jane Austen's art. And overall, the manuscript materials have taken on a new importance with the increasing emphasis on textual studies, an area treated in great detail by Kathryn Sutherland, Professor of Bibliography and Textual Criticism at the University of Oxford, in *Jane Austen's Textual Lives: from Aeschylus to Bollywood* (2005), with its close examination of the working manuscripts and its consideration of what this evidence reveals of the writer's creative process and the form in which her manuscripts may have been delivered to the printer.

Professor Sutherland heads her study with a telling quotation from Virginia Woolf: 'There is Jane Austen, thumbed, scored, annotated, magnified, living almost within the memory of man, and yet as inscrutable in her small way as Shakespeare in his vast one'.[43] Readers will decide for themselves whether the study of the manuscript works, from Chapman to the present day, has rendered the 'inscrutable' Jane Austen to any degree less 'inscrutable'.

Notes

1 *Memoir* (1871), [p. 201].
2 Ibid., pp. [295], 296.
3 Ibid., pp. 181-82.
4 *Spectator*, 22 July 1871, pp. 891-92; *Saturday Review*, 22 July 1871, pp. 118-19; *Nation* (New York), 7 September 1871, pp. 118-19: this was a review of the American edition, published by Scribner.
5 *Athenæum*, 15 July 1871, pp. 71-72.
6 *Cornhill Magazine*, July-December 1871, vol. 24, p. 159.
7 'Sensation' novels, so-called in the 1860's, and otherwise known as 'fast', 'bigamy' or 'adultery' novels, were essentially scandalous tales of modern life, involving mystery and deception, in a familiar, everyday setting.
8 *Academy*, 1 August 1871, pp. 367-68.
9 *North British Review* (April 1870), vol. 52, pp. 129-52; *Blackwoods Edinburgh Magazine* (March 1870), vol. 107, pp. 294-305.
10 *Sincerity and Authenticity* (1972), p. 8.
11 For Example, Goldwin Smith – Regius Professor of Modern History at Oxford (1858-66), then Professor of History at Cornell – wrote a sobre and commonsensical *Life of Jane Austen* (1890), with a short chapter *The Watsons* and *Lady Susan*. The earlier work he sees as a 'mere exercise', with Lady Susan 'a crude and coarse germ of…Mary Crawford'; of *The Watsons*, he remarks that 'it promises well' and he counters Austen-Leigh's suggestion for why it was left unfinished, pointing out that the Watson family are 'gentlefolk' and suffer no social decline (*Life of Jane Austen*, London: Scott, 1890, ch. 8, pp. 182-83).
12 Bradley (1851-1935), at this time Professor of Poetry at Oxford, gave this same lecture to members of The English Association and it was reprinted in the Association's annual volume entitled *Essays and Studies* (Oxford: Clarendon, 1911, vol. 2, pp. 7-36).
13 *Jane Austen and her Art* (Oxford: Oxford University Press, 1939), [p. v].
14 *New Statesman*, 10 March 1923, pp. 662-63: *The Watsons*,

Introduction A.B. Walkley (London: Parsons, 1923); *The Watsons*, concluded by L.Oulton (London: Hutchinson, [1923]).

15 *The Common Reader* (London: Hogarth Press, 1925), pp. 168-83.

16 *Nation & Athenæum*, 21 March 1925, p. 860, reprinted in *Abinger Harvest* (London: Arnold, 1936), pp. 148-52.

17 Gilson, p. 377.

18 *Jane Austen and her Art*, p. 88.

19 Ibid., p. 99.

20 Ibid., p. 39.

21 Ibid., pp. 134-35; pp. 180-81; p. 200.

22 'Jane Austen', *Essays by Divers Hands* (London: Transactions of the Royal Society of Literature, 1928), vol. 7, p. 82.

23 *Scrutiny* (1941), vol. 10, pp. 61-90, 114-42; (1942), pp. 272-94; (1944), vol. 12, pp. 104-19. The 'Critical Theory' was reprinted in *A Selection from Scrutiny*, compiled by F.R.Leavis (Cambridge: Cambridge University Press, 1968), vol. 2, pp. 1-80. The quotations given so far are from *Selection*, p. 1.

24 *Scrutiny* (1941), vol. 10, p. 86. This claim is usefully considered by Roger Gard at the opening of chapter 2, *Jane Austen's Novels: The Art of Clarity* (New Haven & London: Yale University Press, 1992).

25 *Selection*, p. 3.

26 Ibid., p. 35, n. 2.

27 *Scrutiny* (1941), vol. 10, p. 133.

28 Ibid., p. 77.

29 A facsimile is given in MW, facing p. 242.

30 *Jane Austen: Irony as Defense and Discovery* (Princeton: Princeton University Press, 1952), p. 260.

31 The supporters include George Watson, in *The Literary Critics* (Harmondsworth: Penguin, 1962), p. 212: 'a careful and brilliant group of articles'; Robert Liddell, *The Novels of Jane Austen* (London: Longmans, 1963); Graham Hough, *The Listener* (7 November 1963), p. 749; Margaret Kirkham, *Jane Austen, Feminism and Fiction* (1983), pp. 139-42.

32 *Jane Austen*, pp. 260-63.

33 *Jane Austen: A Study of her Artistic Development* (London: Chatto, 1965), p. vii.

34 This book was originally prepared as an Oxford thesis under Miss Lascelles' supervision. At an early stage, Southam planned to write on JA's style. But Miss Lascelles directed him towards this subject. She said that it was a topic that she had once wanted to take up and which still remained to be studied.

35 *Lady Susan, The Watsons, Sanditon*, The Penguin English Library (Harmondsworth: Penguin, 1974).

36 Ibid., 'A Note on the Text', pp. 37-39. Further manuscript information is provided at the head of the end-notes for each of the three works.

37 Alistair M.Duckworth, 'Postscript: *Sanditon*', *The Improvement of the Estate: A Study of Jane Austen's Novels* (Baltimore & London: Johns Hopkins University Press, 1971, 1994); '*Sanditon*: the Seventh Novel', ed Juliet McMaster, *Jane Austen's Achievement* (London: Macmillan, 1976), pp. 1-26; Marilyn Butler, *Jane Austen and the War of Ideas* (Oxford: Clarendon, 1975), pp. 286-89.

38 Sandra M.Gilbert & Susan Gubar, *The Madwoman in the Attic: The Woman Writer and the Nineteenth-Century Literary Imagination* (New Haven & London: Yale University Press, 1979, 2nd edn. 2000).

39 Tony Tanner, *Jane Austen* (Basingstoke: Macmillan, 1986) p. 284. Coincidentally, Forster and Tanner were both, at different periods, Fellows of King's College, Cambridge, in whose Library the manuscript of *Sanditon* had been since 1930. Whether Tanner had ever discussed *Sanditon* with Forster is an interesting speculation.

40 *Northanger Abbey, Lady Susan, The Watsons and Sanditon*, The World's Classics (Oxford: Oxford University Press, 1971, 1990).

41 *Northanger Abbey, Lady Susan, The Watsons and Sanditon*, The World's Classics (Oxford: Oxford University Press, 2003).

42 *Catharine and other Writings*, edd Margaret Anne Doody & Douglas Murray, The World's Classics (Oxford: Oxford University Press, 1993).

43 Sutherland, p. xi.

Lady Susan

Lady Susan	probably c.1793-94
Autograph manuscript	Pierpont Morgan Library
Facsimile	*Jane Austen's "Lady Susan": A Facsimile of the Manuscript in the Pierpont Morgan Library and the 1925 Printed edition* (Garland: New York & London, 1989).

Lady Susan was first published by J.E.Austen-Leigh in the second edition of the *Memoir* (1871). He described it there as 'the chief addition' to the volume.[1] As the original manuscript could not be found at this time, Austen-Leigh made use of a not wholly accurate copy made some years before by Lady Knatchbull (Fanny Knight), who owned the original. This copy was available to Austen-Leigh since Lady Knatchbull had given it to his sister, Anna Lefroy. Neither the copy nor the original manuscript carry a title. But it is likely that *Lady Susan* was the traditional title within the family; whereas, in the case of *The Watsons*, also untitled, Austen-Leigh is careful to explain that the title is of his own devising.[2] The first publication of a text based on the original manuscript was the Oxford University Press edition in 1925, edited by R.W.Chapman.

The manuscript is a fair copy consisting of 79 quarto leaves measuring 7½ x 6 ⅛ in., the pages numbered by Jane Austen 1-158. Leaves 44 and 55 carry the watermark 1805; and it is possible, as some critics suggest, that that the authorial third person 'Conclusion' was added around this time, when Jane Austen made the fair copy. Jane Austen carried out the transcription, through to the end of the 'Conclusion', with care, maintaining a fine, flowing and regular calligraphic hand, uniformly seventeen to eighteen lines per page as if the work was being preserved for posterity and for reading round the family, exactly in the style of the three juvenilia *Volumes*. During the transcription, Jane Austen made a small number of revisions and corrections.

At Jane Austen's death, the manuscript passed to Cassandra, who left it to Fanny Knight, later Lady Knatchbull. It came to light at the time of her death in 1882 and passed to her son, Edward Knatchbull-Hugessen, the first Baron Brabourne. It was auctioned following his death in 1893. The pages were slightly trimmed and mounted, probably when the manuscript was lavishly bound at some time before 1898, when it was re-auctioned at Sotheby's. In 1933, it was sold at Sotheby's from the library of Lord Rosebery and passed through the hands of several owners before its purchase by the Pierpont Morgan Library in 1947. In 1989, the Library published a facsimile of the manuscript with a Preface by Professor Walton Litz.

There are differing views on the date of *Lady Susan*. In the 'Preface' to the *Memoir* text, Austen-Leigh wrote that he was 'not able to ascertain when it was composed. Her family have always believed it to be an early production'.[3] This view remains unchanged in the next family biography, the *Life and Letters of Jane Austen* (1913) by Austen-Leigh's son William (1843-1921) and his nephew Richard (1871-1962), who had access to further Austen papers and traditions; and in the revised version of this work, *Jane Austen: A Family Record* (1989, second edn., 2004), Deirdre Le Faye sees it as 'probable' that *Lady Susan* follows the last of the juvenilia, 'as a first attempt to deal with a serious theme'.[4] This places its composition in the period c.1793-94, the dating proposed by Southam in the second edition of the *Minor Works*,[5] and argued fully on literary and stylistic grounds in chapter three of *Jane Austen's Literary Manuscripts*. Sutherland has 'Probably...1794-5'.[6] However, Gilson, in the standard Austen bibliography, describes *Lady Susan* as 'written about 1805'.[7] This dating seems to stem from a confusion between the date when the work was originally composed by Jane Austen and when she made the fair copy.[8] An even later date, post-1809, is suggested by Marilyn Butler in the Jane Austen entry for the *Oxford Dictionary of National Biography* (2004).[9] Unluckily, Professor Butler seems to have been unaware of Catherine Austen's reference – indirect but unmistakable – to *Lady Susan* as one of the 'betweenities', a composition of the years 'when the nonsense was passing away, and before her wonderful talent had found it's (*sic*) proper channel'[10]– the 'proper channel' referring to the writing of the earliest of the six novels, *Sense and Sensibility* and *Pride and Prejudice*, which Jane Austen began working on in the later 1790's.[11] In this perspective, one has to ask how likely it is that at some time not earlier than 1810-12 – the dating Professor Butler proposes for *Lady Susan* – Jane Austen would revert to epistolary fiction, a form that she had tried and abandoned more than ten years before. 1810-11 was the very time she was preparing the two earliest novels for publication and from about February 1811 onwards she was engaged with *Mansfield Park*. And is it likely that a writer determined on getting into print would spend time on a *novella* when publishers were looking for three-volume novels? Moreover, an epistolary novel, a story in letters, a form by then outmoded? An author with an established reputation and a regular publisher at hand could get away with *novellas*, as Maria Edgeworth was successful with her *Tales of Fashionable Life*, two collections published in 1809 and 1812. But could an unknown? There is a case for arguing that Jane Austen carried out superficial improvements to *Lady Susan* when she made the fair copy around 1805. These could include adding the 'Conclusion', a hasty tying-up of the story's loose ends. It is significant that for this final section, Jane Austen abandons the letter form, – indeed, opens with a joke about the expense of continuing the 'Correspondence'[12] – and turns to direct narrative, a change possibly indicating the distance in time between the body of *Lady Susan* and its ending; and it confirms the family dating, placing its composition ten or twelve years earlier. In this chronology *Lady Susan* stands as a transitional work, a 'betweenity'. Following the last of the juvenilia, which are dated June 1793, it precedes 'Elinor & Marianne', the original version of *Sense and Sensibility*, a novel, according to Caroline Austen, '*first* written in letters, and so read to her family'.[13]

The singular importance of *Lady Susan*, however, is not as a specimen in the history of Jane Austen's development, instructive as it can be from that point of view. For *Lady Susan* stands alone in the body of Jane Austen's work as a highly accomplished and tightly focused study of a single character, a women free of moral constraints and bent on domination, a figure of fascination and wit, in her high moments 'gay and triumphant',[14] commanding the work from beginning to end. In style and finish – its 'frosty sparkle', to quote Mary Lascelles[15] – it is a remarkable accomplishment and in its concentration of focus quite free from the fumblings and uncertainties we would expect to find in apprentice work. Richardson's inordinate length – what Henry Austen called 'the errors of his prolix style and tedious narrative'[16]– was warning enough. The central action of the story, generated by Lady Susan's duplicities and manœuvres, is conducted over a period of only three months and is delivered briskly with a strong dramatic sense. Jane Austen had also taken positive lessons from her close knowledge of Richardson's *Sir Charles Grandison*: that dialogue, even in letters, could be set down as spoken; and, further, that an epistolary structure could be exploited to advantage, playing off one correspondent against another, with facts twisted or concealed, as we see in Lady Susan's duplicitous letters to Mrs Vernon; these, in turn, undercut by the perceptive accounts that Mrs Vernon sends her mother; and further deceptions and plans disclosed in the frank and self-revealing letters Lady Susan sends to Mrs Johnson, her London friend and confidante. This interplay of letter-voices, also involving Reginald and his father, and, once, Lady Susan's daughter, is the opportunity Jane Austen makes to explore a virtuoso range of tones and styles.

Some literary historians believe that Jane Austen was indebted to *La Liaisons Dangereuses* (1782) by Laclos: in the predatory character of Madame de Merteuil, the female rake; and, technically, in the pattern of contrasting voices woven into the correspondence.[17] Lady Susan has also been seen as a type of the 'merry widow' character of Restoration comedy – notably Wycherley, Etherege and Congreve – who reappears later in comedies and novels of the eighteenth-century, plays which Jane Austen herself had seen or taken part in at Steventon and novels which she had read.[18] And these earlier works provided Jane Austen with models or elements that she could use: the sophisticated and charming flirt, the tyrannical mother, the daughter to be sacrificed for a profitable marriage, the foolishly proud young man tempted and deceived by an adventuress, the family concern for his possible disgrace, the judicious ending with the villainess unmasked, her manœuvrings and machinations collapsed, the son of the house wiser for his experience and rewarded with the daughter he has saved. The fashionable world of Lady Susan, Mrs Johnson and Sir James Martin, with its Town values and dissipation, is worsted by the integrity and principle of family life in the country. Nothing here is new. These are the somewhat melodramatic furnishings of sentimental fiction, material to be laughed at, and they confirm *Lady Susan*'s eighteenth-century origin, at a distance from the world of Emma Watson. Yet Jane Austen's central figure is realised in terms which are wholly individual. Lady Susan carries no trace of being a composite or derivative character-type and the nearest hint of a precursor comes in one of Jane Austen's own earlier pieces, 'Leseley Castle: An unfinished novel in letter', dating from 1792, in which there is the outline of 'Cunning' Louisa Burton, a young woman whose 'extraordinary beauty' and other calculated attractions of 'Manners' and 'address' disguise her 'real Character' and 'natural disposition' under a 'mask'. Acting 'plausibly' and 'cautiously' in fulfilling 'her father's schemes', her true nature is unsuspected; and, falling for her wiles, the son of the house is married within a month.[19] But there is no antecedence here; Lady Susan is delivered to us as a character newly-drawn; and it comes as no surprise to find a line of naive supposition, extending from the 1870's onwards, that in order to portray such a figure, Jane Austen must have based Lady Susan on someone known to the family, either a society woman, a tyrannical Mrs Craven from the past;[20] or, from her own time, Eliza de Feuillide, a flirtatious cousin who swept into the Austen household in 1786 and eleven years later married Jane's brother Henry.[21] Other speculation in the critical literature has seen *Lady Susan* as a sketch for *Mansfield Park*, its heroine a proto-Mary Crawford.[22]

Notwithstanding its polish and sophistication, in one respect at least *Lady Susan* does carry a distinct immaturity, a weakness that betrays its proximity to the juvenilia. The later novels are populated with characters substantial enough to challenge and counter the heroine, who is called upon, as part of her progress, to assess and re-assess herself and others around her. In *Lady Susan*, however, no other character is substantial enough to provide such resistance: Frederica, the tyrannised daughter, is given a single letter and Lady Susan can ridicule her schoolgirl rebellion; Reginald is too easily captivated; and Mrs Vernon, deeply prejudiced from the outset, remains a helpless bystander to the end. So although Lady Susan is defeated through the workings of the plot, as a character she remains unchallenged and her character unchanging. In effect, there is no collision of wills, no contest of personalities, no cause on her part for thought or inward reflection. In this young writer's *tour de force*, we are faced with a brilliant character sketch, not a rounded character;

and a figure, moreover, quite out of balance in so wholly dominating the work. As Margaret Drabble puts it, 'Lady Susan does too much of the talking, and runs away with the novel'[23] – entertainingly so, one would add. Nonethless, Jane Austen recognised that *Lady Susan* represented an artistic dead-end, a trial she was not to repeat.

Notes

1   'Preface', *Memoir* (1871), p. vi.
2   Ibid., [p. 295].
3   Ibid., [p. 201].
4   p. 89.
5   [p.ix].
6   *Jane Austen in Context*, ed Janet Todd (Cambridge: Cambridge University Press, 2005), p. 15.
7   According to Gilson, *Lady Susan* was 'written about 1805' (p. 374).
8   The confusion seems to have come about in this way: in Chapman's Oxford edition of 1925, there is no discussion of the dating question, simply the title-page statement: 'Written about 1805'. The nearest he comes to discussing the question is in *Jane Austen: Facts and Problems* (1948). Referring to the 1805 watermark, he explained that this 'really proves no more than that at some time in, or not long after, 1805 Jane Austen was still sufficiently interested in the piece to be at the trouble of making a copy of it', since at a time when paper was relatively expensive, 'it was unlikely that any considerable quantity of it would remain unused in a family given to writing' (pp. 49-50). There can be no mistake, Chapman is talking about the transcription of *Lady Susan*, not about its composition. Unfortunately, this distinction was lost when he next gave a date. In *Jane Austen: A Critical Bibliography* (1954, 2nd edn 1955), the date for *Lady Susan* is given as 'c.1805' (p. 12). Chapman repeats this date in the first edition of the *Minor Works* volume (pp. vii, [243]). Presumably, in giving the 1805 date, Gilson was simply following Chapman's lead. Chapman's theory about the rapid use of paper in the Austen family can be tested against the precise dates we have. These point to Jane Austen's storing paper for up to four

or five years: the paper for the two chapters of *Persuasion* carries the watermark 1812, and Jane Austen gives her beginning and ending dates on the manuscript as 8 and 18 July 1816; some of the paper for *Sanditon* is watermarked 1812, some 1815, and, similarly, Jane Austen gives her beginning date 27 January and 18 March 1817 at the end.

9 Vol. 2, p. 969. Professor Butler argues the same case, with a fuller literary discussion, in the *London Review of Books*, 5 March 1998, p. 6.

10 Letter to James Edward Austen-Leigh, 1 April?1869 (M, p. 186).

11 The record of these versions is in Cassandra Austen's note, reproduced *MW*, facing p. 243 and discussed in *LM*, pp. 52-54.

12 p. 166.

13 'Memory is treacherous, but I cannot be mistaken in saying that Sense and Sensibility was *first* written in letters – *&* so read to her family', Caroline Austen, Letter to James Edward Austen-Leigh, 1 April?1869 (M, p. 185).

14 *MW*, p. 291.

15 *Jane Austen and her Art* (1939), p. 99.

16 'Biographical Notice', p. 7.

17 Laclos' influence is well discussed in Roger Gard, *Jane Austen's Novels: The Art of Clarity.*

18 See Jay Arnold Levine, '*Lady Susan*: Jane Austen's Character of the Merry Widow' (*Studies in English Literature* (1961), vol. 1, no. 4, pp. 23-34.

19 *MW*, pp. 116-19.

20 In 1920, Mary Augusta Austen-Leigh (1838-1922), a daughter of James Edward, declared *Lady Susan* to be a 'Study from Life' (*Personal Aspects of Jane Austen* (1920), p. 104) on the grounds that the young writer would have needed a real-life model in order to draw a character as 'vicious' as Lady Susan (Ibid., p. 100). A somewhat similar line of argument was implied by her brother William (1843-1921) and nephew Richard (1871-1962) in the *Life and Letters* (pp. 80-81). Mary Augusta then quoted an (unidentified) 'family MS.', telling the story of 'the cruel Mrs.—' who tyrannised her daughters (*Personal Aspects*, pp. 100-02). We now know that this was Mrs Craven, the maternal grandmother of Martha and Mary Lloyd, the

second wives of James and Francis Austen. The details are recounted by James's daughter Caroline in her *Reminiscences* (Chawton: The Jane Austen Society, 1986), pp. 7-9).

21 For the Eliza de Feuillide/Lady Susan identification, see *LM*, pp.145-46.

22 Most fully developed in Q.D.Leavis, 'A Critical Theory of Jane Austen's Writings: II "Lady Susan" into "Mansfield Park"' (*Scrutiny* (October 1941, January 1942), vol. 10, pp. 114-42, 272-94).

23 Introduction, *Lady Susan, The Watsons, Sanditon* (1974), p. 14.

*

LETTER 1

1. Lady Susan Vernon: Lady Susan carries a courtesy title as the daughter of an Earl, a Marquess or a Duke of the English peerage. There was an existing Vernon family – notable, of long standing and widespread – resident in Staffordshire, a part-industrial county in the North Midlands famed for its potteries and their product, Staffordshire ware, referred to in *NA* as 'the clay of Staffordshire' (vol. 2, ch. 7). Almost 150 miles from London, JA spoke of it as 'a good way off' (*L*, p. 37). This is the location of Vernon Castle, Lady Susan's former home (Letter 16).

2. My dear Brother: a familiar form of address to a brother-in-law. Lady Susan's late husband, Frederic, was a brother of Charles Vernon.

3. introduced to a Sister: sister-in-law.

4. too much into society…state of mind: Widows were expected to mourn the death of their husbands for not less than two years. Lady Susan is still in the first period, lasting a year-and-a-day, of deep or full mourning, followed by a further year of half or second mourning. These stages were regulated by an elaborate protocol of mourning dress and conduct. In the first year, widows were expected to lead a life of retirement. Hence Lady Susan's comment on the Manwarings' going 'too much into society' for her 'present situation'. The protocol of mourning conduct arises later, in Letter 30.

JA discusses her own mourning dress following the death of Edward Austen's wife, Elizabeth, in Octoberv 1808 (letter to Cassandra, 15-16 October 1808, *L*, pp. 47-48.)

5. your delightful retirement: home of seclusion and privacy.

6. the Governess: usually a poor gentlewoman, employed and resident in a family, often at the level of an upper servant (see Letter 6), charged with the education and upbringing in morals and conduct of the younger children and girls.

7. one of the best Private Schools: were usually small, run for profit and conducted by their owners – in this case, as we hear later, a Miss Summers. Located in Wigmore Street, off Cavendish Square, the school is well placed to attract 'Girls' from 'all of the best Families'. This was a very fashionable part of London just north of Oxford Street: an area, together with Mayfair – south of Oxford Street – of London's 'best addresses' at this time (Pevsner, 1968, p. 412). So it is for social rather than educational reasons that Lady Susan describes the school as one of the 'best', admitting that she has chosen it to provide her daughter with 'good connections' and 'those **accomplishments** which are now necessary to finish a pretty Woman', to train her in the 'Grace & Manner' required of a society woman and wife. Board and education in private schools around London cost between sixteen and thirty-five guineas a year, whereas a school such as Miss Summers', centrally placed and socially elite, would cost upwards of a hundred guineas, plus extras such as an entrance fee to the school and further charges for visiting teachers for dancing, drawing, French etc. Hence Lady Susan's complaint that 'The price is immense'.

8. in Town: London, in particular the fashionable West End, as distinct from the commercial City section to the east.

9. not to be denied admittance: Lady Susan raises the possibility that she will be unwelcome as a guest for reasons of social and family protocol: as we learn in Letter 2, 'The Females of the Family are united against' her on account of her reputation for 'general flirtation'.

LETTER 2

1. to be discreet…to be as quiet as possible: restrained, on account of the protocols of deep mourning.

2. make proposals to me: an offer of marriage.

3. his throwing her off: disowning her, just as Mr Collins advises Mr Bennet 'to throw off' his 'unworthy child' Lydia after her elopement with Wickham (*P&P*, vol. 3, ch. 6). Mr Johnson was Mrs Manwaring's godfather up to the time of her marriage.

4. No.10 Wigmore St.: just north of Oxford Street, presumably this is the address of Miss Summers' school, which Lady Susan is proposing as their rendez-vous. According to Boyle's *Fashionable Court Guide* in 1793, this house was occupied by a Mrs Goddard, the name that JA uses in *E* for the 'mistress' of the school at Highbury (vol. 1, ch. 3).

5. that insupportable spot: that unbearable place.

LETTER 3

1. spending the Christmas with you: amongst the gentry the celebration of Christmas livened up from the 1750's onwards. It was regarded principally as a holiday festival, a family gathering; and with their household enlarged with visitors the Austens at Steventon took the opportunity to put on plays at the Rectory. In a Prologue written by James Austen in 1787, we read of the season's 'social' and 'festive' 'joys', 'the window' decked with 'rustic holly's…sober green' and the season's 'sports' and 'gambols' (James Austen, pp. 18-19). Of Christmas celebrations, JA uses the word 'Gaieties' in a letter of January 1801 (*L*, p. 68); these included carols, presents for the servants and children, charity to the poor and a turkey (the last two mentioned by JA in a letter of November 1813 (*L*, p. 197), Christmas pudding, plum cake, exotic foods such as black butter and preserved ginger and, to quote JA in December 1798, the wishing of 'merry Christmas' (*L*, p. 30). Christmas trees were a later innovation, after JA's time.

2. so speedy a mark of distinction: a polite mark of attention.

3. first in agitation: in prospect.

LETTER 4

1. the most accomplished Coquette: a woman experienced and skilful at winning the admiration and affection of men out of vanity, the appetite to conquer, or for her own amusement. A familiar figure in eighteenth-century drama and fiction.

2. at Hurst & Wilford: these are invented place names.

3. not even Manners: the knowledge of polite behaviour in good society.

4. Where Pride & Stupidity unite,…worthy notice: delivered in a smart, epigrammatic, Johnsonian style, this means that someone proud and stupid is not capable of any deception worth noticing.

LETTER 5

1. She is perfectly well bred: socially skilled and well-mannered, a concept that derives from the mid-eighteenth century notion of 'good breeding'. In turn, this originated in *Some Thoughts Concerning Education* (1693) by the philosopher John Locke: 'that decency and gracefulness of Looks, Voice, Words, Motions, Gestures, and of all the whole outward Demeanour, which takes in Company, and makes those with whom we converse, easie and well pleased' (Section 200). Locke's ideas, influential in forming the social and cultural values of the age, circulated most widely via Lord Chesterfield's *Letters to his Son Philip Stanhope* (1774), republished and soon adapted in such conduct books as *The Principles of Politeness* (1775), *The Fine Gentleman's Etiquette* and *Some Advice on Men and Manners* (both 1776). Chesterfield sent Stanhope a marked-up copy of Locke's book, commending his 'stress' on 'good breeding' which, in turn, is a topic that he retails throughout the *Letters*, a book that became the Bible of manners in society and was constantly reprinted down the eighteenth century and beyond.

In essence, Chesterfield defined 'good breeding' as a matter of diplomacy and social accommodation: of pleasing other people and fitting in with them, of adjusting to the society around one: 'Good breeding is the natural result of common-sense, and common observation. Common sense points out civility [politeness], and observation teaches you the manner of it, which makes it good breeding' (letter dated 23 March 1746, *Letters* (1932), vol. 3, p. 753). In Richardson's *Sir Charles Grandison* (1753-54), Harriet Byron observes good-breeding in the hero's relaxed sociability, his attentiveness to new acquaintance, and his 'easy, yet manly politeness' in 'dress' and 'address' (vol. 1, letter 36).

2. an illiberal spirit: an ungenerous and unforgiving nature.

3. Dignity should be lessened…Family Estate: by the custom of primogeniture the inheritance of family property and estates passed down from eldest son to eldest son. Any departure from this custom – as it would be if Lady Susan's late husband had sold Vernon Castle to his younger brother, Mr Vernon – would reflect badly on both his financial competence and the honour of the family. So the sale of Vernon Castle 'elsewhere' ie to someone unnamed, outside the family, was a last resort, brought about by extravagance on Lady Susan's part (rather than her husband's), since, as we learn in Letter 1, he endured a 'long illness'.

4. his name in a Banking House: as a named partner in a bank, just as JA's brothers Henry and Francis started out in 1801 as named partners in the London banking house of Austen, Maunde & Austen With various partners, Henry prospered and opened branches in Alton and elsewhere, remaining a banker until his concerns were hit by the post-war slump and he was declared bankrupt in the spring of 1816.

5. with the greatest sensibility: in the later eighteenth-century cult, both literary and social, sensibility denoted a refined awareness of one's own feelings and to the feelings of others. Valued highly as the expression of a rare, superior and sensitive nature, it was a quality much celebrated in the heroines of sentimental fiction and sometimes in the heroes as well. In the Juvenilia, JA parodied the absurd and comic extremes to which the cult of sensibility was pushed in contemporary literature and fashionable manners.

6. under cover to you: as an additional sheet within a letter addressed to Mrs Johnson. The letter itself would not come inside an envelope but consisted of a folded sheet or sheets, sealed either with sealing wax or a wafer (a moistened sliver of dried glue) carrying the impress of the sender's seal, and addressed on the outside.

LETTER 6

1. She is really excessively pretty: 'excessively' was then in vogue, meaning very or extremely, but not necessarily indicating any excess whatsoever. In the novels, JA employs the word in dialogue to suggest the looseness and imprecision of a character's language and thought.

2. Symmetry, Brilliancy and Grace: JA may be alluding to a line in 'Bleeding Rock', a popular, anthologised (and now forgotten) poem by Hannah More: 'Hers every charm of symmetry and grace' (1776, 1816, p. 233).

Symmetry was the bodily quality of being well-proportioned, shading into the emotional quality of being well-balanced. It was a conventional requirement for heroines of fiction. Accordingly, that the 'critical eye' of Mr Darcy detects 'more than one failure of perfect symmetry' in her 'form' (*P&P*, vol. 1, ch. 6) redounds to Elizabeth Bennet's credit.

Brilliancy could be considered to be an external or superficial quality, slightly suspect, usually found in a man's 'wit' or a lady's 'eyes' (as in Letter 17). Hugh Blair (1718-1800) one of the leading eighteenth-century authorities on rhetoric, judged 'brilliancy' to be 'affected' or 'false' (*Lectures*, 1783, vol. 1, lecture 2), as in Lady Susan's use of the word reported by MrsVernon in Letter 24.

Grace: here gracefulness, a physical quality of bodily movement, of the limbs and bodily form. Blair refers the reader to *The Analysis of Beauty* (1753) by William Hogarth, the 'Line of Grace', 'a wavering curve', being one of the two lines constituting 'Beauty' (*Lectures*, vol. 2, lecture 5); and Hogarth also described this 'Line' as being the 'only one precise serpentine-line' (1997, p. 51).

3. Her address to me: both a person's manner and physical bearing towards other people, especially upon meeting and mixing with them. Conduct books for young ladies recommend a facial expression conveying openness, amiability, cheerfulness and pleasure at their company; and, for example, towards men of higher rank, a manner of 'calm, dignified respect' – advice that comes in a handbook of Regency etiquette for women, *The Mirror of Graces* (1811, p. 203), which devotes four chapters to the whole area of 'deportment' including 'address'. Chesterfield emphasised gracefulness as an important quality of a gentleman's address.

4. a happy command of Language: a talent traditionally attributed to the Ancients ie the writers of classical Greece and Rome, and valued highly by period's two authorities on rhetoric, George Campbell (1719-96) and Hugh Blair. Lady Susan exhibits this skill in making 'Black appear White' and in her elegant and forceful turn of phrase.

5. left in Staffordshire: See Letter 1, note 1. In this passage, JA's readers would identify a recurrent theme in eighteenth-century literature: the contrast between the simplicity and probity of country living and the gay frivolity and excess of fashionable London life.

LETTER 7

1. by sending her to Edward S^t: the rather awkward phrasing here can be re-worded: 'by sending to Edward St. for her'. Edward Street is now Langham Place, running due north of Oxford Circus.

2. the grand affair of Education: female education was the subject of much philosophical and political discussion at this time. Beyond the 'practical', 'domestic' and 'useful' skills in preparation for married life and for conducting a household, did girls need any education beyond the three r's? Or did they deserve, equally with men, a training and broadening of the mind, what Lady Susan describes, derisively, as 'the prevailing fashion of acquiring a perfect knowledge in all the Languages Arts & Sciences'? Or was its main purpose to provide a grooming for marriage, for mixing in society, and for attracting the right man, with an emphasis upon ornament, performance and display, upon polishing and 'perfecting' the **'accomplishments'** identified here by Lady Susan as 'now necessary to finish a pretty Woman....French, Italian, German, Music, Singing, Drawing'?

The voices of opposition included Catharine Macaulay – 'Confine not the education of your daughters to what is regarded as the ornamental parts of it' (*Letters on Education*, 1790, p. 50) – and Mary Wollstonecraft, arguing that boys and girls should be educated together. In the 1790's the debate on these issues can be followed in the pages of the *The Lady's Magazine* and other women's periodicals of the time. Two or three years earlier, in the opening pages of 'Catharine' (1792), in *Volume the Third*, JA mounted her strongest attack on 'accomplishments' both directly and in the person of Camilla Stanley.

3. *my* hand & arm, & a tolerable voice: it was accepted that for an unmarried young woman, playing a harp or piano, and singing at a social gathering was as much an opportunity for showing off her physical charms as displaying musical abilities.

4. a perfect knowledge: Lady Susan was not alone in fearing that a young lady with such mastery of a subject would be regarded as an immodest female 'prodigy', an object of wonder, curiosity and even fearfulness among likely suitors, rather than admiration. It was view shared by some of the leading 'conduct' writers of the time, including Dr John Gregory (*A Father's Legacy to his Daughters*, 1774), Hester Chapone (*Letters on the Improvement of the Mind Addressed to a Young Lady*, 1777) and Jane West (*Letters to a Young Lady*, 1806).

5. to her list: at a ball, a lady kept a written list of gentlemen who had engaged in advance to dance with her.

6. his application by a Line: a proposal of marriage with an encouraging letter.

7. overture: an early step in making a proposal of marriage.

LETTER 8

1. open weather: a sportsman's term for fine, dry and frost-free weather, ideal for the hounds following the fox's scent and giving the horses firm going across country.

2. Sussex: an agricultural county south of London, good for hunting.

3. send for his Horses: a hunting man would maintain his own stable of trained horses – referred to here properly as 'Hunters' – at his country home and would bring several with him when staying elsewhere in fox-hunting country during the season. This lasted from the beginning of November to the end of March.

4. a degree of fascination: as we see in Johnson, a word carrying considerable force: 'The power or act of bewitching; enchantment; unseen inexplicable influence'.

5. neither to Delicacy: regard for another's feelings.

LETTER 9

1. certainly entailed: the effect of the entail was to settle the estate's line of inheritance, legally and unalterably, on a specified heir, con-ventionally the eldest son, or, as in *P&P*, the nearest male relative young enough to continue the line with his own prospective children. The many complexities of this arrangement are indicated by Guenter Treitel in *Jane Austen and the Law* (2006).

2. *his* emancipation: freedom; here, Mr Manwaring's freedom from the bonds of marriage. Johnson gives us 'The act of setting free; deliverance from slavery'; and since Jane Austen was probably at work on *LS* in the 1790's, when the emancipation movement was in full swing, we cannot rule out the possibility of a veiled *double-entendre* here, quite within Mrs Johnson's compass to make such a joke with an intimate such as Lady Susan.

LETTER 10

1. the immediate influence of Intellect: intelligence.

LETTER 12

1. do not admit of: do not allow.

2. You must be sensible: aware.

3. most interesting to your connections: in the archaic sense of 'of concern to' your relations and friends.

4. an absolute engagement: a firm, definite engagement.

5. want of character: bad name

6. deep Art: profound artfulness. Johnson defines 'deep' as 'Full of contrivance' and 'art' as 'cunning'.

7. out of my power...the family Estate: see Letter 9, note 1. The entail is effected by a legal instrument, known as a 'strict settlement' which is irrevocable.

8. My ability of distressing: in the quasi-legal sense of depriving him of financial support. During his father's lifetime, it was usual for the eldest son or heir of a landed gentleman to receive an allowance, so freeing him from the need to take paid employment.

9. every comfort of my life: in Johnson's sense of 'Consolation; support under calamity or danger'.

10 that honest Pride: in Johnson's definition: 'just, righteous'.

11. Mr Smith's intelligence: news, information.

LETTER 13
1. the late shocking reports: recent.

LETTER 14
1. I can have no veiw: no purpose, or intention. The 'ei' spelling is JA's.

2. her conduct have been doubtful: not in the modern sense of being dubious or suspect but as Johnson puts it, 'not yet determined or decided... uncertain'.

3. on the catch for a husband: on the look out.

4. make a worthy Man completely miserable: a play on the saying 'the happy man' for a man whose marriage proposal has been accepted or a husband newly-married, a phrase that JA used as the sub-title for her little dramatic skit *Sir Charles Grandison* written in the early 1790's as a joke on her favourite novel, Richardson's *The History of Sir Charles Grandison* (1753-54).

5. must acquit her on that article: excuse her on that point or accusation. Derived from legal terminology: a formal indictment is drawn up in individual articles or charges.

6. every Mind of common candour: according to Johnson, 'candour' is 'Sweetness of temper; purity of mind; openness...kindness'. 'common candour' can be understood as the fairness or impartiality normally to be expected.

LETTER 15

1. to have been unexceptionable: perfectly satisfactory.

2. a perverse girl: obstinate and self-willed.

3. strolling along the Shrubbery: an area of the garden close to the house given over to a display of ornamental trees, flowering bushes and shrubs and flowers, many of them exotica, reflecting the botanical interests of the period. Designed for relaxation, shrubberies had rapidly-draining gravelled paths which allowed for walking in all weathers, a quality which JA emphasises in the novels: *S&S* draws attention to 'the dry gravel of the shrubbery' (vol. 3, ch. 6); and when Sir Thomas Bertram finds Fanny Price in her attic-room, shivering and fireless in mid-winter, with 'snow on the ground', he suggests that she 'go out for an hour on the gravel' 'as the dryest place' (*MP*, vol. 3, ch. 1).

4. commit the event to a Higher Power: leave to the workings of Providence, the earthly operation of the divine will. JA may be alluding satirically to similarly melodramatic invocations of the 'Higher Power' in two contemporary novels by Ann Radcliffe: *A Sicilian Romance* (1790), vol. 2, ch. 9 and *The Mysteries of Udolpho* (1794), vol. 4, ch. 9. In *NA*, Henry Tilney claims to 'have read all Mrs.Radcliffe's works, and most of them with great pleasure' (vol. 1, ch. 14).

LETTER 16

1. liberal spirit of Manwaring: 'liberal' carries no political significance and denotes someone with the education and outlook befitting a gentleman, in this situation being open-minded and generous in his views.

2. He has been teizing me: bothering.

3. into this country: a phrase commonly used in hunting circles for an area designated as the territory of a hunt; or, more loosely, 'this part of the country'.

4. lodging somewhere near me *incog*: a colloquial abbreviation of incognito, identity concealed or disguised, usually found in the context of comedy. The essayist Joseph Addison included *incog*. in a list of words 'miserably curtailed' according to the fashion of the time. Although

Addison first made this pronouncement in the *Spectator* long ago (no. 135, 4 August 1711), the journal was familiar to Austen's readers. Much reprinted, its contributors were highly regarded as providing models of good English style and giving sound advice. In *The Philosophy of Rhetoric* (1776) George Campbell repeated Addison's judgement, placing 'incog.' in a list of 'barbarisms' and 'affected terms' arising 'from the abbreviation of polysyllables' (vol. 1, bk. 2, ch. 3, sect. 1).

LETTER 17

1. in her Academy: since the word was normally applied to societies of the learned and distinguished – the Royal Academy, Academie Francaise – this was a somewhat pretentious, yet widely used, term for a school to employ.

2. This pathetic representation: Johnson: 'public exhibition'; performance.

3. neither so fair: a pale complexion was valued as a social indicator: it signalled the facial care of the toilette and the unexposed life of the lady, in contrast to the exposed and sunburnt complexion of the lower orders.

4. blooming as Lady Susan's: healthy in appearance.

5. her temper is untractable: an obsolete form of intractable, unmanageable.

6. nothing satisfactory transpires: emerges. Johnson: 'To escape from secrecy to notice: a sense lately innovated from France without necessity'.

7. The small Pianoforte: as distinct from the large or grand piano, the 'small' version, sometimes known as the square piano, was the invention of Johannes Zumpe c.1760, with later technical developments from the 1770's onwards, many of them introduced by John Broadwood. Some models were built disguised as side- or dressing-tables. The 'square pianoforte' that arrives for Jane Fairfax comes from 'Broadwood's'(*E*, vol. 2, ch. 8).

LETTER 19

1. proceeding directly by the stage: stage coach, so-called because the horses were changed at coaching-inns at stages every twelve miles or so along the road. There, travellers could board or leave the coaches or take refreshments.

2. it was atchieved: JA's spelling.

3. most flattering prognostics: the sarcastic tone of Lady Susan's remarks in these lines can be gauged by the fact that 'prognostics', predictions, was a term usually found in a medical context relating to symptoms.

4. parade of propriety: an excessive display of social sensibilities.

5. a peice of nicety: scrupulousness. The 'ei' spelling is JA's.

6. all this Lenity: lenience; Johnson, 'mercy'.

7. & canvassed by: debated, discussed.

LETTER 20

1. in the breakfast room: or breakfast parlour ('parlour' indicating a room occupied by the family), for less formal meals, or fewer people than warranted the use of the dining-room. It was also used as a morning sitting room.

2. his person & address: the 'person' is the appearance, bodily figure; for 'address', see Letter 6, note 3.

3. put on our Pelisses: sometimes known as greatcoats, 'pelisses' were outdoor cloaks, loosely-fitting, with or without sleeves, knee- to ankle-length and cut to follow the high-waisted line of a woman's dress fashionable at this time. Usually of silk or velvet, they could be made of heavier materials and lined and trimmed and worn all year round. In 1800-04 they returned to fashion with sleeves and a collar.

4. of an amiable disposition: Johnson gives 'pleasing', not the modern 'friendly.'

5. too much of the *Rattle*: someone who chatters 'incessantly in a lively or thoughtless manner' (*OED*). Italicised by JA possibly because she had in mind a character in Fanny Burney's *Cecilia* (1782) – chapter 6, entitled 'A Rattle', in which the rattler, Lady Honoria Pemberton, is introduced.

6. from any cause in suspense: Johnson: 'Held in doubt; held in expectation'.

7. who in connection: a family 'connection'.

8. to a fortunate Establishment: settlement in marriage.

9. I am not apt to deal in professions: given to producing ready declarations.

10. **sacrificed to Policy**: expediency.
11. **the greatest consciousness**: self-consciouness.

LETTER 21

1. **no better than equivocation**: deceit.
2. **the unspeakable great kindness**: quite the opposite of the modern sense of being 'unspeakably bad'.

LETTER 22

1. **tho' extremely gallant**: polite and attentive, as in the manner of a gentleman courting.
2. **Sir James was no Solomon**: a sensible or wise man, from the ancient King Solomon of Israel (d. c.930 BC) who became a by-word for justice and wisdom.
3. **a Chit, a Child**: a belittling term for a girl, conveying a degree of contempt or superiority.
4. **afterwards sufficiently keen**: Johnson: 'Severe; piercing'.

LETTER 23

1. **his mind is interested**: he is concerned.

LETTER 24

1. **your interrupting the Diabolical scheme**: Lady Susan's language begins to take on religious overtones, soon to be deepened in her reference to 'everlasting Misery', this being the torments of hell and to 'Earthly Duty', describing a mother's care for her child as a duty enjoined by God. 'diabolical schemes' were also employed in the plotting of popular melodramatic novels, a notable example being *Charlotte: A Tale of Truth* (1791), a best-seller by Susanna Rowson (vol. 2, ch. 27). JA uses 'diabolical' only once again, in one of the melodramatic chapters of S&S (vol. 3, ch. 8), the scene of Elinor's interview with Willoughby.
2. **any application to you**: approach.
3. **this Heroine in distress**: Frederica characterized as the distressed heroine, a familiar stock figure out of sentimental or Gothic fiction.
4. **would have sensibly hurt me**: deeply, intensely.
5. **to my own Character**: reputation.

LETTER 25
1. **condescension was necessary**: submissiveness.

LETTER 26
1. **unadvisable for them to meet**: the first two definitions of 'unadvisable' given in Johnson carry the idea of antagonism: 'To encounter; to close face to face.' 'To encounter in hostility.' This meeting might be to enter upon a duel.
2. **he is going for his health to Bath**: the ancient spa town of Bath, in Somerset (now in Avon), its mineral waters thought curative for many conditions, including **gout**. This was an extremely painful joint inflammation, commonly of the big toe, caused by the deposit of sodium urate, and usually attributed to drinking wine and beer.
3. **laid up with**: incapacitated with.
4. **Drawingroom-apartment**: a set of furnished rooms, including a formal reception room for visitors.
5. **Upper Seymour St**: running westwards off Portman Square, north of Oxford Street. The Square was developed 1764-84, with house by the leading architects of the day, including Robert Adams and James Wyatt, and the streets leading off were equally fashionable, including Upper Seymour Street, whose householders in 1794 included the Bishop of Rochester, a General, three Colonels, a Baron and three titled Ladies. A reference to 'our charming House in Portman-square' in the juvenilia ('Lesley Castle', 1792), suggests that JA had personal knowledge of this part of London
6. **One title I know**: a member of the aristocracy, carrying a title.
7. **might have had**: by marriage.
8. **besides Baronets**: as well as baronets, the lowest of the hereditary titles, ranking as a commoner and taking precedence over all knights except Knights of the Garter.

LETTER 27
1. **for the benefit of Masters**: visiting teachers of deportment, dancing, drawing, music, French and other subjects and accomplishments beyond the basics of reading, writing and arithmetic.
2. **but her Principles**: moral principles.
3. **in Town this winter**: the Winter social season was the early months

of the full season which ran from 1 January to June, the month of the King's official birthday. During this period the landed gentry would customarily spend some time in London.

LETTER 28

1. to the Lakes: the English Lake District in Cumbria, a poplar tourist destination in north-east England since the mid-eighteenth century.

2. scarcely command myself: keep my temper.

LETTER 29

1. to be formal: punctilious, even stiff and stuffy, in matters of behaviour.

2. too old to be agreable, & too young to die: the wit and balance of these lines suggest that Lady Susan is invoking a well-known Augustan quotation. However, the closest literary source is a line from the Cavalier poet Thomas Carew (?1595–?1639): 'He is too faultless, and too young to die' ('To my Lord Admiral, on his Late Sickness, and Recovery').

2. I was even stagger'd: the past participle of to stagger; in Johnson: 'To hesitate; to fall into doubt; to become less confident or determined'.

LETTER 30

1. The convention was that a man and woman of marriagable status would need to be engaged before writing directly to one-another. By this measure, Lady Susan's letter to Reginald carries the presumption of considerable intimacy.

2. they require a delicacy: scrupulousness.

3. He has the right to require a woman of fortune in his daughter in law: refers to the expectation that a bride would bring a dowry proportionate to the fortune the groom has or will inherit. In the opening lines of MP, we are told that Maria Ward, the future Lady Bertram, 'with only seven thousand pounds', is calculated to be 'at least three thousand pounds short of any equitable claim to' Sir Thomas's 'handsome house and large income' (p.3).

4. so early a second marriage: at this point, Lady Susan has been a widow for ten months. As a year-and-a-day was the required period of deep mourning, and the mourning period extended for no less than two years, she has convention on her side in arguing for delay. See Letter 1, note 4.

5. Cruel as this sentence may appear: a pun on Lady Susan's part, referring back to the previous grammatical sentence and forwards to 'pronouncing it', as a judge would pronounce sentence upon a guilty defendant; a neat piece of word-play on JA's part, providing more evidence of the 'command of language' Lady Susan has been credited with.

6. & whose Sensibilities: delicacy of feeling, a stronger term than mere 'feelings', the word JA originally used in the ms.

7. seek amusement abroad: out and about, meeting people in company.

LETTER 33

1. This Eclaircissement: in origin, a French term used in the theatre referring to a crisis point or denouement, carrying with it the idea of a sudden dramatic revelation. By this time, it was well-established in English as a literary usage and employed with some frequency by Richardson. However, according to Campbell, its appearance in English was an example of 'Barbarism' and he cites it as one of those French words which 'lately introduced…greatly corrupt the simplicity of our tongue'; 'such words with us, look rather like strays than any part of our own property' (*Rhetoric*, 1776, vol. 1, bk. 2, ch. 3, sect. 1, part 2). The 8th edition of Johnson's *Dictionary* (1799) continues to classify it as a French word, meaning 'Explanation; the act of clearing up an affair by verbal expostulation'.

2. by such Manoeuvres: borrowed from French at the end of the 1750's, the word was first employed in English as a technical military term to describe deceptive tactics in sea and land warfare. By 1780, it was still in use at sea, but now more colloquially for a deceptive gambit, a ploy or subterfuge. Its earliest recorded use in an English social context, as here, is in a letter of 1792. Regarded as a thoroughly French loan-word, it did not find a place in the Johnson edition of 1799.

LETTER 35

1. to stagger your Esteem: literally, to make someone or something stagger, as we would say shake or undermine.

LETTER 40

1. **at no great distance**: lapse of time, soon.

CONCLUSION

1. **Post office Revenue**: postal charges, paid by the recipient, were calculated according to the distance and the number of sheets. Within London, prior to 5 April 1801 there was a penny letter post for a single sheet, thereafter after 2d. Outside London, charges were 3d. for a single sheet to an address up to 15 miles, rising to 17d. for the furthest inland distance of 700 miles.

2. **such unexampled attention**: unprecedented.

3. **alarm of an Influenza**: regarded as a highly infectious epidemic illness, its severity ranging widely, from the mild to the fatal. It was also known as 'catarrhal fever', which may explain Lady Susan's anxiety about 'her daughter's constitution'.

4. **talked, flattered & finessed**: the *OED* quotes *LS* as the earliest literary example: 'to bring or modify by finesse or delicate handling'. It probably came from the term 'finessing' used in card games for 'the endeavouring to gain an Advantage by Art and Skill' (Hoyle, 1745, p. 64). 'Finesse' is classified in Johnson as French and described as 'an unnecessary word which is creeping into the language'.

5. **abjuring all future attachments**: 'abjuring' was normally used in a legal context for disclaiming, repudiating.

6. **detesting the Sex**: short for 'the fair sex', a somewhat arch circumlocution for women, derived from the Anglo-French usage, 'le beau sexe', a fair or beautiful one. The English phrase was in general use from the seventeenth-century onwards.

The Watsons

The Watsons	probably 1804 to early 1805
Autograph manuscript	Part in Queen Mary College, University of London and part in Pierpont Morgan Library
Facsimile	No facsimile has yet been published. A page is reproduced as 'Manuscript Pages' I. A page is reproduced as the frontispiece of Chapman's Oxford edition (1927) and a page in Sutherland (2005), p. 138.

The Watsons was first published by James Edward Austen-Leigh in the second edition of the *Memoir* (1871). He was able to base his text on the original manuscript as it was then in the possession of his sister Caroline. Austen-Leigh found 'some obscurities and inaccuracies of expression… which the author would probably have corrected' and which he now took upon himself to correct.[1] These changes are not considerable. They amount to a tidying up and modernising in the presentation of the text, including the removal of irregularities and eccentricities in Jane Austen's spelling and punctuation, the introduction of paragraphing and the separation of dialogue. Austen-Leigh's edited text held sway until the Oxford University Press edition of 1927. For this, the editor, R.W.Chapman, returned to the original manuscript. Like *Lady Susan*, the manuscript is untitled and Austen-Leigh explains that *The Watsons* is of his own devising, 'for the sake of having a title by which to designate it'.[2] (During Jane Austen's lifetime, the as-yet unpublished *Persuasion* was known to the family as 'The Elliots' and Austen-Leigh seems to be following that precedent).

The manuscript is an uncompleted first draft, about 17,500 words. The pages are unnumbered, there are no chapter divisions, nor regular indication of paragraphing or dialogue. As a whole, the text is written in a small, neat, even hand, uniformly twenty-five lines to the page. The quantity of correction and revision varies from page to page, some pages are unchanged, others carry heavy alteration. The 44 leaves (the final verso is blank) are gathered in a bifolium (a single sheet folded in two) and eleven quires numbered by Jane Austen 1 to 11. The two leaves of the bifolium, written landscape, measure 5¼ x 7½ in., the remainder 7½ x 4¾ in. The paper is watermarked 1803. In quires 7, 9 and 10 there are three loose sheets (formerly pinned, possibly by Jane Austen), also watermarked 1803. One of these replaces a section of cancelled text, the other two are extensions to the existing text. Some pages have been irregularly trimmed along the top edge, with the loss of the upper strokes of letters.[3]

The manuscript was left by Jane Austen to Cassandra. On her death in 1845, it went to Caroline Austen (1805-80), younger daughter of James Austen, who left it to her nephew William Austen-Leigh (1843-1921). He divided the manuscript, donating the first twelve pages – six leaves, a bifolium and a quire of four leaves – to a Red Cross charity sale held at Christies in April 1915. From 1915-25, these leaves were owned by Alice, Lady Ludlow. In 1925, they were purchased by the London dealer Charles Sawyer, who tried, unsuccessfully, to re-unite them with the remainder of the manuscript. In December 1925, the six leaves were purchased by Pierpont Morgan and taken into the Library. On William Austen-Leigh's death in 1921, the larger part of the manuscript – thirty-eight leaves, in ten quires – went to his nephew Lionel and his three sisters. This section remained in family ownership until its sale at Sotheby's, 'The Property of Joan Austen-Leigh',[4] in July 1978, to be purchased by the British Rail Pension Fund. It was re-sold at Sotheby's in September 1988 to Sir Peter Michael who placed the manuscript on deposit with his old College, Queen Mary's, University of London.

Initially, with 'only the internal evidence of the style to guide me', Austen-Leigh felt unable to date the composition of *The Watsons*. However, he advised readers of the *Memoir*, 'on a close inspection of the original manuscript, the water-marks of 1803, and 1804, were found' and on that basis he supposed 'that it was composed at Bath, before' Jane Austen 'ceased to reside there in 1805'[5] – the actual date was 2 July 1806. In 1883, Austen-Leigh's niece, Fanny Caroline Lefroy (1820-85), was to provide a more precise dating: 'Somewhere in 1804' Jane Austen 'began "The Watsons", but her father died early in 1805 [27 January] and it was never finished'.[6] This statement is likely to be accurate if Fanny Lefroy was quoting Cassandra, who talked about *The Watsons* to her nieces, an item of information we gather from Austen-Leigh in an after-word added to the text.[7]

> When the author's sister, Cassandra, showed the manuscript of this work to some of her nieces, she also told them something of the intended story; for with this dear sister – though, I believe, with no one else – Jane seems to have talked freely of any work that she might have in hand. Mr. Watson was soon to die; and Emma to become dependent for a home on her narrow-minded sister-in-law and brother. She was to decline an offer of marriage from Lord Osborne, and much of the interest of the tale was to arise from Lady Osborne's love for Mr. Howard, and his counter affection for Emma, whom he was finally to marry.[8]

Given the story's promising start and Jane Austen's clear sense of the lines along which it was to continue, we are left wondering why *The Watsons* was abandoned at this early stage, perhaps a fifth of the way into the novel. There is the expectation of a 'merry widow' high comedy in Lady Osborne's pursuit of Mr Howard, almost twenty years her junior – 'very handsome' she is, and with 'all the Dignity of Rank'[9]– and further comedy, the sparks already flying, in Lord Osborne's clumsy pursuit of Emma (not unlike Darcy's early approaches to Elizabeth Bennet), and Tom Musgrave, Osborne's go-between, is an unpredictable and amusing loose cannon; and with three other unmarried sisters and brother Sam hopeful of Miss Edwards, there is plenty to anticipate in the way of marriage complications. Although Austen-Leigh admitted that he could give 'no satisfactory answer' to this question, nonetheless, he came up with his own 'guess, that the author became aware of the evil of having placed her heroine too low, in such a position of poverty and obscurity as, though not necessarily connected with vulgarity, has a sad tendency to degenerate into it' and he foresaw 'circumstances likely to be unfavourable to the refinement of a lady'.[10] Inevitably, Austen-Leigh's notions of 'vulgarity' and the ladylike are Victorian and they place both Jane Austen and Emma Watson in a false light. Jane Austen had no problem in placing Fanny Price in the 'poverty' of her Portsmouth home, in daily contact with a drunkard and foul-mouthed father and she returns to Mansfield Park no less ladylike in her ways than when she left. Neither is Emma Watson lowered by the impoverishment of her father's home at Stanton. Nor by the suburban vulgarity of her sister-in-law, Mrs Robert Watson: 'pleased with herself…for being now in possession of a very smart house in Croydon, where she gave genteel parties, & wore fine cloathes', 'pert & conceited' in her 'manners', and with 'continual smiles & very slow articulation…her constant resource when determined on pleasing', and eyeing Emma 'with much familiar curiosity & Triumphant Compassion'.[11] Nor by the aristocratic vulgarity of Lord Osborne, 'a very fine young man', attending the ball 'only because it was judged expedient for him to please the Borough', who distresses Emma with his attention, his staring and gaping 'without restraint';[12] and it is left to Emma to remark that he could be 'better bred' and behave in a more gentlemanly way.[13] Breaching good manners, he makes an unannounced social call on the Watsons; and in the face of his urging her to employ her female persuasiveness in obtaining a horse, Emma behaves, to borrow Austen-Leigh's term, with the full 'refinement of a lady', delivering a polite but silencing rebuke, in a 'manner…neither sententious nor sarcastic': 'Female Economy will do a great deal my Lord, but it cannot turn a small income into a large one.'[14]

Fanny Lefroy's wording for the date of *The Watsons* – 'but her father died early in 1805 and it was never finished'– suggests a direct connection between the abandonment of the novel and Mr Austen's death. It may be that this loss and the reduced circumstances of the Austen household in Bath – Mrs Austen now alone with her two unmarried daughters – were too painfully close to the fictional prospect of *The Watsons*. The death of their invalid father – like Mr Austen, a clergyman – leaves the four unmarried Watson daughters facing homelessness and poverty, with the grim alternatives of husband-hunting or finding work, subjects heatedly discussed in the fragment. Jane Austen may have felt unhappy with this degree of biographical/circumstantial proximity and disinclined to continue the story at this point in time. Her heroine is a girl of spirit and resilience, self-confident and no slave to convention, as we witness at the ball when she takes the hand of Charles Blake, a 'little scene' that Virginia Woolf found 'moving out of all proportion to its surface solemnity'.[15] But the closing pages of the fragment, with

Emma in her father's sick-room and at leisure to 'read & think',[16] sound a very different note – 'from being the life & Spirit of a House, where all had been comfort & Elegance, & the expected Heiress of an easy Independance, she was become of importance to no one, a burden on those, whose affection she c[d.] not expect, an addition in an house, already overstocked, surrounded by inferior minds with little chance of domestic comfort, & as little hope of future support.'[17] 'It was well for her that she was naturally chearful', Jane Austen adds.[18] But this comment does nothing to lift the melancholic mood; all that faces Emma is an invitation to Croydon; and it is easy to understand why Jane Austen should lay the manuscript aside at the time. This is an explanation that satisfied Mary Lascelles, probably Jane Austen's most thoughtful and well-informed biographer and critic. In Mr Austen's death, Miss Lascelles also saw 'the loss of his' much needed 'encouragement', and she referred to a further 'grievous' blow in the unexpected death of her friend and mentor, Mrs Lefroy, who had been killed in a riding accident only six weeks before.[19]

Yet these circumstances do nothing to explain Jane Austen's failure to return to the manuscript, just as she did to add a rounding-off 'Conclusion' to *Lady Susan*. Of course, the completion of *The Watsons* would have been a task of a different order. But over the next four or five years Jane Austen certainly had the time to carry this through. Until the family arrived at Chawton in July 1809, she had no major work in hand and there was ample time and opportunity to finish what would have been her fourth novel – *Sense and Sensibility* and *Pride and Prejudice*, the first and second, were prepared for publication at Chawton, and Benjamin Crosby, a London publisher, had already purchased the third, *Northanger Abbey* (under the name of *Susan*), in Spring 1803. So there was every incentive to continue the work.

One theory is that Jane Austen abandoned *The Watsons* altogether because she found the similarities between this fragment and her works-in-progress too close; for example, the aristocratic ill-manners of the Osbornes and, in *Pride and Prejudice*, Lady de Bourgh and Darcy, and a further likeness in the shaping of the plot, involving the awkward encounters between the high-born young man and the heroine, the latter with her bevy of unmarried sisters and an absent or near-absent father, all these features common to both novels. There is also the suggestion that Jane Austen saw material in *The Watsons* which could be salvaged and used to better advantage elsewhere. This was an idea that Austen-Leigh stamps on so emphatically in the 1871 *Memoir* that one suspects that it had already got an airing in the family: 'It could not have been broken up for the purpose of using the materials in another fabric'; and he gives as his opinion that, apart from a similarity between Mrs Robert Watson and Mrs Elton, 'it would not be easy to trace much resemblance between this and any of her subsequent works'.[20] In 1913, in the *Life and Letters*, the Austen-Leighs glanced at the idea of re-use, only to reject it as being 'a procedure…contrary to Jane Austen's invariable practice.'[21] But later critics persisted with this line of speculation. Dr Chapman judged that '*The Watsons* may with some plausibility be regarded as a sketch for Emma',[22] a supposition elaborated by Q.D.Leavis in 'A Critical Theory of Jane Austen's Writings: 1' (1941); and in a subsequent letter to the *Times Literary Supplement*, Mrs Leavis declared it as her belief that this method of re-cycling material was 'a process by which Jane Austen habitually worked'.[23] To their disadvantage, neither, it seems, were informed by Anne Thackeray's perceptive account of *The Watsons*, published in 1871, in which she recognises the integrity and individuality of the fragment as a forebear, not a material source, of *Pride and Prejudice* and *Emma*.[24] In the present day, Kathryn Sutherland has expressed her belief that 'Incidents and themes from the aborted fragment *The Watsons* are transported or recycled in *Mansfield Park* and *Emma*' and she supposes that *The Watsons* may not have been 'taken up and finished at a later date because it had been so effectively absorbed elsewhere.'[25]

We should not rule out the possibility that Jane Austen was simply dissatisfied with what she had done and regarded any attempt at its continuation as unrewarding. Virginia Woolf suggests that possibility when she concluded that 'the stiffness and bareness of the first chapters [of *The Watsons*] prove that she was one of those writers who lay their facts out rather baldly in the first version and then go back and back and back and cover them with flesh and atmosphere' with the aim of achieving what is not yet achieved here, 'another of those exquisite and apparently effortless introductions'.[26] Mary Lascelles also detected some difficulty: 'Jane Austen seems to be struggling with a peculiar oppression, a stiffness and heaviness that threaten her style', a problem she tries to shake off in moving towards 'shorter, more colloquial words' in the correction of the narrative and dialogue.[27]

The Watsons is the earliest of Jane Austen's pieces for which we have the working manuscript; and, as such, it has considerable value in revealing her procedures of composition. Whether she planned the work first on paper and established its outline and characters, or carried these elements in her head, we don't know, since no evidence of this kind survives. But at least we can judge from the state of the text and the general nature of the corrections and revisions that the story-line, plotting and characterisation were clearly planned from the outset. Including the section replaced and the two extensions, there are few changes to the text which seem to depart from what we can identify as the original scheme. Overall, allowing for some degree of brotherly *in memorialism*, this comes sufficiently close to Henry Austen's testimony that 'Every thing came finished from her pen; for on all subjects she had ideas as clear as her expressions were well chosen'.[28]

The fact that the manuscript is unpaginated, largely unparagraphed and without chapter divisions and the normal arrangement of dialogue, should not necessarily be taken as indications that it stands in a primitive state. The chapter divisions could be introduced when Jane Austen was further on with the text, perhaps soon after this opening section, and certainly by the time she came to make the fair copy. At that stage, her paramount concern would be for the legibility and correctness of the manuscript. Decisions on the text presentation would be made by the printer, remembering that many were printer-publishers, who expected to undertake far more in the way of formalising the text than is the practice to-day, a responsibility that could be left safely to the printing-house, since the compositors were used to such work and educated readers were employed to check the proofs for precisely these points.

Looking at the detail of the manuscript, we are able to distinguish between corrections, that is instant changes, made at the time of writing and entered neatly, along the line, and revisions, probably made soon after and entered, equally neatly, above the line, and indicated by caret marks. Examples of the immediate, along-the-line change can be seen in the transcription, f.10ᵛ: Jane Austen was in the act of writing 'he *poured* her wine' or perhaps 'a glass of wine' when she changed this to 'he *helped* her to wine', a word which is both more precise and more indicative of an appropriate politeness, given that Emma is a guest in the house; and eight lines below, 'a *better* rubber' becomes 'a *fairer* rubber', providing a more sharply defined quality to the conduct of the card-game. Many more revisions were made slightly later, probably when Jane Austen was reading over to herself the pages just completed. Also on f.10ᵛ: 'they were *set in for* their Desert' becomes 'they were *drawn round the fire to enjoy* their Desert' – here the rather abstract becomes spatial, localised and descriptive; and nine lines below, 'I *think* he wᵈ. enjoy it." *very much.*' becomes '*how much* he wd. enjoy it."'– a curtailment that brings an evident gain in expressive force, catching the energy and emphatic weight of Mr Edwardes' (elsewhere spelt Edwards) speaking voice. Belonging to this same category of recent revision are lines inserted into the existing text, as in f.11ʳ, line 8: 'The Osbornes are to be no rule for us', a curt and snappish reprimand to Mr Edwardes, delivered by his wife. Clearly, Jane Austen intended that their disagreements should provide part of the comedy of the story. A further category of revision can be identified. These changes are made in a scrawled hand, often heavily inked, and probably entered when Jane Austen was later re-reading the fragment from beginning to end. An example of this can be seen on f.31ʳ, lines 5-13. Jane Austen's main purpose at this point is to establish Elizabeth Watson's interest in Tom Musgrave. With this in view, she cancels the lines extraneous to this purpose and heightens the admiration Elizabeth expresses for the young man, adding that in comparison with Lord Osborne, he is 'the *smartest*' as well as 'the…most fashionable' of the two. Finally, in a category of its own, is the relatively large-scale passage which Jane Austen cancelled and replaced with new text pinned over the old. The original 16 lines on f.30ʳ is a rather flat sequence of dialogue between Emma and Lord Osborne during his embarrassing mid-afternoon call at Stanton Rectory. Osborne's earlier attempt at flattery – half-boots to set off 'a neat ancle', a horse to show off a woman, and her persuasive powers to obtain one – are rather crude, as she points out, and he stammers an apology for his awkwardness. The replacement – 20 lines on f.30aʳ – transforms the scene into a genuinely dramatic engagement in which Emma challenges Osborne, compelling his appreciation and respect. Jane Austen may have made this replacement when she paused at the end of the fragment in order to read through her composition to the end of its opening section. At this time, she may also have decided to enlarge slightly on the existing text at two points towards the end, attaching two further leaves to the existing leaves f.35ᵛ and f. 40ʳ. The first extension, of 31 lines, reveals more of Robert Watson's unfeeling nature as he probes Emma on the loss of any financial support from her aunt; and the second, of 20 lines, is significant in revealing the first sign of Emma's interest in Mr Howard, a development which was to lead in time to their marriage.

What we learn from the manuscript is that while Jane Austen was able to set down much of *The Watsons* in a fully-formed and apparently finished state, she was prepared to go over the text again to revise heavily where this was called for and to return to the text yet again to carry out still further revision and enlargement. And as we move towards the end of the manuscript, there is nothing to suggest any flagging of attention or energy. The level and style of correction and revision remain constant, the hand is as firm and well-shaped as we see it in the opening pages and she maintains the uniform 25 to 26 lines per page. All this suggests that whatever brought *The Watsons* to an end it was not a decline in interest or inspiration; and why, during the empty pre-Chawton years at Southampton, Jane Austen chose not to continue this fourth novel remains an open question.

Notes

1 Preface to *The Watsons*, M (1871), [p. 295]).
2 Ibid.
3 A detailed description of the manuscript is given in Sutherland, pp. 128-47.
4 Sotheby's Catalogue of Sale, 25 July 1978, p. 248.
5 *Memoir* (1871), [p.295]. JEAL's mention of an '1804 watermark' is curious, since no such watermark is to be found in the extant manuscript. Was he (or someone) simply misreading or misreporting the '1803'? Or could there have been further leaves with that watermark? If so, they disappeared, unobserved and without subsequently coming to light, before he had time to include them in his *Memoir* text – all of which seems unlikely.
6 'Is it Just?', *Temple Bar* (1883), vol. 67, p. 277.
7 One of these girls was Jane Austen's niece Catherine Anne (1818-1877), the eighth child of Francis Austen. In 1842, she married John

Hubback, a London barrister, who suffered a mental breakdown. To support herself and her three children, she turned to writing and her first novel, *The Younger Sister* (1850), published under her married name, is based upon her recollection of having heard *The Watsons* read to her by her aunt Cassandra. According to her eldest son, John Henry (1844-1939), she 'had studied this manuscript with her Aunt Cassandra so effectively that when she began to publish on her own account she was able to reproduce from memory the text of this manuscript almost word for word' (*Cross Currents in a Long Life*, 1935, p. 5). The novel is dedicated 'To the Memory of her Aunt THE LATE JANE AUSTEN...by the Authoress who...was from childhood taught to esteem her virtues and admire her talents'. She felt sufficiently knowledgeable on family matters to send some comments to James Edward Austen-Leigh for the second edition of the *Memoir*. Well-known in her time, Mrs Hubback published a further nine novels.

8   *Memoir* (1871), p. 364.

9   *W*, p. 38. Noting that Lady Osborne was 'nearly fifty' (p. 38), Chapman thought that her name was 'Doubtless a slip for *Miss Osborne*' (p. 121).

10 *Memoir* (1871), p. 296.

11 *W*, pp. 86-88.

12 Ibid., pp. 38,39,45.

13 Ibid., pp. 66-67.

14 Ibid., pp. 79.

15 'Jane Austen', *The Common Reader: First Series* (London: Hogarth, 1925, 1975), p. 174.

16 Ibid., p. 118

17 Ibid., p. 118-19.

18 Ibid., p. 119.

19 Lascelles, p. 19.

20 *Memoir* (1871), p. 296.

21 *Life and Letters*, p. 175.

22 *Facts and Problems*, p. 51. I place this ahead of Mrs. Leavis's 'Critical Theory' because, when challenged by her, Chapman claimed that this part of his book was already written by 1940, before her *Scrutiny* articles appeared (see correspondence in the *Times Literary*

Supplement: RWC, 20.11.1948, p. 653; QDL, 4.12.1948, p. 681;
RWC, 18.12.1948, p. 713).

23 *Scrutiny* (1941), vol. 10, pp. 61-90 and letter in *TLS*, 4.12.48, p.
681. Southam countered the 'Critical Theory' in *LM*, 'Appendix',
pp. 141-53.

24 See p. 13 above.

25 *Jane Austen in Context*, ed Janet Todd (Cambridge: Cambridge University Press, 2005), p. 20.

26 'Jane Austen', *The Common Reader: First Series*, p. 173.

27 Lascelles, pp. 99-100.

28 'Biographical Notice of the Author', *NA&P,* p. 8.

*

1. The first winter assembly: it was usual for large coaching-inns in market towns to provide rooms for an 'assembly', a public social event, paid for by subscribers, at which the local gentry could get together for dancing, playing cards, promenading, gossiping and making new acquaintance. Their facilities – which usually included a ball-room, rooms for billiards, cards, concerts and refreshments and chairs set out for spectators and gossips – provided entertainment and the opportunity for circulation and social intercourse for those of all ages, not least marriageable young ladies hoping that the Master of Ceremonies would introduce them formally to eligible young men – just as Catherine Morland is introduced to Henry Tilney on her first visit to the Old Assembly Rooms at Bath (*NA*, ch. 3). Following such an introduction, they could then dance together and converse with propriety. Here, in 'D', the assembly was held in 'the Assembly-room' of the White Hart inn, the winter assemblies running from September or early October to March.

2. Town of D. in Surry: as the only town with an initial 'D.' in Surrey (JA omits the 'e'), this is almost certainly Dorking, an ancient Surrey market-town, twenty-three miles south of London; in 1805, it had a population of just over three thousand, with 580 houses. This identification fits the geography of *W* as other Surrey towns are named or mentioned by initials. Moreover, Dorking's famous old coaching-inn, the White Horse – corresponding to 'D.'s' 'White Hart', mentioned a few pages into the story – was the point at which the Austens are likely to have broken their journey in travelling eastwards from Hampshire into Kent, to Sevenoaks or Godmersham, in order to visit other members of the family. As their route would also have taken them through Guildford and Reigate, also mentioned in *W*, it was an area with which JA had some familiarity. And nearby Dorking was Box Hill, the celebrated Surrey beauty spot where JA placed the picnic scene in *E*. Another familiar place, only five miles to the north of Dorking, was Great Bookham, a village where the Rector was JA's godfather, the Rev Samuel Cooke, the husband of Mrs Austen's cousin, Cassandra Leigh.

3. Tuesday Octr ye 13th: 'y^e' was an archaic form of 'the' sometimes preserved, as here, in dates and other traditional formulations.

Speculative attempts are sometimes made to relate the composition of JA's works to the fictional dates she gives in the novels. In this instance, in the early years of the nineteenth-century the 13th of October fell on a Tuesday in the years 1801, 1807 and 1812. But it is equally possible that there is a private family joke here, just as 16 December 1810, the date of Mary Elliot's marriage to Charles Musgrove (*P*, vol. 1, ch. 1), could be deliberately chosen by JA as a light-hearted reference to the day and month of her own birth, 16 December 1775.

4. Country Families: families of the local landed gentry.

5. kept their coach: ownership of a coach or carriage was a claim to social status. A coach could cost around £300, with a further £350 a year for maintenance. To support this outlay called for an income of at least £800-1000 a year. About 1798, Mr Austen set up a carriage bearing the Austen family coat-of-arms, probably relying on horses and a driver borrowed from a local farm. Even then, with an income of five to six hundred pounds, he found the costs too high and kept the carriage only a year, JA announcing to Cassandra that her father has 'laid down the carriage' (17-18 November 1798, *L*, p. 20).

6. no close carriage: a carriages with full sides joined to a roof, and therefore fully enclosed, a feature the Watsons were too 'poor' to afford.

7. to dress: change into her ball dress.

8. on every monthly return: each month.

9. Aunt who had brought her up: it was common practice for children in large families to be brought up by richer or childless relatives, just as Fanny Price comes to the Bertram household in *MP* and JA's brother

Edward joined the childless Knight family at their country house at Godmersham.

10. her first public appearance: ie at a public event.

11. the old chair: the lightest, smallest and most economical of all horse-drawn vehicles, unenclosed and drawn by a single horse.

12. lose his money at cards: at an assembly, while the dancing was going on, some of the men (and women too), in particular those past the age for dancing, or disinclined to watch, chose to play in the card-room, usually for small sums of money.

13. some comfortable soup: a comforting, refreshing soup, in winter often substantial too when it was a rich, thick soup fortified with wine and spices. Elizabeth mentions this to her sister to reassure her that she can count on something to eat after the journey back from the assembly. Whereas at a private ball a buffet or a meal would be laid on, at a public assembly it was quite usual for no more than tea and spiced wine to be provided.

14. quite independant: with an income sufficient to support himself.

15. my Father cannot provide for us: Mr Watson is 'sickly' and his family's use of the Rectory and his income will continue only as long as he is able to perform his clerical duties – and, according to Cassandra's account of how *W* was to continue – this crisis was not far off since 'Mr. Watson was soon to die' (*Memoir*, 1871, p. 364).

16. grow old...laughed at: Elizabeth Watson, unmarried at 28, imagines her spinsterhood continuing into old age – rendering her a figure as vulnerable as Miss Bates in *E*.

17. Chichester: the ancient county town of West Sussex, forty miles south west of Dorking.

18. Stanton: in England, there were a number of places with this name but none in the neighbourhood of Dorking

19. for the sake of Situation: material circumstances.

20. Teacher at a School: "at a school' to distinguish this from the occupation of being a teacher (usually called a governess) resident in a private home. Emma Watson's strong view reflects the low esteem in which women teachers were held at this time. Armed with experience of teaching, Mary Wollstonecraft wrote that 'A teacher at a school is only a kind of upper servant, who has more work than the menial ones. A governess to young ladies is equally disagreeable' (*Thoughts on the*

Education of Daughters, 1787, edn 1989, vol. 4, p. 25). In *E*, we find these views echoed: Emma Woodhouse remarks to Harriet that 'pride or refinement' are not to be expected 'in the teacher of a school' (vol. 1, ch. 7) and Jane Fairfax regards the 'situation' of a governess as a form of slavery (vol. 2, ch. 17).

21. Croydon: a Surrey market-town seventeen miles to the north of Dorking and of a similar size. It was a place that JA passed through more than once.

22. Not for the Universe: an emphatic variant upon the colloquial saying 'Not for the world' and commonly found in later eighteenth century plays and novels

23. more than once: ballroom etiquette – often incorporated in assembly 'Rules' – laid down 'A change of partners every two dances, if agreeable' (Chivers, p. 37); and other contemporary commentators regarded two dances with the same partner to be the respectable limit. This was not an arbitrary notion but was 'designed to facilitate social mixing, to involve strangers, and to prevent anyone being monopolized by a single partner (whether or not they wished to be)' (quoted in Stafford, p. 304).

24. Shropshire: a west midlands county, approximately 160 miles north west of London.

25. our great wash: a single weekly boiling of the household's accumulated linen.

26. Guildford: the ancient county town of Surrey, twelve miles to the west of Dorking.

27. Mr.Curtis won't often spare him: see note 29.

28. ten thousand pounds: known as her marriage 'portion', this was the sum of money that a bride would bring with her to the marriage; similarly the reference below to 'Robert', his 'good wife & six thousand pounds'.

29. only a Surgeon: many country doctors were known as surgeon-apothecaries. Originally, apothecaries were druggists, dispensing chemists. However, during the course of the eighteenth-century they increasingly moved into medical practice and by JA's day, a so-called surgeon or surgeon-apothecary was expected to be a trained surgeon-physician plus oculist, functioning as a general practitioner, a term that came into use around this time indicating that he handled all aspects of medicine, often supplying his own medicines. The reference above to Mr Curtis not sparing him suggests that Sam is the junior partner in practice with him, a more experienced medical man.

30. to the Turnpike: the turnpike gate at which a toll or fee was collected for the passage of wheeled vehicles and cattle (local cart traffic and funerals were exempt) along a section of main road. The money was used for the road's upkeep. The name 'turnpike' is derived from the pike-like shape of the toll bar.

31. entered on the pitching: the cobblestone surface of a paved road.

32. at the Milleners: the millinery shop principally selling hats alongside other fancy goods such as ribbons, lace and other small decorative items of women's clothing.

33. Shrubbery & sweep: the sweep is an economy drive for a town house close to the road. Shaped in a tight half-circle, it maintains some claim to the house's dignity in allowing a carriage-and-horses to enter at one gate and leave at another; and a shrubbery (see *LS*, letter 15, note 3), suggestive of country-house life, was another embellishment of town houses; both of these features designed to advance Mr Tomlinson's pretensions to owning a house 'in the Country'.

34. posts and chain: JA represents 'the Town of D.' as a market-town and these are obstacles to prevent visitors to the town from parking carts, carriages, drays or any other vehicle immediately in front of the house, which would normally be built right up to the narrow pavement, without the protective distancing that a forecourt or front garden would provide.

35. Man in Livery with a powder'd head: a uniformed servant, his hair whitened with a dusting of powder (see note 174).

36. a reserved air: according to Trusler (1794), 'Mien rather relates to our look; carriage to our frame…air, to both' (p. 31).

37. ormal Civility: courtesy according to the formalities of politeness.

38. genteel looking: with the appearance and manner of a gentle-woman.

39. hair in papers: in curl-papers: sheets of soft paper in which to shape and set the hair in curls.

40. Horses…ordered from the White Hart: these are horses supplied by the local inn which maintained a stock of carriage-horses, usually known as post- or hack-horses, available for hire in the neighbourhood and for coaches travelling along the main road that ran east and west through Dorking.

41. lounge: a period of strolling or relaxation in the town. However, the tone of the word could carry a hint of disapproval. At a far extreme were the notorious 'Bond Street loungers', a distinctive social type, upper-class idlers with time on their hands and nothing better to do than comment on the passers-by. As for Mr Edwards, we learn later that 'He had lived long enough in the Idleness of a Town to become a little of a Gossip...'.

42. to the parlour: a sitting-room used by the family.

43. good humoured Gallantry: a style of male courtesy appropriate to courtship; so, in this instance, with a mildly exaggerated and ironic manner.

44. his complexion...rather too much exposed to all weathers: because country doctors usually did their rounds on horseback, their faces could take on a bronzed and weather-beaten appearance associated with farm-labouring life. This was a particularly sensitive point at a time when doctors were trying to shake off their apothecary-tradesman associations and establish themselves firmly as professional men. Hence the importance Mr Perry in *E* attaches to being able to give up his horse and travel round his practice in the dignity of a carriage. So Mary Edward's suggestion of a likeness between Emma Watson and her brother Sam is quite unflattering; it may be a dig at her 'very brown' complexion (see notes 64, 189).

45. enjoy their Desert: served at dinner, the dessert was a separate course of little delicacies, many of which, such as dried fruit, nuts, and sweet and spicy confections could be eaten using one's fingers and away from the table. It could also include more elaborate items, such as fresh fruits, ices, jellies etc and a sweet dessert wine.

46. in a social way: for pleasure, not serious playing cards for money.

47. a fairer rubber: a rubber of whist was a set of three or five games.

48. little Whist club: whist clubs were a male preserve usually meeting, as here, at the local inn. There is a similar whist club in *E*.

49. dinner at midnight: dinner could be served as early as 3 pm in the country (as it seems to be with the Edwards and Watsons, as we learn later), and at any time up to around 6.30. In the London season and in fashionable spa towns such as Bath and Tunbridge Wells, it was served up to about 8 pm and could last two to three hours. So, even allowing for some humorous exaggeration on Mr Edwards' part, to be finishing dinner 'at midnight' indicates a dinner of some proportions, pretensions and style. Later, we hear Tom Musgrave boast of 'going home to an 8 o'clock dinner'.

50. old...Bath: the Old or Lower Assembly Rooms at Bath, sometimes known as Wiltshire's, dated from 1709. They were located near the Abbey and Pump Room. Continuing, in rivalry, alongside the New or Upper Rooms, which were opened in 1771, the Lower Rooms were the scene of Catherine Morland's introduction, via the master of ceremonies, to Henry Tilney (*NA*, vol.1, ch. 3). From about 1805, the Old Rooms began to lose favour; they fell into a decline and were destroyed by fire in 1820.

51. into *that* Country: spoken in tones of contempt, since among the English Ireland was seen as a wild and outlandish spot; time spent there a period of endurance, exile and deprivation; its inhabitants uncouth and uncivilized; and its young men were widely represented in plays and novels – including Fanny Burney's *Cecilia* (1782) and *Camilla* (1796), Robert Bage's *Hermsprong* (1796) – as fortune-hunters preying upon English womanhood.

52. no resisting a Cockade: a 'cockade' was a regimental emblem, such as a rosette, worn by army officers on their head-gear; the word is used here metonymously to stand for the officer himself.

53. when an old Lady plays the fool: a variant on the popular saying 'when a wife plays the fool' in entering upon a second marriage. Although the solemn undertakings of the Church marriage ceremony, the marriage vows, were – in the words of the service – binding only 'till death do us part', nonetheless, a second marriage was often regarded as an act of betrayal on the part of the widow against her deceased first husband, an indulgence of lustfulness, quasi-adulterous, on her part. In this instance, the act of folly is in falling for an Irish officer.

54. the Tea things: this term included the entire range of items required for serving tea – the 'ceremony' mentioned a few lines below – a silver tea tray (called a table) on a mahogany stand; the teapot; a tortoiseshell tea caddy holding black and green tea; tea kettle or urn (for hot water), placed on a stand with a spirit burner below; the cream jug; sugar basket and tongs; cups, saucers, plates and spoon

55. a dish extraordinary: additional, more than usual.

56. an additional muffin: a 'muffin' was a small form of bread, sometimes made with the addition of butter and eggs. In this form, it was like the modern tea-cake.

57. a short gallery: a passageway.

58. they were accosted: addressed; here, in a perfectly neutral sense.

59. in a morning dress: worn through the extended 'morning' until 3 or 4 pm. Sufficiently formal for walking out and paying visits but without the further formality required of evening dress or, a degree more, of full evening dress.

60. 8 or 900£: an unearned income providing for a very comfortable life-style.

61. accessions of portly Chaperons: the arrival of stout 'chaperons', older women, usually married, who escorted younger unmarried women to public events to ensure both that they behaved with propriety and, in turn, were treated with propriety. JA's novels are notable for presenting a succession of neglectful or otherwise unsuitable chaperons whose carelessness contributes to the comedy.

62. Empressément: an 'animated display of cordiality' (OED). It was understood to signify a proper and polite degree of earnestness or eagerness in attending to people. However, as JA employs the word here, it seems to shade over into self-importance. A notable usage comes in Fanny Burney's *Cecilia* (1782). Captain Aresby, much given to producing French words and expressions, is anxious to avoid committing 'any faux pas by too much empressément' (vol. 4, bk. 7, ch. 9).

63. Emma in the meanwhile…introduced by Capt. Hunter: One of the standard rules or conventions of assemblies was that the honour of opening the first dance should lie with brides recently-married or strangers to the neighbourhood. So the emphasis in this passage on the attention given to Emma Watson as an attractive 'new' face may carry the implication, fully understood by JA's readers, that she did indeed open the first dance with Captain Hunter's 'Brother officer'. This convention is echoed in *E* at the Crown inn when Emma Woodhouse has to 'submit to stand second' to the bride, Mrs Elton, who takes precedence at a ball Emma has come to consider as 'peculiarly' her own (vol. 3, ch. 2).

64. Her skin was very brown: later in the story, after the ball, Emma's 'brown skin' becomes a matter of debate: some saw her as faultless, while others judged it to be 'the annihilation of every grace', since conventional beauty called for a fair complexion. Other of JA's heroines share such a distinctive, *un*conventional appearance: Marianne Dashwood is 'very brown' (*S&S*, vol. 1, ch. 10); and following her summer tour of the Peak district Elizabeth Bennet is judged by Louisa Bingley to have become 'so brown and coarse' while Darcy sees her as 'rather tannned' (*P&P*, vol. 3, ch. 3). See note 189 and *LS*, letter 17, note 3, for the issues relating to a fair, untanned complexion.

65. & expression to make that beauty improve: expressiveness.

66. Mr Howard formerly Tutor: JA may have borrowed the name 'Howard' out of local knowledge. Three-quarters of the Manor of Dorking was owned by Charles Howard, Duke of Norfolk. The christian name, too, may be common to both, since Mr Howard's sister's eldest son is named Charles, which suggests that it is a Howard family name. Such jokey borrowings are not unusual in JA.

67. Tutor…now Clergyman: it was common practice for the son of a wealthy or aristocratic family to be educated at home by a private tutor, until 12 if he was going on to one of the public schools. The tutor would almost invariably be an Oxford or Cambridge educated clergyman who also carried responsibility for his pupil's moral upbringing. Mr Howard has been rewarded with the living of the Castle parish. In *S&S*, Robert Ferrars attributes his brother's 'extreme *gaucherie*' to 'the misfortune of a private education', ie being only tutored, and his own man-of-the-worldliness to 'the advantage of a public school' (vol. 2, ch. 14).

68. had by much the finest person: appearance, figure.

69. a very fine young man: in this clichéd phrasing, 'fine' is used by JA with a degree of irony, neatly caught in Fielding's account of the word: 'An Adjective of a very peculiar Kind, destroying, or, at least, lessening the Force of the Substantive to which it is joined: As *fine* Gentleman, *fine* Lady, *fine* House, *fine* Cloaths, *fine* Taste; – in all which *fine* is to be understood in a Sense somewhat synonymous with useless' ('Modern Glossary', *Covent-Garden Journal*, no. 4, 14 January 1752).

70. to please the Borough: by strict definition, this means that 'D.' has a royal charter, a municipal corporation, and is represented by a Member of Parliament. More broadly, we are to understand that Lord Osborne's presence at the assembly is for public relations and has a political motive:

that of keeping on good terms with the local gentry. Alongside him, they are likely to have considerable voting power and influence in the town's corporation and the Parliamentary constituency.

71. dance down every couple: in the English country-dance of this period, the dancers were ranged in couples lengthways in two parallel lines, the gentlemen on one side, the ladies on the other. According to the figures of the dance, in turn the couples traced an interweaving pattern down their respective lines and back up again, so completing one circuit of the dance with each other couple in succession, and returning to their original place. Dancers who wanted to rest could move to the bottom of the lines, whereas Charles visualises himself and Emma on the move throughout. A dance would last about thirty minutes.

72. to order the dance: it was customary for the highest placed socially of the couples to stand at the head of the lines as the 'top couple' – in this case Colonel Beresford ('the smartest officer of the sett') and Miss Osborne – with the right to 'call': the lady of the leading pair had the privilege of nominating which tunes were to be played as well as the figures of the dance, which were sometimes well-known and associated with a particular tune. Her partner conveyed her 'call' to the musicians. The places of the remaining ladies and their partners were usually according to the numbers that they drew from the Master of Ceremonies on entering the ballroom. At the conclusion of the first dance, the 'call' would then pass on to the second lady and so on down the line.

73. not keeping my engagement: in this, Miss Osborne commits the ballroom's one unforgivable offence – of putting off an agreed partner in favour of someone else. The dire consequences that could follow such behaviour were graphically drawn in Fanny Burney's *Evelina* (1778): the naïve heroine, unaware of ballroom etiquette, unwittingly turns down her partner in favour of the hero and for the remainder of the novel finds herself persecuted by the rejected partner.

74. with Colⁿ Beresford: a 'Colonel' was the officer with command of a regiment; and we can take it that he is the senior officer present.

75. to begin the set: in this usage, the 'set' was the formation in which the figures of the dance were performed. At large assemblies, where there was insufficient room to accommodate all the dancers in a single pair of long lines, the company as a whole could be divided into sets, a sub-grouping, usually made up of four pairs.

76. been interesting to Emma: this was a key term in literature, in sentimental fiction most of all, with a range of meanings, usually romantic. Johnson brings out the sentimental-romantic aspect: 'To Interest...To affect; to move; to touch with passion; to gain the affections: as, this is an *interesting* story'. In this instance, it indicates Emma's fascination for the feelings to be read in the boy's expression; and a few lines later she behaves with the impulsiveness of a truly sentimental heroine: she 'did not think, or reflect; – she felt & acted –.' When Margaret later tells Emma that Tom Musgrave is 'interesting to me', the word is used with its full sentimental-romantic meaning. Elsewhere, it carries the more conventional meaning of fascinating or intriguing (see note 117).

77. was more diffuse: extensive, widely expressed.

78. condescending a kindness: generously accommodating.

79. provided with his gloves: it was *de rigeur* for gentlemen to wear white gloves whilst dancing.

80. with nearly equal complacency: satisfaction.

81. as she turned him: changed or reversed positions with him according to the pattern of the dance.

82. talking to Charles: for periods in the country dance, the couples were at rest, and conversation with bystanders became possible.

83. his Uncle at Wickstead: no place of that name is mentioned in contemporary gazeteers

84. taught him Latin: probably in preparation for his entrance to one of the great public-schools, for which the ability to translate the simplest Latin authors was the single academic entry requirement.

85. Ld Osborne's Hounds: hunting dogs. Increasingly, down the eighteenth-century, these were likely to be foxhounds. The Vine Hunt, local to the Austens in Hampshire, replaced their pack of harriers – for hunting hare, until then the principal quarry – with foxhounds in the 1790's. James Austen and his son, JAEL, both hunted with the Vine.

86. her proper station: more than position, this carried, with the faintest hint of mockery, the further idea of the appointed place in which she is required to be, as a sentry at his post; in this instance, attentive to Mrs Edwards.

87. within the Cardroom: beyond.

88. passage was straightened: straitened, narrowed.

89. Lady Osborne's Cassino Table: a fashionable and perfectly respectable card game in polite society. The ten of diamonds, counting two points, is called great casino/cass and the two of spades little casino/cass, one point, the winners being the first pair to reach a total of eleven points.

90. to receive his Uncle's suffrage: approval.

91. I am not acquainted: having not been formally introduced.

92. a monstrous curious stuff'd Fox: 'monstrous'. Johnson describes this as 'A cant term' (here, a kind of fashionable slang), and gives the definition, 'Exceedingly; very much'.

93. requesting Mrs E. aloud to do him the honour of presenting him… Watson: social protocol required Tom Musgrave to seek an introduction to Emma through Mrs Edwards, her chaperon for the evening.

94. Lord or Commoner: a standard wording found in ancient charters and legal documents, meaning that all ranks and levels of men are equal in the eyes of the law.

95. the rules of the Assembly: we can take this as a mild joke on Tom Musgrave's part. Whereas established assembly rooms in fashionable resorts such as Tunbridge Wells, Brighton and Bath had their 'Rules', the so-called assemblies held at country-town inns were not regulated with such formality. The 'Rules' set down in the *New Bath Guide*, 1802, for the 'New Assembly-Rooms' established what was required 'to enforce regularity of conduct' and 'uniform decency of manners' and included such details as the powers of the 'Master of the Ceremonies', the times of balls, the charges, the dress code, the regulation of card-playing and gambling, when boots could and could not be worn, the exclusion of 'all' socially 'improper company' (pp. 89-92). According to the dress code, gentlemen were not usually allowed to wear gaiters nor carry sticks or canes within the Rooms. In this instance, Tom Musgrave is invoking one of the unwritten rules – that a lady and a gentleman should not monopolise each other's company.

96. never be patronized: tolerated, allowed. Tom Musgrave's wording is designed both to flatter and mock Mrs Edwards, since it carries the suggestion that she is a patron of the Assembly ie one of the local people of importance whose names add lustre to the event. Lurking in the background is Johnson's definition: 'Commonly a wretch who supports with insolence [contemptuous pride], and is paid with flattery'.

97. She is by much too nice: strict, in the archaic sense of particular or scrupulous.

98. a judge of Decorum to give her license: Musgrave continues his lightly mocking flattery, employing the vocabulary of law, in which a 'license' is an agreement.

99. such a dangerous Particularity: a bad example of a special case.

100. a very sad neighbour: unsatisfactory.

101. at Howard's elbow during the two dances: Lord Osborne's proximity is possible because while one couple is dancing down the line, the remaining couples are at rest, allowing them to talk between themselves or, as in this case, with a bystander.

102. the Osbornes & their Train: JA's ironic use of 'Train' conveys something of the Osbornes' importance and self-importance, a 'train' usually being an entourage, a processional retinue or body of retainers accompanying someone of high rank on a ceremonial occasion.

103. Barrel of Oysters: oysters were then not an expensive delicacy and it was quite usual for an oyster-lover to consume a small barrel or keg of fifty or one hundred at a sitting.

104. famously snug: 'famously', a colloquial form, uniting extremely and enjoyably with 'snug', the idea of being comfortably out of the way.

105. a look of complacency: in a secondary, social meaning, 'complacency' signifies a range of recognition, from the merest acknowledgement, acquiescence or consent, to satisfied approval.

106. imagine him mortifying: a layered verbal joke. Amongst the meanings for 'mortifying' are the ideas of being emotionally pained and the practice of self-denial. In its derivation from the French word *mort*, it also carries the idea of putting to death. While Tom Musgrave is literally 'mortifying' the oysters in eating them alive, there is little hint of self-denial in his enjoyment of an entire barrel of oysters on his own.

107. fresh Negus: a drink named after its inventor Colonel Negus (died 1732), often served at balls and other social occasions and made from port or sherry, hot water, sugar and spices.

108. surrounded by Red coats: soldiers (here referring solely to officers) were known by the distinctive colour of their regimental dress tunics.

109. her brown skin: see note 64.

110. the annihilation: a word in use from c.1750 onwards. In political, religious and scientific works, the word meant total destruction; and it became a vogue-word following its use in Richardson's *Clarissa* (1748); Fanny Burney's *Evelina* (1778), *Cecilia* (1782) and *Camilla* (1796); and it appears no less that nineteen times in Mary Robinson's *Walsingham, or the Pupil of Nature* (1797), a novel well-known at the time as an account of the social constraints placed upon women, a context in line with this part of *W.* JA continues her own distinctive handling of the word twice in the second paragraph of the final chapter of *S&S* (vol. 3, ch. 14) and in *MP* (vol. 2, ch. 4 and vol. 3, ch. 15).

111. a neat Curricle: a fashionable two-wheeled carriage, light and speedy, drawn by two horses harnessed abreast.

112. to use no ceremony: the rules of politeness would require Emma to delay reading the note until the visitors had left.

113. attending the Visitation: a formal visit of enquiry by the diocesan bishop – for Dorking the Bishop of Winchester – or his representative, the Archdeacon of Surrey, with the purpose of examining the spiritual and temporal affairs of the parishes, including the state of repair of the churches and church property. The term also extended to the meeting at which the enquiry took place. There may be a family reference here: Mrs Austen's sister Jane Leigh married a clergyman, Edward Cooper. His eldest son, Edward junior, also a clergyman, was a productive writer of hymns and sermons. One of these, published in 1802, he delivered to the clergy of the Archdeaconry of Walsall assembled there for the Archdeacon's triennial visitation – Walsall was about twenty miles from his own Staffordshire parish of Hamstall Ridware. This sermon went into a collection, published in 1804, of which he sent JA a copy.

114. from R.: almost certainly the old town of Reigate, six miles to the east of Dorking.

115. what a famous Ball: 'famous', like 'monstrous', a piece of fashionable slang, in this instance meaning enjoyable.

116. not critically handsome: judged according to the strict criteria of beauty Miss Osborne is not exactly 'handsome'.

117. a most interesting little creature: fascinating or intriguing.

118. *naïve*: innocent and unaffected. A word that Blair identified as French and spoke of approvingly: it 'shows us a man's sentiments and turn of mind laid open without disguise…undisguised openness' (*Lectures*, 1783, vol. 2, lecture 39). JA's only use of this word.

119. piquante: 'stimulating': one of the definitions given by Johnson. As a French word, it associations could suspect, as in Mary Wollstonecraft, *A Vindication of the Rights of Women* (1792): 'Their husbands leave home to seek for a more agreeable – may I be allowed to use a significant French word? – *piquant* society'. JA's only use of this word.

120. **better bred**: see *LS*, letter 5, note 1. The essence of what Lord Chesterfield set down as the essence of 'good breeding' is contained in Emma Watson's next remarks about Lord Osborne's need to improve his powers of 'pleasing'.

121. **pelisse**: see *LS*, letter 20, note 3.

122. **for the obligation**: with a much stronger force than 'obligation' carries to-day; coveying clear-cut sense of indebtedness: that in exchange for the lift, Emma would be required, in turn, to grant a favour to Tom Musgrave.

123. **to be too nice**: to be too particular.

124 **interest with Mary**: sentimental or romantic 'interest' or attraction for Mary.

125. **air**: see note 36.

126. **his address rather**: see *LS*, letter 6, note 3.

127. **my heart did misgive me me**: I was afraid.

128. **You talked so stoutly**: firmly, robustly.

129. **your Brag**: boasting.

130. **without any Theatrical grimace or violence**: this passage touches one of the heated contemporary issues of church practice. Mr Howard's straightforward and undramatic manner of reading and preaching, so admired by Mr Watson, is in the sober mainline Anglican tradition, firmly established in the eighteenth century and supported by the rhetoricians. In his *Lectures* (1783), Blair warns 'against taking the model of preaching from particular fashions that chance to have the vogue' (Lecture 29) and against 'all affectation' in 'delivery' (Lecture 33). The 'Theatrical grimace…the studied air & artificial inflexions of voice' employed by 'your very popular and admired Preachers' is Mr Watson's scathing account of the pulpit 'enthusiasm' and 'zeal' displayed in the histrionics of Methodist, Nonconformist and, within the Church of England, evangelical styles of preaching. What they had in common was an active, demonstrative manner that attracted many worshippers just as it affronted conservative churchmen such as Mr Watson. As we see from her letters, JA's own preferences lay distinctly with the sober Anglican

tradition and it was a position she was able to promote in *MP*.

    Discourse: any address, including a sermon, in which a subject is explored at some length.

131. He related the dishes: in a typical dinner of two or three 'full courses', for the first course upwards of ten different dishes would be on the table for the diners to choose from. Following that there would be a light intermission of cheese, celery and salad etc. For the following course, the table was re-laid, with some dishes remaining and some new dishes of lighter and sweeter foods brought in. For the dessert (from the French *desservir*, to clear the table), a further course, the table was cleared again and the cloth removed (see note 45).

132. partridges were high: it was considered that the flavour of the meat was enriched if the birds were hung from four to seven days, depending on their age and readiness for eating. Beyond this first stage of decomposition, partridges that were 'pretty high' could be referred to as 'stinking' (as JA does in 'The first Act of a Comedy', *Volume the Second*).

133. my gouty foot: see *LS*, letter 26, note 2.

134. the Knife-case: knives came in sets of a dozen or more fitted upright in a case, sometimes of plain leather, sometimes decorated with an elaborate design and fit to be displayed on a sideboard.

135. the honour of waiting on Mr Watson: paying a first social call of introduction to the head of the family, a necessary step for a **stranger** (someone not yet introduced), before introducing himself to any of the daughters.

136. all the inconsistency: Johnson: 'incongruity': the disparity between the humbleness of Mr Stanton's home and the social standing of these guests.

137. the convenient Mr Musgrave: in the sense that his presence in the room allows Lord Osborne to sit next to Emma and talk to her on her own.

138. You should wear half-boots: a style of boot for ladies, varying in height from just above the ankle to half-way to the knee. With thin leather soles and flat wedge-like heels, they were considered unsuitable for rough ground. Nonetheless, they could be sufficiently robust for Emma Woodhouse to make a call down Vicarage-lane in mid-winter (*E*, vol. 1, ch. 10).

139. nankin: the front-laced uppers were made of nankeen, a distinctive type of Chinese cotton, naturally yellow, named after Nanking, its place of origin. Close-textured, the material was durable and hard-wearing.

140. galoshed with black: the boot was protected from mud and water by an edging of black leather where the sole was joined to the upper; and it could be more extensively protected with an additional layer of black leather.

141. or the means: keeping a lady's horse involved appreciable costs: stabling, fodder, saddlery, in addition to the cost of the horse itself. During the war, the cost of feeding and maintaining a single horse had doubled to approximately £40 a year. That this was a considerable expenditure is made clear in *S&S*, at the opening of ch. 12, when Marianne Dashwood reveals to Elinor that Willoughby has made her the financially burdensome gift of a horse.

142. Female Economy will do a great deal: Emma's readiness with this answer is completely in line with eighteenth-century feminist thinking. Since the 1770's, advice to 'young ladies' had stressed the importance of practising and understanding 'economy'. According to Hester Chapone, it was a subject 'so important…that it ought to have the precedence of all other accomplishments' (*Letters*, 1773, Letter VII 'On Economy', vol. 2, p. 48) and in 1806 Jane West laid down that 'every girl ought to possess a competent knowledge of arithmetic. It is also desirable that this knowledge be practical as well as theoretical; that she should understand the value of commodities, be able to calculate expenses, and to tell what a specific income will afford' (*Letters to a Young Lady*, vol. 3, pp. 259-60). A fragment of evidence survives – a page from a personal account book for 1807 – indicating that JA was herself scrupulous in recording the Austen household expenditure and her own personal expenses down to the last ½ penny.

143. by Nanny's approach: 'Nanny' is a child's name for her nurse and the former nurse in the Watson family has stayed on as a household servant.

144. he be'nt to have his dinner: in the ms, JA wrote 'he ben't'. In Nanny's mouth, this is the countrywoman's version of the question 'is he not?' or 'isn't he?'.

145. take up the Fowls: 'fowls' was a term covering all types of edible bird, including geese, ducks and wild-fowl.

146. will be hunting: the hunting season proper begins 1 November. In the time-scheme of the *W*, it is still October and the hunting would be 'cub hunting' of the young foxes; likewise the pack would include young hounds.

147. this Country: a hunting man, Lord Osborne speaks in hunting terminology, in which a 'country' is the precisely defined area within which a hunt is permitted to operate. The hunt local to Dorking – bordered by three other hunts – was the Surrey Union (formed from joining two private packs in 1798/99), its country covering much of Surrey – extending ten miles west beyond Guildford, beyond Reigate to the east, four miles north of Leatherhead and beyond Cranleigh in the south. The Surrey Union had six 'meeting' points – the 'meet' being the horses, riders and hounds that composed the hunt – in the immediate vicinity of Dorking.

148. throw off: in hunting parlance, to unleash the hounds and set them in pursuit of their quarry.

149. drawn out: to draw out is to force the fox out of its lair.

150. good wishes in person: before the hunt set out, it was customary for the members of the hunt and their friends and supporters to have an alcoholic farewell drink, a so-called stirrup cup, wishing the hunt success.

151. smartest & most fashionable: here, as elsewhere, for the comparative, JA employs what we regard to-day as the superlative form.

152. which carried quite as much Impertinence: a nobleman calling unannounced at the home of a penurious clergyman in bad health cannot be construed as an everyday social visit, since protocol now places on Mr Watson the notional obligation, an onerous one if carried out, of paying a return call upon Lord Osborne at Osborne Castle, a point of etiquette explored to the end of this paragraph.

153. such an alienation: estrangement, keeping at a distance.

154. was an Attorney: a solicitor.

155. he had been Clerk: articled (apprenticed) to a solicitor.

156. she gave genteel parties: Johnson gives 'Polite; elegant in behaviour; civil'. But these positive meanings, as at note 38, were just beginning to be undermined, with an alternative and subversive sense of pretentiously making a show of these qualities, a characteristic of the rising middle classes, those who were not born to the gentry but aspired to it and aped the gentry's ways. An attorney's wife, Jane Watson falls into this category and JA complements her use of the subversive 'genteel' with the equally subversive 'very smart' and 'fine', continuing this characterisation to the end of the paragraph. Also see S, ch.11, note 2.

157. & rather wanted Countenance: Johnson: 'Confidence of mien, assurance of aspect'; a calmness and composure in her looks.

158. who threw herself away on an Irish Captain: see notes 51-53. Following this, Robert Watson reflected to himself that through this folly Emma's aunt has left him, as a lawyer, unlikely 'to have any property...to get the direction of', a train of thought that continues, see note 169.

159. settling with the Post-Boy...Posting: posting was travelling with post-horses hired from licensed posting-house inns conducted by post-masters, as opposed to travelling with other fare-paying passengers on a stage-coach which kept to the main roads only. In the vicinity of London, the standard charge was usually one shilling a mile for a pair of horses, twice that for four, half for a single horse. The postboy or postillion, at around 3d a mile, rode on the near-side horse of a leading pair of four or more horses, or of a pair when there was no driver. The posting rates were rising at this time. Hence Robert's complaint at the 'advance'. Dorking's two inns – the Red Lion and the White Horse – were both posting houses and the innkeepers listed as 'Country Post Masters'. Like the Crown Inn at Highbury, they would keep post-horses 'more for the convenience of the neighbourhood than from any run on the road', the 'road' being the main or turnpike road to London.

160. a doubtful halfcrown: the half-crown was a silver coin of two shillings and sixpence (12½ p); this one is 'doubtful' ie suspect because it appears to be counterfeit, coined of base metal.

161. I would endite it: in modern spelling, to indict is to bring a legal charge.

162. Who is Surveyor now: whereas turnpike roads were run by trusts, local and village roads were the responsibility of the parishes they passed through. To give him his full title, The Surveyor of Highways was one of the propertied men in the neighbourhood elected to this office by the village constables and churchwardens.

163. your Raillery: Johnson defines as 'Slight satire; satirical merriment'.

164. they are rather too mixed: public events where people of various classes and occupations, professional and commercial, might be found intermingled, gatherings which Jane Watson looks down on in contrast to the genteelism of her own 'select' private 'parties'. The full force of 'mixed' comes across in two lines from Byron's *Beppo* (1818): 'The company is "mixed" (the phrase I quote is/ As much as saying, they're below your notice' (stanza 58).

165. seven Tables: for playing cards.

166. her most languishing tone: 'expressive of sentimental emotion' (*OED*). A cliché term long established in the literature of sensibility. Its satirical application was formed in *The Female Quixote* (1752) by Charlotte Lennox. The heroine, Lady Arabella, uses a similar 'languishing tone' and, a few lines later, throws herself into a chair 'in a languishing posture' (vol. 2, bk. 5, ch. 2). Other sentimental languishings commonly involved 'eyes', 'looks', 'airs' and 'glances', all of them expressive of a devoted lover, or a beloved one, overcome by emotion.

167. the tone of artificial Sensibility: see *LS*, letter 5, note 5.

artificial or 'false' 'Sensibility' was by this time a familiar concept, widely discussed. Readers in the 1790's would be familiar with *Letters on the Improvement of the Mind* (1773) by Hester Chapone; Mary Wollstonecraft took a key passage from Letters IV-V, 'On the Regulation of the Heart and Affections', giving it the title 'False Sensibility' and reprinting it in a didactic anthology aimed at girls, *The Female Reader; or Miscellaneous Pieces...For the Improvement of Young Women* (1789, pp. 86-88). Later, in *E*, JA was to draw genuine 'sensibility': for example, the 'tone of great sensibility' with which Knightley comforts Emma, thinking her to have been jilted by Frank Churchill (vol. 3, ch. 13); and the 'look of true sensibility' that crosses Emma's face as she admits to Frank Churchill a similarity in their being connected to 'two characters so much superior to our own' (vol. 3, ch. 18).

168. we never eat suppers: supper was a light and informal refreshment, rather than a meal, usually served at the end of the evening around 10 or 11 pm.

169. settled something on you: conveyed money or property to her, for her immediate or future use.

170. Liberal & enlightened Minds: see *LS*, letter 16, note 1.

171. provided decently...at her mercy: this refers to the fact that in the normal way a widow held only a life interest in whatever share of her late husband's estate came to her at his death; and that if she remarried, that life interest came to an end. Instead of this, the property that came to Emma's aunt from the late Mr Turner was left to her unconditionally and with her marriage has now passed into the hands of Captain O'Brien. For a fuller explanation of property rights in marriage see *S*, chapter 3, note 3.

172. a sad break-up: the disposal of his property.

173. had a thousand...pounds: a dowry bringing this sum into the marriage.

174. fresh powder in your hair: the practice of using whitening or slightly coloured hair powder, made from refined wheat or starch, and sometimes perfumed, came into fashion for formal dress wear in the later decades of the eighteenth-century as the fashion for wigs went out. But its use began to decline with the Hair Powder Act of 1795 which imposed an annual tax of one guinea. Although hair powder continued to be worn as a patriotic and anti-Gallic Tory gesture, by 1805 it was outmoded, lingering on only amongst a few traditionalist die-hards until the 1840's.

175 putting up your last new Coat: shortening.

176. It has been excessively admired: 'excessively', fashionable slang for very much. JA uses the word, making a joke of it, in a letter to Cassandra (*L*, p. 202).

177. chiding Eliz^th...I beseech you: this passage refers to the customary practice for each course of the meal to consist of a quantity of dishes – 'the profusion' – laid out on the table together (see note 131); in this case, all except the hot dish, the 'roast Turkey', about whose arrival Jane Watson makes such a fuss.

178. if we make a round game: a card game so-called because each player takes a turn (a 'round'); and, as distinct from whist and other such games involving partners, any number of players could take part, joining and leaving the game at will, each playing for him- or herself in competition with the others.

179. Speculation is the only round game: according to the *OED*, the main point of Speculation was 'the buying and selling of trump cards, the holders of the highest trump card in a round winning the pool'. Austen herself seems to have particularly enjoyed the noisy business of bidding for unturned cards where the speculative element was to the fore (see *L*, pp. 163-64, 167). In *MP* (vol. 2, ch. 7), the progress of a game is an extended metaphor for the interests of the various players.

180.   to play at Cribbage: a card game in which the 'crib' is comprised of the cards discarded by the players and passed on to the dealer.

181.   certainly a postchaise: a 'chaise' was a light, covered, carriage; in this case, as there was only one passenger, it would have been drawn by two rather than four horses. 'post' indicates that it was hired from the stables at the local inn.

182.   the wrap of a Travellor: an additional outer garment worn by travellers as a protection against wind and rain.

183.   at extraordinary seasons: with the sense, now obsolete, of times of day.

184.   the best Pembroke Table: an elegant side-table with slender, tapering legs and one or two fitted drawers. It could be extended by raising either or both of the two hinged side drop-leaves; supported by brackets, they turned out from the central table top. Fashionable from the 1760's onwards. The name Pembroke possibly derived from the Welsh town of that name. When to 'general contentment' several new tables arrived at Steventon at the end of 1800, JA described to Cassandra the positioning of 'The Pembroke…by the sideboard,' writing that it gave Mrs Austen 'great delight in keeping her Money and papers locked up' (letter 8-9 November 1800, *L*, p. 55)

185.   as he came avowedly from London: Johnson: 'In an open manner'.

186.   chatting at the Bedford: located under the Piazza at Covent Garden, this was one of the most famous of London coffee houses. Its clientele, largely literary and artistic, included Pope, Fielding, Sheridan, Garrick, William Collins, William Hickey and Zoffany. At its heyday in the 1760's, according to a contemporary, it was famed as 'the emporium of wit, the seat of criticism, and the standard of taste' and in terms of London's cultural geography stood at 'the centre of gravitation between the court and city' ('By A Genius', *Memoirs*, 1763, pp. 1, 3). It was the coffee-house patronised by John Thorpe, where he boasted of having met General Tilney 'for ever' ie regularly (*NA*, vol. 1, ch. 12).

In the ms of *W*, having second thoughts, JA wrote 'Horse Guards' above 'Bedford', apparently intending this as a replacement. But she then cancelled this revision and reverted to the 'Bedford', possibly because the Horse Guards coffee-house, much patronised by the military – it stood on Whitehall, the rear of the building overlooking Horse Guards Parade – had an unsavoury reputation for disorder and as a haunt of prostitutes, associations which would have taken Tom Musgrave's affected raffishness a step too far.

187 Fine open weather: dry, frost-free weather, providing the horses with a firm but not frozen surface, and ideal for hunting.

188. Charming season for Hunting: the fox-hunting 'full season' opened around 1 November and ended around mid-March or April, while the 'Autumn hunting' of cubs was from late August onwards.

189. convert to a brown complexion: as the following passage makes clear, a fair complexion was fashionable, as it implied attention to the skin and a ladylike care to keep out of the sun, whereas a brown skin was associated with the vulgarity of working life and exposure to the weather (a point also urged against Sam Watson). Nonethless, JA determinedly challenges this convention, giving Emma Watson a 'very brown' skin.

190. to your Condescension: consideration.

191. in such Dishabille: informal dress and thus unsuitable for paying a social call. Directly from the French *déshabillé* (undress). So widely used in English that Johnson was happy to accept it as a word thoroughly Anglicized.

192. the fish & counters: fishes were small flat pieces of bone or ivory, in the shape of a fish, used in card games as a counter or in place of money. Also, scores were kept with boards and pegs of French origin and this English peg-fish was derived from the French *fiche* meaning peg.

193. from the beaufit: an eighteenth-century spelling of buffet, the side-table or sideboard where food was laid out.

194. Vingt-un is the game: an abbreviated form of vingt-et-un, a card game in which the aim is to hold cards with a points value of as close as possible to twenty-one. To exceed twenty-one is to **overdraw**. If a player is dealt two aces for his initial two cards, he is allowed to split them, so in effect gaining the advantage of playing with two separate hands. So the sight of Lord Osborne overdrawing himself 'on both his own cards' is something of a spectacle, given his implied irascibility.

195. in the business...of the game: the 'business' of the game is the way in which it is ordered according to the rules; the '**course**' is the actual playing of the game.

196. maintained little complaisance: decorum, politeness.

197. Bason of Gruel: a common spelling for basin. In *E*, 'gruel' is Mr Woodhouse's constant dietary comfort; and sometimes the 'basin' is mentioned as well.

198. I shoot with L^d. Osborne: shoot game birds.

199. made a confidante: a standard character in sentimental and romantic fiction, an intimate female friend with whom the heroine could share her innermost thoughts and feelings, particularly in matters of love.

200. some very inapplicable reply: inappropriate.

201. found the continuance... short: unusually with JA, the meaning of these lines is not immediately evident. From the context, it seems that Margaret has stopped behaving 'properly' towards Emma, who finds the time over which Margaret bothers to maintain her 'gentle voice' in addressing her is even shorter than she had expected.

202. mortifications of unequal Society: the painfulness of having for company people who were inferior to her (intellectually, we are to understand, and in terms of Emma's qualities of good sense and good taste).

203. an untoward Disposition: according to Johnson, 'untoward' has the meaning 'Froward [he defines as 'Peevish; ungovernable; angry; perverse']; perverse; vexatious; not easily guided, or taught'.

204. the dissipation of unpleasant ideas: dispersal, relegation.

205. the expected Heiress of an easy Independance: this is the inheritance of '8 or 9000£' mentioned so painfully by Robert a few pages earlier. Placed in Government funds – the most secure form of investment – interest at around 5% would produce an annual income of £400-450. After Mr Austen's death in 1805, Mrs Austen and her two daughters lived together on an income of £460 and in *NA* £400 is the value of the living offered to James Morland. It was a sum sufficient for a single woman to live on comfortably.

Prayers

Prayers	probably post-1805, possibly 1809
Manuscript	Mills College, Oakland, California
Facsimile	Prayer III, *Three evening prayers* (San Francisco: The Colt Press, 1940).

The existence of the Prayers was first made known in 1927 in a letter from Dr Chapman to the *Times Literary Supplement* reporting the sale and distribution of a collection of Austen letters, manuscript items and memorabilia. The manuscript of the Prayers is listed as item 18.[1] The Prayers were first published in a limited, collector's edition as *Three evening prayers* (San Francisco: The Colt Press, 1940).[2] Unfortunately, the design of the book involved printing the text in capital letters throughout and the punctuation was part-modernised. The Introduction, signed by William Matson Roth – the purchaser of the Prayers and a partner in the Press – outlines the history of the manuscript. At the back is an inserted a facsimile of the third Prayer. The Prayers were reprinted in the *Minor Works* volume, 1954, a text not based on the manuscript but on the Colt Press edition. In the headnote, Dr Chapman explained that as the Colt edition was 'printed throughout in capitals' he was not able 'to reproduce the capitals on the MS'[3] – although, of course, for the third prayer, he could have consulted the facsimile. Instead, throughout the text he used capitals only for 'God', 'Christian(s)', 'Father', 'Lord', 'Heaven' and 'Heavenly'. A lightly annotated text appeared in Jane Austen, *Catharine and Other Writings*, edd. Margaret Anne Doody and Douglas Murray (Oxford: Oxford University Press, 1993). According to the editors, this text is based on a transcription which 'appears to be the typed transcription made by' Roth for The Colt Press edition; and they reported that an examination of the facsimile 'shows...that Roth eliminated almost all capitals from the pieces transcribed'.[4]

The text given here, transcribed from a photographic reproduction, is the first to present its precise detail.

The manuscript is on two separate sheets, each sheet folded once, giving a total of four leaves. The leaves of the first sheet, with the watermark 1818, measure 9 1/8 x 7 5/16 in. The leaves of the second sheet, which is undated, measure 9 7/8 x 7 13/16 in. On f.2^v of the first sheet is written 'Prayers Composed by my ever dear Sister Jane'. According to Deirdre Le Faye (private communication), identifying the three hands, the inscription is in the hand of Charles Austen and was probably added by him when the Prayers came into his possession at the time of Cassandra's death in 1845. On the first sheet, ff.1^r-2^r, is the first Prayer, entitled 'Evening Prayer'. On the second sheet, f.1^{r-v}, is the second Prayer, untitled and unnumbered; and, on f.2^{r-v}, the third Prayer, also untitled and unnumbered. The first and second Prayers, and the third Prayer down to the penultimate line of f.2^r, are in the hand of James Austen; then, at the last line of f.2^r, Cassandra takes over, continuing until the end of the third Prayer on f.2^v.[5] According to Gilson, Prayer I was 'possibly written by JA's sister Cassandra'; 'the second, and the first part of the third, are thought to be written by Henry Austen' (Gilson, 1982, p. 384).

It is Deirdre Le Faye's supposition that the originals of the Prayers were written out separately and that soon after Jane's death Cassandra copied them out as a 'collection', to join her sister's memorabilia. Her clergyman brother James was recruited to help in this. However, in poor health by 1818 – he died the following year – James was unable to finish the task and the copying was completed by Cassandra. Le Faye also points out that until her father's death in 1805, there would be no call for Jane Austen to compose such prayers and suggests that a possible occasion could be January 1809, when bad weather prevented the household from attending their local parish church in Southampton on two consecutive Sundays.[6]

In 1845, Charles's eldest daughter, Cassandra Esten Austen (1808-97), assisted her father in the execution of Cassandra's will, and the Prayers and other memorabilia came into her possession. She died unmarried and these heirlooms passed on to her five nieces, the daughters of Charles Austen jnr. In 1927, they were sold at Sotheby's as the property of Jane Austen (1849-1928) and Emma Florence Austen (1851-1939). The Prayers subsequently passed through a number of hands before their purchase by William Roth. A Trustee of Mills College, Roth presented the manuscript to the College in 1957.

In composing the three evening Prayers, Jane Austen's drew upon The Book of Common Prayer, widely known as the Prayer Book. This contains the official liturgy of the Church of England, the services and forms of prayer with which she was familiar from childhood, and which preserved a heavily cadenced and ritualistic form of English, its liturgical style, deriving from the text originally prepared under Archbishop Cranmer and issued in 1549. This text was modified in 1552, 1559 and 1604; it was revised after the Stuart Restoration in 1660; and reissued in 1662. These later modifications and revisions largely related to matters of doctrine and content rather than to the style of expression, which essentially remains that of the mid-sixteenth century; and the quotations given here and in the notes are taken from the Clarendon Press edition of 1818.

It is clear that Jane Austen found no difficulty in handling the language of the Prayer Book – its traditional diction, formulations and prose rhythms. This was regarded as the authentic language of prayer and in an Anglican household, any considerable departure from the main elements of this liturgical style would not have been acceptable, a principle echoed in Johnson's declaration that he knew 'of no good prayers but those in the *Book of Common Prayer*'.[7] In many households it was customary to gather for morning and evening prayers using the collect (prayers appropriate to a specific day or occasion) of the Prayer Book and this would have been the practice of the Austens as a clerical family: Mr Austen was a clergyman, as was Jane's brother James, and from 1816, her brother Henry. We remember Fanny Price's energetic endorsement in the Chapel at Sotherton: 'A whole family assembling regularly for the purpose of prayer, is fine!'.[8]

Some latitude was permissible in the language of prayers for 'Domestic' or 'Family' use within the privacy of the home, as distinct from 'Public' prayers read in church or on some official occasion, such as a military or civic parade. While clergymen were expected to use the existing forms given in the Prayer Book, that requirement did not extend to lay people in their own homes, whether they were holding prayers *en famille*, or whether these were 'Solitary', the private prayers of someone on their own. Nor were the laity unguided. There were many books of 'Family Worship', providing morning and evening prayers for every day of the week. In *Female Education* (1799), Hannah More, the leading Christian educationalist of the time, provided extensive 'Hints...for furnishing young persons with a scheme of prayer', spelling out the various sections – 'adoration, self-dedication, confession, petition, thanksgiving, and intercession' – for which she advocated the qualities of 'plan, and design, and lucid order'.[9] A few years later, in *Practical Piety* (1811), in chapter 5 on 'Prayer', she offered encouragement to all: 'It is not eloquence, but earnestness' which should prevail; and chapter 12 is devoted to the subject of 'Self-Examination', a discipline prominent in the first of Jane Austen's Prayers.[10]

Beyond religious-educational works and the Prayer Book itself, it seems likely that Jane Austen found direct inspiration in *A Serious Call to a Devout and Holy Life* (1728) by William Law. In its 20th edition by 1816, it was standard reading amongst the clergy and far beyond and we can be sure that there was a copy in Mr Austen's library. Its likely appeal to Jane Austen can be judged from Johnson's tribute – that his reading the *Serious Call* was the first occasion of his 'thinking in earnest of religion, after I became capable of rational enquiry'.[11] Law's influence on Johnson seems to be confirmed in his *Dictionary*, where the two illustrative quotations from Law in the first edition of 1755 had risen to almost two hundred by the 4th edition of 1773. And beyond the words and phrases we find in both Law and Jane Austen (these are specified in the notes), there is also a shared emphasis upon wider themes – the duty upon us of universal love and benevolence and the importance of self-examination – both as a doctrine, and as a duty for the end of the day. There are elements of style, too, which seem to place Jane Austen's prayers closer to the tighter and less elevated forms of Law than to the Biblical resonances of the Prayer Book, with its long, rolling cadences, its strings of sonorous doublets and near-repetitions – those very 'redundancies and repetitions' in 'Our liturgy' which, according to Henry Crawford, 'require good reading not to be felt'.[12] Accordingly, sometimes we seem to overhear an unritualised near-speaking voice as Jane Austen asks, in Prayer I, 'Have we thought irreverently of Thee, have we dis-obeyed thy

Commandments, have we neglected any known Duty, or willingly given pain to any human Being?'; or, in Prayer III, when she offers thanks 'for every hour of safety, health & peace, of domestic comfort & innocent enjoyment. We feel that we have been blessed far beyond any thing that we have deserved…'; and again in Prayer I: the petition offered up in the Prayer Book, 'That it may please thee to preserve all that travel by land or by water', is re-rendered: 'and heartily do we pray for the safety of all that travel by Land or by Sea'. This new wording is in tune with Edmund Bertram's comment on modern reading and preaching: 'It is felt that distinctness and energy may have weight in recommending the most solid truths…'.[13] We can well imagine that Jane Austen wanted to ensure that the household, including the servants and any visiting nephews and nieces, was not lulled by familiar sonorities but kept wide awake with language more emphatic and down to earth and meanings more colloquially expressed.

The Prayers help us understand how it was that, having spoken of his sister's genius as a writer, her 'intuitive, and almost unlimited' 'power of inventing characters', Henry Austen – the failed banker turned clergyman – could devote the crowning paragraph of the 'Biographical Notice' to her Christian belief, the single 'trait' that 'makes all others unimportant. She was thoroughly religious and devout'.[14] For modern readers, these issues may have little or no bearing on their experience of the novels. But it is worth remarking that Richard Whately – whose 1821 review of both *Northanger Abbey* and *Persuasion* stands as a milestone in the criticism of the novels – identified Jane Austen as 'evidently a Christian writer', an author whose religious concerns were 'not at all obtrusive,' 'rather alluded to, and that incidentally'; and Whately, who was to become Archbishop of Dublin, rejoiced in the fact that, in preaching no sermons, she kept apart from her moralising contemporaries.[15] It is also worth saying that Jane Austen trod the truly Anglican path of this time in preserving a strict reticence about religious experience and in avoiding the least hint of theological debate.

Notes

1. 'A Jane Austen Collection', *The Times Literary Supplement*, 14 January 1926, p. 27.

2. The *New York Times Book Review* describes this as 'a dainty rubricated edition' bound in 'a flowered brocade damask', the text set 'by hand in Centaur capitals with a dignified clarity of arrangement that befits the beauty and reverence of the prayers' (21 April 1940).

3. *MW*, p. 453.

4. *Catharine*, p. 283.

5. Deirdre Le Faye has identified these hands (private communication). Until now, the accepted identifications have remained those proposed by R.W. Chapman: the inscription on f.2ᵛ he first attributed to Charles Austen (*Jane Austen: Facts and Problems*, 1948, p. 165), revising this in 1954 to 'almost certainly?– Cassandra's'. He judged that the hand of the first two Prayers and the first part of Prayer three 'may be Henry Austen's' and he reported that the remainder of Prayer three is in a hand 'thought by experts to be JA's own' (*MW*, p. 453).

6. For the suggestion of Law's influence, and a stimulating and enlarging correspondence on this point, I am most grateful to George Westhaver, then Chaplain of Lincoln College, Oxford..

7. *Boswell's Life of Johnson*, ed G.B.Hill, rev L.F.Powell (Oxford: Clarendon, 1934), vol. 4, p. 293.

8. *MP*, vol. 1, ch. 9.

9. Hannah More, *Strictures on the Modern System of Female Education* (London: Cadell, 1799), ch. 12, vol. 1, pp. 257-74; vol. 1, p. 266; 12ᵗʰ edn., 1818, vol. 1, p. 452.

10. Hannah More, *Practical Piety; or, the Influence of the Religion of the Heart on the Conduct of Life*, (London : Cadell, 1811, 11ᵗʰ edn 1817), vol. 1, p. 103; ch. 5, pp. 103-30; ch. 12, pp. 266-98.

11. *Boswell's Life of Johnson*, vol. 1, p. 68.

12. *Mansfield Park*, vol 3, ch. 3.

13. Ibid.

14. 'Biographical Notice', *N&P*, pp. [3], 8.

15. *Quarterly Review* (January 1821), vol. 26, pp. 359-60.

*

The text that follows is taken from the original family manuscript and is printed here by permission of Special Collections, F.W. Olin Library, Mills College

There are some oddities or anomalies of capitalisation and phrasing. For example, in Prayer (III), we would expect the final words to be 'for them ourselves' – 'them' referring back to 'our fellow-creatures'– rather than the word 'men' in the manuscript. Such an example may reflect a usage of the time or, possibly, an error or deliberate change made in the act of transcribing Jane Austen's original manuscript text, which has not survived and from which the family copies were made after her death.

(I)
Evening Prayer

Give us grace,[1] Almighty Father, so to pray, as to deserve[2] to be heard, to address thee with our Hearts, as with our Lips.[3] Thou art every where present, from Thee no secret can be hid;[4] may the knowledge of this, teach us to fix our Thoughts on Thee, with Reverence & Devotion that we pray not in vain. –

Look with Mercy on the Sins we have this day committed, & in Mercy make us feel them deeply, that our Repentance may be sincere,[5] and our Resolutions stedfast of endeavouring against the commission of such in future. – Teach us to understand the sinfulness of our own Hearts,[6] and bring to our knowledge every fault of Temper[7] and every evil Habit in which we may have indulged to the dis-comfort of our fellow-creatures, and the danger of our own Souls. – May we now, and on each return of night, consider how the past day has been spent by us, what have been our prevailing Thoughts, Words and Actions during it, and how far we can acquit[8] ourselves of Evil. Have we though irreverently of Thee, have we dis-obeyed thy Commandments, have we neglected any known Duty, or willingly given pain to any human Being? – Incline[9] us to ask our Hearts these questions Oh! God, and save us from deceiving ourselves by Pride or Vanity.

Give us a thankful sense of the Blessings[10] in which we live, of the many comforts of our Lot; that we may not deserve to lose them by Discontent or Indifference.

Be Gracious[11] to our Necessities,[12] and guard us, and all we love, from Evil this night.[13] May the sick and afflicted, be now, & ever thy care; and heartily do we pray for the safety of all that travel by Land or by Sea, for the comfort & protection of the Orphan & Widow, & that thy pity may be shewn, upon all Captives & Prisoners.[14]

Above all other blessings Oh! God, for oursleves, & our fellow-creatures, we implore Thee to quicken[15] our sense of thy Mercy in the redemption[16] of the world, of the Value of that Holy Religion in which we have been brought up, that we may not, by our own Neglect, throw away the Salvation Thou has given us, nor be Christians only in name. –

Hear us Almighty God, for His sake who has redeemed us, & taught us thus to pray.–

Our Father which art in Heaven &c.

(II)

Almighty God! Look down with Mercy on thy Servants here assembled & accept the petitions[1] now offer'd up unto thee.

Pardon Oh God! the offences of the past day. We are conscious of many frailties; we remember with shame & contrition, many evil Thoughts & neglected duties, & we have perhaps sinned against Thee & against our fellow-creatures in many instances of which we have now no remembrance.[2] – Pardon Oh God! whatever thou hast seen amiss in us, & give us a stronger desire of resisting every evil inclination & weakening every habit of sin. Thou knowest the infirmity of our Nature, & the temptations which surround us. Be thou merciful, Oh Heavenly Father! to Creatures so formed & situated.

We bless thee for every comfort of our past and present existence, for our health of Body & of Mind & for every other source of happiness which Thou hast bountifully[3] bestowed on us & with which we close this day, imploring their continuance from Thy Fatherly Goodness,[4] with a more grateful sense of them, than they have hitherto excited. May the comforts of every day, be thankfully felt by us, may they prompt a willing obedience of thy Commandments & a benevolent spirit towards every fellow-creature.[5]

Have mercy Oh Gracious Father! upon all that are now suffering from whatsoever cause, that are in any circumstance of danger or distress – Give them patience under every Affliction,[6] strengthen, comfort & relieve them.

To Thy Goodness we commend ourselves this night beseeching thy protection of us through its darkness & dangers. We are helpless & dependant; Graciously preserve us – For all whom we love & value, for every Friend & Connection, we equally pray; However divided & far asunder,[7] we know that we are alike before Thee, & under thine Eye.[8] May we be equally united in Thy Faith & Fear,[9] in fervent devotion[10] towards Thee, & in Thy merciful Protection this Night. Pardon Oh Lord! the imperfections of these our Prayers, & accept them through the mediation of our Blessed Saviour, in whose Holy Words we farther address thee; our Father.

(III)

Father of Heaven! whose goodness has brought us in safety to the close of this day,[1] dispose our Hearts in fervent prayer.

Another day is now gone, & added to those, for which we were before accountable.[2] Teach us Almighty Father, to consider this solemn Truth, as we should do, that we may feel the importance of every day, & every hour as it passes, & earnestly strive to make a better use of what Thy Goodness may yet bestow[3] on us, than we have done of the Time past.

Give us Grace to endeavour after a truly christian Spirit to seek to attain that temper of Forbearance[4] & Patience,[5] of which our Blessed Saviour has set us the highest Example, and which, while it prepares us for the spiritual Happiness of the Life to come, will secure to us the best enjoyment of what this World can give. Incline us Oh God! to think humbly of ourselves, to be severe only in the examination[6] of our own conduct, to consider our fellow-creatures with kindness, & to judge of all they say & do with that Charity which we would desire from men ourselves.

We thank thee with all our hearts for every gracious dispensation,[7] for all the Blessings that have attended our Lives, for every hour of safety, health & peace, of domestic comfort & innocent enjoyment. We feel that we have been blessed far beyond any thing that we have deserved; and though we cannot but pray for a continuance of all these Mercies,[8] we acknowledge our unworthiness of them & implore Thee to pardon the presumption[9] of our desires.

Keep us Oh! Heavenly Father from Evil this night. – Bring us in safety to the beginning of another day & grant that we may rise again with every serious & religious feeling which now directs us.

May thy mercy be extended over all Mankind, bringing the Ignorant[10] to the knowledge of thy Truth,[11] awakening the Impenitent, touching the Hardened.[12] – Look with compassion upon the afflicted of every condition, assuage the pangs of disease,[13] comfort the broken in spirit.

More particularly do we pray for the safety and welfare of our own family & friends wheresoever dispersed, beseeching Thee to avert from them all material & lasting Evil[14] of Body or Mind; & may we by the assistance of thy Holy Spirit so conduct ourselves on Earth as to secure an Eternity of Happiness with each other in thy Heavenly Kingdom. Grant this most merciful Father, for the sake of our Blessed Saviour in whose Holy Name & Words we further address Thee.[15]

Our Father &c. &c

*

Quotations
The quotations from The Book of Common Prayer are taken from
the edition published at Oxford: The Clarendon Press, 1818 and the
Biblical quotations are taken from the Authorised Version, the King
James Bible of 1611.

(I)

1. grace: 'The free and unmerited favour of God as manifested in the
salvation of sinners and the bestowing of blessings' (*OED*).
2. deserve: an unusual application. Both in the Old and New
Testaments 'deserve' almost invariably relates to punishment or death
while in the Prayer Book the word is several times used of God's gifts
(Collect for Trinity 12) or blessings. In the third Prayer, paragraph 4, JA
has 'deserved'.
3. Hearts…Lips: cf. the General Thanksgiving: 'that we may shew
forth thy praise not only with our lips, but in our lives'.
4. from…hid: cf. the collect that opens the Communion Service:
'Almighty God, unto whom all hearts be open…and from whom no
secrets are hid…'.
5. that our Repentance may be sincere: cf. 'grant us true repentance',
The Absolution, or Remission of sins, at Morning and Evening Prayer.
6. the sinfulness of our own Hearts: cf. Matthew 15:15 'For out of the
heart proceed evil thoughts, murders, adulteries, fornications, thefts,
false witness, blasphemies.'
7. Temper: Johnson, quoting Law, gives one definition as 'Disposition
of mind'. cf. Law, *A Serious Call*, ch.23, 'He therefore who knows himself
most of all subject to anger and passion must be very exact and constant in
his examination of this temper every evening. He must find out every slip
that he has made of that kind, whether in thought or word or action; he
must shame and reproach and accuse himself before God for everything
that he has said or done in obedience to his passion. He must no more
allow himself to forget the examination of this temper than to forget his
whole prayers….if you find that vanity is your prevailing temper…never
spare or forget this temper in your evening examination…'.
8. acquit: clear or free. The force of this word comes from its origin in
the idea of settling with a creditor.

9. incline: carries the literal sense of bending as a force applied by God to those praying.

10. Give…Blessings: cf. the General Thanksgiving: 'And we beseech thee, give us that due sense of all thy mercies, that our hearts may be unfeignedly thankful'.

11. Gracious: compassionate, generous towards.

12. Necessities: urgent needs or wants.

13. guard…night: cf. the collect for Aid against all Perils, from the service of Evening Prayer: 'by thy great mercy, defend us from all perils and dangers of this night'.

14. May…prisoners: cf. the Great Litany: 'That it may please thee to preserve all that travel by land or by water, all women labouring of child, all sick persons and young children, and to shew thy pity upon all prisoners and captives….That it may please thee to defend and provide for the fatherless children and widows, and all that are desolate and oppressed'.

If, as it has been suggested, the Prayers were written between late 1806 and spring 1809, while the Austens were living at Southampton, in referring to 'all prisoners and captives', JA may have had particularly in mind the French prisoners confined in the town's ancient Wool House.

15. quicken: make alert and alive.

16. redemption: 'Being justified freely by his grace through the redemption that is in Jesus Christ' (Romans, 3:24). 'Deliverance from sin and its consequences by the atonement of Jesus Christ' (*OED*).

(II)

1. petitions: formal requests made within the body of a prayer.

2. many…remembrance: cf. 'Who can tell how oft he offendeth: O cleanse thou me from my secret faults' (Psalms, 19:12).

3. bountifully: 'with generosity and liberality: I will sing unto the Lord, because he hath dealt bountifully with me' (Psalms, 13:6).

4. Fatherly Goodness: cf. a post-communion prayer: 'we thy humble servants entirely desire thy fatherly goodness…'.

5. benevolent…fellow-creature: cf. Law, *A Serious Call*, from the heading to ch. 20: 'Universal love is here recommended to be the subject of prayer at this hour' [midday]; within ch. 20, 'using…prayers, for the common good of all his fellow creatures'; ch. 21, also headed as treating 'universal love'; and within ch. 21, 'benevolent to all our fellow creatures as creatures of God…'.

6. Give…Affliction: cf. A Collect or Prayer for all Conditions of men: 'giving them patience under their sufferings, and a happy issue out of all their afflictions'.

7. divided & far asunder: in the family circle, this might be understood as attaching particularly to the welfare of the sailor brothers. During the Southampton years, Francis's duties took him as far afield as China, and Charles, who was patrolling offshore North America, encountered French naval vessels.

8. thine Eye: the 'eye of god' is a frequent image in the psalms of the Coverdale translation of the Bible (1535), preserved in the Book of Common Prayer.

9. Faith & Fear: cf. Prayer for the whole state of Christ's Church Militant here in earth: 'And we also bless thy Holy name, for all thy servants departed this life in thy faith and fear'. 'Fear', in this devotional context, combines dread and reverence.

10. fervent devotion: 'fervent', originally the term for burning material or boiling liquid, as in 'the elements shall melt with fervent heat' (2 Peter, 3:10); also applied figuratively to the force of devotion or prayer, as in 'The effectual fervent prayer of a righteous man availeth much' (James 5:16).

(III)

1. Father…day: cf. the opening of The third Collect, for Grace in the service of Morning Prayer: 'O Lord, our heavenly Father, Almighty and everlasting God, who hast safely brought us to the beginning of this day'.

2. accountable: as men and women are accountable for their lives before God on the Day of Judgment.

3. bestow: give freely.

4. Forbearance: associated with the quality of 'longsuffering' attributed to God in refraining from punishing sinful mankind and allowing time to find their way to repentance: 'Or despisest thou the riches of his goodness and forbearance and longsuffering: not knowing that the goodness of God leadeath thee to repentance?' (Romans, 2:4).

5. Patience: both a human and a divine characteristic: 'the God of patience' (Romans, 15:5), 'your patience and faith in all your persecutions and tribulations' (2 Thessalonians,1:4).

6. examination: self-examination to ascertain one's sins, weaknesses and failings.

7. dispensation: here, a divine giving out or bestowing, as in the phrase 'the dispensation of the grace of God' (Ephesians, 3:2)

8. continuance of all these Mercies: 'continue such thy mercies towards us' (Thanksgivings, For Peace and Deliverance from our Enemies).

9. presumption: disrespect, effrontery, impudence, immoderation, self-wilfullness: 'Presumptuous are they, selfwilled' (2 Peter, 2:10); 'And the man that will do presumptuously, and will not hearken unto the **priest' (Deuteronomy, 17:12).**

10. Ignorant: heathen, unenlightened.

11. knowledge…Truth: cf. A Prayer of St Chrysostom, at the conclusion of the service of Evening Prayer: 'granting us in this world knowledge of thy truth…'.

12. Hardened: as in the question 'who hath hardened himself against' God 'and prospered?' (Job, 9:4).

13. assuage the pangs of disease: cf. 'to asswage the contagious sickness wherewith we lately have been sore afflicted' (Thanksgivings, For Deliverance from the Plague, or other Common Sickness).

14. avert from them all material & lasting Evil: cf. 'turn from us all those evils that we have most righteously deserved' (from a prayer at the end of The Litany).

15. Words…Thee: referring to the Lord's Prayer which concludes each of these Evening Prayers. In the Sermon on the Mount, Jesus instructs the people in the way they should pray and the words they should use: 'After this manner therefore pray ye…' leading directly into the words of the Lord's Prayer (Matthew, 6: 9-13), of which JA writes out no more than the opening two words.

Plan of a Novel

Plan of a Novel	probably written spring 1816
Autograph manuscript	Pierpont Morgan Library
Facsimile	*Plan of a Novel* (Oxford: Clarendon Press, 1926); the first page is included here as 'Manuscript pages' II.

A version of the *Plan* was published in chapter 7 the 1870 *Memoir* (pp. 161-65). At many points, Austen-Leigh slightly re-worded the text towards more formal prose and several sections were omitted. Although he noted that the names of some of the 'advisers are written on the margin of the manuscript,' no names are given.[1] His version of the text was accompanied by extracts from the correspondence between Jane Austen and James Stanier Clarke which provided some of the circumstances of the *Plan's* composition. The complete text, with some minor changes to the punctuation, was given in the *Life and Letters* (1913, pp. 337-40), accompanied by the names of those supposedly supplying the 'hints'.[2] In 1926, the Clarendon Press published Chapman's full text, a facsimile of the manuscript, and Jane Austen's three letters to Clarke (15 November, 11 December 1815, 1 April 1816) together with his replies.

The manuscript is a lightly and neatly corrected fair copy written on the four sides of two quarto leaves (both 14¾ x 9⅛ in.). The sheets carry the watermark of a hunting horn and the date 1813. The names of the persons from whom the 'hints' supposedly came are numbered and written in the left-hand margin alongside the matching numbered 'hints' in the text.

The *Plan* was among the manuscripts that came to Cassandra at her sister's death in 1817. Cassandra left the manuscript to her brother Charles, whose eldest daughter, Cassandra Esten Austen (1808-97), assisted her father in the execution of Cassandra's will in 1845, when the *Plan* and other memorabilia came into her possession. She died unmarried and her Jane Austen collection passed to her five nieces, the daughters of Charles Austen jnr. The *Plan* was one of the items in this collection purchased by Chapman in 1924 from the three daughters who remained unmarried. This manuscript he sold on to the Pierpont Morgan Library in December 1925.[3] The *Plan* is listed as item 4 in a description of the collection that Chapman sent to the *Times Literary Supplement* in January 1926.[4]

In the *Memoir*, the *Plan* is presented in a strongly biographical framework, as belonging to the single episode in Jane Austen's life when her 'Seclusion from the literary world' was interrupted and a 'mark of distinction…bestowed upon her', this being the interest of the Prince Regent in her work, his permission for her next novel to be dedicated to him, and her conducted tour of Carlton House, the Prince Regent's official residence in London.[5] Her guide on this visit, which took place on 13 November 1815, was the Regent's Librarian, the Rev James Stanier Clarke. Austen-Leigh provided extracts from the correspondence that passed between Jane Austen and Clarke. However, his editing had the effect of obscuring the full comedy of the *Plan*, since he cut most of Clarke's suggestions, including the main section of advice given in the letter of 21? December 1815;[6] equally, he omitted from the text of the *Plan* those suggestions that Jane Austen had quoted from Clarke either directly or near *verbatim*. This very point was noticed by Caroline Austen. Writing to congratulate her brother on the publication of the *Memoir*, she commented, 'I see you have been very merciful to Mr. Clarke in omitting the most ridiculous parts of his letter'.[7] In truth, Austen-Leigh could hardly be expected to treat the *Plan* any more generously than he did, since with the scene-setting and the quotations from Clarke, even in this truncated form it occupied almost one-tenth of the *Memoir*.

It is no surprise that even at this late stage in her career Jane Austen turned so readily to literary burlesque. Far from ending with the juvenilia or the early version of *Northanger Abbey* – which had been accepted for publication in 1803 – this was a style of family entertainment that she kept alive for the next generation of nephews and nieces. On her visits to Chawton, James's daughter Anna could remember borrowing novels from a circulating library at Alton to read and then 'relate the stories to

Aunt Jane….Greatly we both enjoyed it, one piece of absurdity leading to another'. One such favourite was *Lady Maclairn, the Victim of Villainy* (1806) by Rachel Hunter, 'an exceedingly lengthy affair' in which 'the same story about the same people, most of whom I think had died before the real story began was repeated 3 or 4 times over',[8] altogether a lachrymous tale in which all the characters contributed to a rising flood of tears. When she returned home to Steventon, Anna sent her aunt a Hunteresque letter, to which Jane Austen replied in kind, with a missive in which 'Miss Austen's tears have flowed'.[9] Jane Austen also encouraged her niece to write a 'mock heroic story' in which the daily coach to Southampton, named Falknor's, was re-named, with ominous Gothic echoes, as 'The Car of Falkenstein';[10] as Mary Lascelles termed it, this was a 'partnership in burlesque invention'.[11] It also seems likely that the juvenilia notebooks were being read and re-read to the younger generation. Certainly, details were being up-dated. In 'Catharine', *Coelebs in Search of a Wife* (1809), the novel by Hannah More, replaces a reference to 'Seccar's explanation of the Catechism', and, a 'Regency walking dress' is added, a reference which could not have preceded the Regency Act of 1811. Three or four years later, Anna's brother James Edward was making his own attempt to complete 'Evelyn' and 'Catharine', the two unfinished stories in *Volume the Third*.[12] And beyond her own writing Jane Austen continued to find amusement in other people's burlesques. A notable example is Eaton Stannard Barrett's *The Heroine, or Adventures of a Fair Romance Reader* (1813), one of the most entertaining and widely-read novels of the day: 'a delightful burlesque', Jane wrote to Cassandra, 'particularly on the Radcliffe style'[13] – which she was to draw on heavily in writing *Sanditon*. Eight months later, in November 1814, she told Anna that she was planning to write a burlesque of her own, 'a close Imitation' of Mary Brunton's *Self Control* (1810), a moralising tale, which, a year before, she had found 'excellently-meant, elegantly-written' and 'without anything of Nature and Probability in it'.[14]

So it seems that for Jane Austen burlesque was virtually a habit of mind and the family provided an alert and appreciative audience close to hand. We know from Caroline Austen's memoir that when her aunt returned from her visit to Carlton House, 'the little adventure was talked of for a while with some interest, and afforded some amusement'.[15]

The memory of that visit was kept alive by the correspondence that followed, Clarke's suggestions continuing into his third and final letter, written from Brighton Pavilion on 27 March 1816.[16] At the beginning of May, Fanny Knight arrived at Chawton. She was a favourite niece – 'almost another Sister...quite after one's own heart'– Jane Austen described her to Cassandra;[17] and since Fanny is credited with no less than four of the fifteen 'hints', it seems likely that the *Plan* was largely composed during her three weeks' stay. Clarke had himself put forward this very suggestion – 'make all your friends send Sketches to help you'– four months earlier, back in December 1815.[18] In practical terms, then, there was ample time for Jane Austen to have contacted the others identified as supplying 'hints'. Mary Cooke, a second cousin and lifelong friend, named for three, sounds a very credible source. But how likely is it that she would have approached William Gifford, a famed classical scholar, John Murray's principal literary advisor, and, as editor of the *Quarterly Review*, something of a literary panjandrum? Gifford read the manuscript of *Emma* in September 1815 and recommended its publication, at the same time offering to revise it. But there is no record that Jane Austen accepted this offer or that she ever met or communicated with Gifford, either directly or through Murray. His 'hint' sounds like a joke, an opportunity for Jane Austen to get her own back for his intrusive suggestion of touching her work. Similarly, it may be a retaliatory joke on Mr Sherer, the Vicar of Godmersham, the principal parish in her brother Edward's Kent estate. She knew and admired him as a clergyman. However, as she noted in her 'Opinions of *Emma*', he 'did not think' Emma 'equal to either *MP*...or *P&P*'. To make matters worse, he was 'Displeased with my pictures of Clergymen'.[19] Mrs Craven and her daughter also passed 'Opinions' on *Emma*: Jane Austen noted that they 'liked it very much, but not so much as the others'.[20] And the remaining two, Mrs Pearse and Mr Sanford, were so far outside the family circle that one feels prompted to ask: if them, why not Cassandra or their long-term companion, Martha Lloyd? Would they not have been invited to join in? And where is a 'hint' from Mrs Austen, famed in the family for her humorous verses and her 'sprack wit'?[21] The likely answer is that the elaborate numbering and naming of these 'various quarters', the supposed sources of the 'hints', are a spoof, an extension to the central joke.[22]

In composing the *Plan*, Jane Austen was turning Clarke's suggestions and the man himself into a family entertainment, a joke that embraced many of the elements she found ridiculous in popular fiction – black and white characters, episodic plots and melodramatic action, structural incoherence, moralising and propaganda, mannerisms of language and style and so on. As a novel-reading family, the Austens would be attuned to these elements of parody and burlesque; and we can be sure that Jane Austen alerted at least her closest circle to the transparent absurdity of the suggestions emanating from Mr Clarke. At the same time, Jane Austen's contact with the Librarian, and the exchange of letters that followed, was a collision of significance. As well as inspiring the *Plan*, it provoked Jane Austen to a statement of her artistic principles, an announcement that she would not be tempted to 'Historical Romance' by 'Profit or Popularity'– seemingly a dig at Sir Walter Scott as well as Clarke. Her metier, as she understood it, was not in dealing with the courts and courtiers of Clarke's suggestion but with 'pictures of domestic Life in Country Villages'– precisely the locale of *Emma* – and she was not to be deflected from her 'own style' and her 'own Way'.[23] Now far into *Persuasion*, her sixth novel, it was an assertion she could make with confidence.[24]

Notes

1 *1870 M*, p. 161.

2 *Life and Letters*, pp. 337-40.

3 In these transactions, Chapman revealed an unexpected commercial streak. In an article published in 1950, he recalled that thirty years earlier he first made the acquaintance of the American millionaire-collector, Pierpont Morgan – 'an ardent Austenian' Chapman calls him – then building his collection of Austen letters. On a subsequent occasion, Morgan asked Chapman 'if there were any chance of acquiring a scrap of her manuscript'. This 'modest ambition', Chapman explained, 'I was able to satisfy'. Without going into detail, he recounted that 'A family collection of Jane Austen's remains became available. I bought it, as honorary middleman, for what was thought a fair price, and divided the spoils at my leisure,' selling items on to the British Museum and to Morgan ('Manuscript-Hunting in Two Continents', *The New Colophon* (vol. 2, pt. 8, 1950), pp. 370-78). Chapman itemised the 'family collection' – from the sisters, the

three daughters of Charles Austen jnr, their identity undisclosed throughout – in a letter entitled 'A Jane Austen Collection' (*Times Literary Supplement*, 14 January 1926, pp. 26-27).

4   'A Jane Austen Collection', *The Times Literary Supplement*, 14 January 1926, pp. 26-27.

5   *1870 M*, pp. 142, 146.

6   Letter 132 (A), *L*, p. 307.

7   Letter of 16 December 1869, *M*, p. 192.

8   Anna Lefroy, 'Recollections of Aunt Jane' (1864), *M*, p. 159.

9   Letter 76 (C),?29-31 October 1812, *L*, p. 195.

10 *FR*, p. 191.

11 Lascelles, p. 36.

12 See Peter Sabor's Introduction to the Cambridge edition of the *Juvenilia* (2006).

13 Letter of 2-3 March 1814, *L*, p. 256.

14 Letter of?24 November 1814, *L*, p. 283; to Cassandra, 11-12 October 1813, *L*, p. 234.

15 Caroline Austen, *My Aunt Jane Austen: A Memoir* (Jane Austen Society, 1952, new edn., 1991), p. 13.

16 Letter 138 (A), *L*, p. 311.

17 Letter of 7-9 October 1808, *L*, p. 144.

18 Letter 132 (A), 21 December 1815, *L*, p. 307.

19 *MW*, p. 437.

20 Ibid.

21 'Mrs Austen herself attributed her cleverness to "my own Sprack wit", a brisk Old English country phrase denoting a lively perception of the character and foibles of others' (George Holbert Tucker, *A Goodly Heritage: a History of Jane Austen's Family*, Manchester: Carcanet New Press, 1983, p. 66).

22 Kathryn Sutherland takes a different view, seeing in this feature of the *Plan* 'clear evidence that habits of confidential collaborative writing and circulation persisted throughout Austen's career' (Sutherland, p. 231).

23 Letter of 1 April 1816, *L*, p. 312. Are we to suspect that it was in JA's mind that she wrote this letter on All Fools' Day?

24 According to Cassandra's record of the dates of composition of the novels (reproduced in *MW*, facing p. 242), *Persuasion* was begun on 8 August 1815 and completed on 6 August 1816.

*

The 'various quarters'
JA identifies by name the 'various quarters' from which the 'hints' for the 'Plan' supposedly came. In the ms, the names are numbered as here, and written in the margin, in line with the 'hint'

1. Mr. Gifford: William Gifford (1756-1826), classical scholar, critic and editor of the *Quarterly Review* – published by John Murray – was also Murray's professional reader, advising him in the choice of new books for his list. Gifford read *E* in manuscript and in September 1815 recommended its publication, offering to revise it. There is no record that such revision did take place nor of JA's ever having met or communicated with Gifford either directly or through Murray.

2, 4, 11, 13. Fanny Knight: 1793-1882, the eldest of JA's brother Edward's eleven children, her favourite niece, valued by her as 'almost another sister' (letter to Cassandra, 7-9 October 1808, *L*, p. 144). That Fanny is credited with no less than four 'hints' suggests her intimacy with the 'Plan', which could have been drafted during her three weeks' stay at Chawton Cottage in May 1816.

3, 5, 10. Mary Cooke: 1781-?1818, a second cousin of JA's and a lifelong friend from childhood.

6. Mr. Clarke: Rev James Stanier Clarke (1767-1834), the Prince Regent's Librarian whose suggestions to JA for the subject of her next novel, to follow *E*, formed the inspiration for the *Plan*.

7. Mr. Sherer: Rev Joseph Godfrey Sherer (1770-1824) was known to JA as Vicar of Godmersham (1811-24), the parish in which her brother Edward's Kentish property lay. In 1813, JA wrote to Cassandra that he was man she liked 'very much' (23-24 September 1813, *L*, p. 226) and a day or two later, she reported that he gave 'an excellent sermon' (25 September, *L*, p. 230). In 'Opinions of *Emma*', JA noted that he was 'Displeased with my pictures of Clergymen' (*MW*, p. 437).

9. Many critics: those friends and family members supposedly soliciting a Gothic-style 'wandering' story in which the heroine and her companion travel far and wide.

12. Mrs. Pearse: Anne Pearse (née Phillimore) was the wife of John Pearse (1760-1836) who purchased Chilton Lodge – on the Bath road near Hungerford, Berkshire – in 1796. Pearse was MP for Devizes 1818-32 and a Director of the Bank of England for thirty-four years between 1790-1828, Deputy Governor 1808-10, Governor 1810-12. He was almost certainly known to Henry Austen from his own banking activities; and it is through Henry that JA, on one of her London visits, is likely to have met Mrs Pearse.

14. Mrs. Craven: née Catherine Hughes (d.1839), second wife of Rev John Craven (1732-1804), invariably mentioned in JA's letters to Cassandra as 'Mrs Craven'. In 'Opinions of *Emma*', JA noted that 'Mrs Craven & Miss Craven [seventeen year-old Charlotte Elizabeth] – liked it very much, but not so much as the others. – ' (*MW*, p. 437).

15. Mr. H. Sanford: Henry Sanford was a friend of Henry Austen and possibly a business connection at Albany, in Piccadilly, where Henry's bank operated 1804-07 and where Sanford occupied an apartment. JA got to know him well, enjoyed his friendship and found him amusing company. When staying with Henry in November 1814, JA wrote to her niece Fanny Knight that Sanford was 'to join us at dinner, which will be a comfort, and in the even^g while your Uncle & Mss Eliza play chess, he shall tell me comical things & I will laugh at them, which will be a pleasure to both' (30 November 1814, *L*, p. 287). In 'Opinions of *Mansfield Park*' Sanford is on record as being 'extremely pleased with it' (*MW*, p. 434).

The 'hints'

a. Scene to be in the Country...settled in a Curacy: cf. Clarke's suggestion: 'to delineate in some future Work the Habits of Life and Character and enthusiasm of a Clergyman – who should pass his time between the metropolis & the Country' (to JA, 16 November 1815, *L*, p. 296). Clarke's suggestions, here and later, derive from his own life. He spent much time in the 'metropolis' of London as Domestic Chaplain and Librarian to the Prince of Wales at Carlton House, and had his own pied-à-terre at 37 Golden Square (just north of Piccadilly Circus). His 'Country' visits were to Petworth House in Sussex, the family seat of his patron, the third Earl of Egremont; and to Chiddingstone near Sevenoaks. There, as he wrote to JA, he 'had been hiding himself from all bustle and turmoil – and getting Spirits for a Winter Campaign' (*L*, pp. 306-07).

Curacy: a term meaning, in this context, the position of parish priest.

b. the most excellent Man: 'most excellent' men and women abound in Richardson: this superlative appears seventeen times in *Clarissa* (1748), thirty times in *Sir Charles Grandison*, and recurs in *S&S*, *P&P*, and *MP*.

c. Heroine a faultless Character: a reminder of 'the lovely young Woman' in 'Jack and Alice' (*Volume the First*) 'possessed of Youth, Beauty, Wit & Merit' (*MW*, pp. 20-21).

d. very highly accomplished...singing in the first stile: the heroine comes equipped with the standard range of accomplishments (see *LS*, letter 7, note 2).

e. dark eyes & plump cheeks: amongst the many fictional heroines who fit this description is Madeline in *Clermont. A Tale* (1798) by Regina Maria Roche, one of the titles on Isabella Thorpe's list of 'horrid' novels (*NA*, vol. 1, ch. 6): she is 'tall...delicately made' with 'eyes, large and of the darkest hazel' and a 'beautifully rounded cheek' (vol. 1, ch. 1). The same dark eyes and plump cheeks feature strongly in Ozias Humphrey's portrait of JA as a girl, a picture likely to be well-known to JA's friends and relations.

f. a tone of high, serious sentiment: Johnson defines 'sentiment' as 'Thought; notion; opinion'.

g. to relate to her the past events of his Life: This was a regular bulking-out device in fictional narrative, often of little or no relevance to the main story. cf. the recounting of 'Life & Adventures' in chapters 3 to 5 of 'Jack and Alice' (the phrase itself is in *MW*, pp. 16, 20).

h. going to sea...about the Court: cf. Clarke's suggestion: 'Carry your Clergyman to Sea as the Friend of some distinguished Naval Character about a Court' (to JA,?21 December 1815, *L*, p. 307). Between 1795 and 1799, Clarke served at sea as a naval chaplain under Captain John Willett Payne RN. A crony of the Prince of Wales, Payne had held a number of official appointments in the Prince's household during the 1780's and 90's, including some years as his Private Secretary.

i. a great variety of Characters: regarded by writers and critics alike as an important feature of literature of all kinds, from epic poetry downwards to the novel. For this reason JA later mentions the point again, reassuring the reader that the heroine's wanderings 'will of course exhibit a wide variety of Characters'.

j. many interesting situations: these would be adventures of all kinds, situations in which his qualities could be put on display, and were regarded as an important aid to displaying character, see Blair, *Lectures*, vol. 2, lecture 37. Clarke's suggestion was that JA should 'bring foreward like Le Sage many interesting Scenes of Character & Interest' (*L*, p. 307). Le Faye suggests that Clarke is referring to Le Sage's *Gil Blas* (1715-35) of which Smollett's translation appeared in 1749.

k. Benefits to result…the respect due to them: cf. Clarke's suggestion: 'shew dear Madam what good would be done if Tythes were taken away entirely, and describe him burying his own mother – as I did – because the High Priest of the Parish in which she died – did not pay her remains the respect he ought to do' (*L*, p. 307). This is the sort 'of solemn specious nonsense – about something unconnected with the story' that JA had facetiously proposed to Cassandra as an improvement to *P&P* (letter of 4 February 1813, *L*, p. 203).

Tythes: the ancient customary right of a Church of England clergyman to receive a tenth of the annual produce of the cultivated land in the parish (by this time, most tithes of produce had been commutated to payments in money). Like many rural clergy, Clarke found tithes burdensome to collect. But the agents he employed to collect them 'were dishonest and cheated him' and taking on the work himself he found 'a time-wasting exercise and deeply frustrating' (Viveash, 2006, p. 13). JA was familiar with the tithing system: just before the Austens left Steventon for Bath she noted that Mr Austen was 'doing all in his power to encrease his Income by raising his Tythes &c' and her expectation was that he might be 'getting very nearly six hundred a year' (letter to Cassandra, 3-5 January 1801, *L*, p. 69).

High Priest: a title in the Old Testament for officials of the temple; and sometimes used of God. Here, Clarke is using the term disparagingly to suggest that the parish clergyman was too superior, too much above himself, to conduct his mother's funeral. This detail is autobiographical. At his own mother's funeral in 1802, Clarke interrupted the Rector of the parish, accused him 'of not showing his mother's earthly remains the respect they demanded', ordered him out of the church and continued the service himself (Viveash, 2006, p.36).

l. of a very literary turn, an Enthusiast in Literature: cf. Clarke's suggestion: 'Fond of, & entirely engaged in Literature' (*L*, p. 297). This would fit Clarke himself. As well as being Librarian to the Prince of Wales, from 1812 he held the post of Historiographer to the King; in 1799 he established the *Naval Chronicle*; and, amongst other works, was co-author (with John M'Arthur) of the official biography of Nelson, *The life and Services of Horatio, Viscount Nelson, from his Lordship's Manuscripts* (2 vols., 1809).

Enthusiast: a term originally applied in the seventeenth-century to those possessed by religious 'enthusiasm', a possession of the spirit that could be worthy and beneficent or extreme and delusive. JA seems to be using the word here in same neutral tone as when she referred to her brother Edward as 'no Enthusiast in the beauties of Nature. His Enthusiasm is for the Sports of the field only' (to Francis Austen, 25 September 1813, *L*, p. 230). The possessed enthusiast is Sanditon's promoter, Mr Parker, to whom JA attaches the word (*S*, ch. 2, note 1).

m. nobody's Enemy but his own: JA slyly rewords Clarke's suggestion 'no man's Enemy but his own' (*L*, p. 297) so that it becomes, verbatim, Sophia Western's description of Tom Jones (Fielding, *Tom Jones*, 1749, bk. 4, ch. 5).

n. most zealous in the discharge of his Pastoral Duties: following the description of Mrs Norris as being 'most zealous' in promoting the marriage of Maria Bertram and Mr Rushworth (*MP*, vol. 1, ch. 4), this epithet would not have a positive ring for JA's readers.

Pastoral Duties: these were the duties of a parish priest in caring for his parishioners: conducting regular Sunday services, baptisms, marriages, funerals etc.

o. an exemplary Parish Priest: a testimonial turn of phrase commonly found in obituaries, on gravestones and other celebratory locations.

Parish Priest: Clarke's own church office as Rector of two Sussex parishes, Preston-cum-Hove and Tillington, near Petworth.

p. light eyes and fair skin: a 'fair skin' was highly valued. See the discussions of this issue in *LS*, letter 17, note 3 and *W*, note 189.

q. a striking variety of adventures: many novelists boasted this as a feature of their works, see for example *The Female Quixote* by Charlotte Lennox, 1752 (vol. 1, bk. 4, ch. 6). It was book JA enjoyed. She wrote to Cassandra in 1807 that it 'makes our evening amusement; to me a very high one, as I find the work quite equal to what I remembered' (7 January 1807, *L*, p. 116).

r. Heroine & her Father...together in one place: that the Heroine and her Father are companion-wanderers may be a reminder of the opening of the most famous of Gothic novels, Ann Radcliffe's *The Mysteries of Udopho* (1794) in which Emily St Aubert accompanies her father on a health-seeking journey to Languedoc and Provence – a journey which Catherine Morland mentions to Henry Tilney (*NA*, vol. 1, ch. 14). JA may also be intending a sly reference to *The Wanderer, or Female Difficulties* (1814), Fanny Burney's most recent novel. There is not an exact parallel since Juliet's father is not with her during her travels and she is alone in her attempts to earn a living. But the closeness of the father-daughter relationship in the *Plan* may be seen as JA's mockery of Burney's sentimental heroines and their devotion to their fathers, mirrored in real life by Burney's own devotion to Dr Burney and declared in the pages-long dedication to him of *The Wanderer*. In Mary Brunton's *Self-Control* (1810), father and daughter travel together from Scotland to London so that Laura can work to salvage their financial plight. When JA read the novel for a second time in 1813, her 'opinion' was 'confirmed of its' being an excellently-meant, elegantly-written Work, without anything of Nature or Probability in it' (Letter to Cassandra, 11-12 October 1813, *L*, p. 234); and a year later, JA told her niece Anna Lefroy that she intended to write 'a close imitation of "Self-control" as soon as I can' (Letter of?24 November 1814, *L*, p. 283).

s. driven from his Curacy...& pursuing her: JA's glance at the persecution theme commonly found in novels of the 1790's and continued in the novels of Mary Brunton and others.

t. a wide variety of Characters: see note i.

u. there will be no mixture: following the position set out by Johnson in *The Rambler* (no. 4, 31 March 1750): that as novelists had a responsibility towards their young and impressionable readers, so they should exhibit 'the highest and purest' 'idea of virtue' 'that humanity can reach' and that 'Vice...should always disgust; nor should the graces of gaiety, or the dignity of courage, be so united with it, as to reconcile it to the mind.' Johnson's targets seem to have been the notably 'mixed' title-heroes of two recent novels, Smollett's *Roderick Random* (1748) and Fielding's *Tom*

Jones (1749). As JA points out in *NA*, a pastiche of the Johnsonian line was followed in Gothic fiction: 'Among the Alps and Pyrenees, perhaps, there were no mixed characters. There, such as were not as spotless as an angel, might have the disposition of a fiend. But in England it was not so; among the English, she [Catherine Morland] believed, in their hearts and habits, there was a general though unequal mixture of good and bad' (vol. 2, ch. 10). 'mixed' is also found in the text-books of rhetoric and belles lettres, as in Hugh Blair's *Lectures* (1783), the lecture on 'Tragedy': 'Mixed characters, such as in fact we meet with in the world, afford the most proper field for displaying...the vicissitudes of life....Such subjects both dispose us to the deepest sympathy, and administer useful warnings to us for our own conduct' (vol. 2, lecture 46).

v. all the Good will be unexceptionable: JA gives this word highly equivocal undertone, employing it six times in *LS* ; equally, in *MP*, in the face of Edmund's objections both Tom Bertram and Mr Yates use 'unexceptionable' in arguing for the qualities of *Lovers' Vows* (vol. 1, chs. 13, 15); and Sir Thomas and Lady Bertram also employ 'unexceptionable' in commending Crawford's proposal to Fanny Price (vol. 3, ch. 2).

w. there will be no foibles: according to Campbell, *The Principles of Rhetoric* (1770), these were 'caprices, little extravagancies, weak anxieties, jealousies, childish fondness, pertness, vanity, and self-conceit' (vol. 1, bk. 1, ch. 2, sect. 2).

x. all perfection of course: this 'hint' would have a private meaning at this time for JA and Fanny Knight. In 1814, the aunt was writing a letter of advice to her niece touching at length on the idea of an ideal partner for her, the 'one in a Thousand, as the Creature You & I should think perfection' (18-20 November, *L*, p. 280).

y. only prevented...by some excess of refinement: the prime example is in Richardson's *Sir Charles Grandison*: Grandison feels himself constrained from declaring his love for Harriet Byron because he judges himself to be honour bound by an existing quasi-engagement to an Italian lady, Clementina Porretta, 'scruples' (see below) which are only overcome when Clementina emerges from a bout of madness with the realisation that as a Roman Catholic she cannot marry an Anglican 'heretic'. The pains and complications of the argument constitute the 'excess' that spins the novel out to such a length, these matters occupying no less than four of the work's seven volumes.

z. first applied to: an order of events dictated by the social proprieties.

aa. by the anti-hero: Richard Steele uses this term in *The Lover* (No. 2, 27 February 1714) referring to 'brutes, who have no sense of any thing but what indulges their appetites'; and to an 'abandoned wanderer', marked by 'his restless following of every woman he sees'. Down the eighteenth-century, *The Lover*, together with Steele's other popular essay-journals, was many times reprinted in his collected works – a set of volumes regarded as essential to a gentleman's library – and they may well have been read by JA in her father's library at Steventon and in Edward Austen's library at Godmersham, where Fanny Knight too could also have met the term. JA elaborates this 'anti-' formulation in S with Mr Parker's recital of quasi-medical terminology in ch. 2 and Sir Edward Parker's 'anti-puerile' in ch. 8.

bb. to support herself...work for her Bread: in Mary Brunton's *Self-Control*, the heroine is determined to provide for herself and her father by her own efforts following his financial ruin: 'Could she but hope to obtain a subsistence for her father, she would labour night and day, deprive herself of recreation, of rest, even of daily food, rather than wound his heart, by an acquaintance with poverty' (vol. 1, ch. 15). And in Brunton's next work, *Discipline: A Novel* (1814), the heroine, who terms herself 'as friendless as...a wanderer', is seen as dependent on her 'own labour' for 'shelter or subsistence' (vol. 2, ch. 18). In calling up the topics of female employment and independence, JA is touching on one of the key debates conducted in women's writing at this time.

cc. to retreat into Kamschatka: a peninsula of north-east Siberia, at the furthest extremity of Russia's Far Eastern Empire. A place of exile, it was a byword for remoteness, arctic cold and endurance. This could be a dig at one of the grosser improbabilities of *Self-Control*, the heroine's abduction to the wilds of North America, a feature that JA made a joking vow to 'improve upon' with a heroine who paddles her way home across the Atlantic '& never stop till she reaches Gravesent' (letter to Anna Lefroy,?24 November 1814, *L*, p. 283). It could also be a dig at *Elizabeth; or, The Exiles of Siberia* (1806), a very popular short French novel by Sophie de Cottin, published in English in 1807 and often reprinted. According to the Author's Preface, the daughter 'conceived the glorious design of delivering a father from exile...in defiance of the various obstacles which opposed her filial heroism…' (edn 1815, [p.i]). Three thousand miles further east, for hardship and remoteness JA's Kamschatka far surpasses Mme.Cottin's relatively mild and civilized starting point in southern Siberia; and the suggestion for this distant location may have come to her from John Bell's *Travels from St Petersburg in Russia, to Divers Parts of Asia*, 2 vols. (London: Robert Bell, 1764), a copy of which carries her signature and the date '1799'.

dd. Heroine inconsolable for some time: Richardson set the fashion for this extreme degree of sorrowing or grief. In the first edition of *Clarissa* (1748), he used eight 'inconsolables' for the heroine, adding another two for the revised edition of 1751.

ee. The clutter of events that concludes the 'Plan' is typical of the rapid and totally unrealistic endings to many of the adventure-romance novels weighed down with complex and melodramatic plots.

ff. Tenderest & completest Eclaircissement: see *LS*, letter 33, note 1; and very recently it had become a literary vogue word among both reviewers and novelists: JA used it again in *MP* (vol. 2, ch. 2) and Scott in three of his current novels: *Waverley* (1815), *Guy Mannering* (1815) and *The Antiquary* (1816).

gg. Throughout the whole work…living in high style: perhaps a direct answer to an unsigned note from 'An admirer', someone who lamented of *MP* 'that his acquaintance with persons so amiable and elegant in mind and manners is of so short duration' (Chapman, 1953, p. 21). Chapman (p. 20), who dated the note '?1815', thought the writer might have been her brother James's son, James Edward (later, Austen-Leigh), at the time aged 17.

Sanditon

Sanditon	January-March 1817
Autograph manuscript	King's College, Cambridge
Facsimile	*Sanditon: An Unfinished Novel* (Oxford: Clarendon Press, 1975) Two pages are reproduced as 'Manuscript Pages' III and IV.

Sanditon first appeared in a summary version, entitled 'The last work', chapter 13 of the second edition of the *Memoir* (1871).[1] This text, about one-tenth of the original twenty-four thousand words, was silently corrected by Austen-Leigh. He linked the extracts with five hundred words of summary, explaining his text in this way:

> Such an unfinished fragment cannot be presented to the public; but I am persuaded that some of Jane Austen's admirers will be glad to learn something about the latest creations which were forming themselves in her mind; and therefore, as some of the principal characters were already sketched in with a vigorous hand, I will try to give an idea of them, illustrated by extracts from the work.[2]

This remained the only version available until Chapman provided a full text, together with a record of the manuscript changes, in the Clarendon Press edition, 1925. The title-page announced the work as *Fragment of a Novel*, while the spine carried *Sanditon*. According to the *Life and Letters* (1913), this was the title 'given to the twelve chapters by the family', a point that Chapman repeated.[3] According to another family tradition, however, Jane Austen intended the title to be 'The Brothers'[4] – words that appear together twice in the manuscript text, in chapter 2, referring to the Parker brothers, Arthur, Sidney and

Thomas.[5] The 1925 text, without the record of manuscript changes but with one or two corrected readings, was used in the *Minor Works* volume (1954). A facsimile of the manuscript, entitled *Sanditon: An Unfinished Novel* (Oxford: Clarendon Press), Introduction by B.C.Southam, was published in 1975; and there is a transcription taken directly from the manuscript: Arthur M. Axelrad, *Jane Austen Caught in the Act of Greatness* (1st Books, 2003).

The untitled manuscript is a first draft, in places heavily revised. Like the manuscript of *The Watsons*, the pages are unnumbered and there is no regular indication of paragraphing or dialogue; however, there are chapter divisions. There is variation in the writing: in some areas there are 21 lines to the page, with the hand open and free-flowing; in others, approaching 30; and on the last page of chapter three (f.16^v) – where Jane Austen wanted to be able to finish the chapter within the space of the page – as many as 37 lines, the hand more compressed and tightly formed. As it turned out, her text just overran the page and rather than start a new quire, she added the final words – 'the Loveliness was complete' – to the space available at the bottom of the first page, f.1^r. One section of chapter 7 (ff.19^{r-v}), amounting to 13 lines, JA wrote first in pencil, presumably at a time when she was unable to work with a pen, later inking over these lines. Other than this, in its appearance the manuscript conveys no sign of Jane Austen's physical weakness.

The 80 leaves are gathered in three quires. When Chapman saw them, the first and second quires were sewn together, but he gives no indication when this may have taken place. The leaves of the first and second quires measure 7½ x 4¾ in. and carry the watermark KENT 1812. The leaves of the third quire measure 6⅜ x 4 in. and have the watermark JOSEPH COLES 1815. The first quire is of 16 leaves, chapters 1-3; the second quire is of 24 leaves, chapters 4-8 and part of 9. The third quire is of 40 leaves and contains the rest of chapter 9 (opening 'with a thousand regrets', the first line of f.41^r) to the end of the written text at f.60^v. The remainder of the quire, folios 61 to 80, is blank.[6]

Jane Austen kept a precise record of her progress, dating the manuscript at its beginning and end: 'Jan: 27. – 1817' and the number '1' at the top of the first page of the first quire, f.1^r; 'March 1.st'and the number '2' at the top of the first page of the third quire, f.41^r; 'March 18' under the last line of the text, the third quire, f.60^v.

After Jane Austen's death, the manuscripts went from Cassandra, to Jane Austen's niece Anna Lefroy and was available to her brother James Edward Austen-Leigh for the second edition of the *Memoir* (1871). It remained in the Lefroy family after Anna's death in 1872 and when Chapman edited the manuscript for the Clarendon edition of 1925, it belonged to Mary Isabella Lefroy (1860-1939), a grand-daughter of Anna. In 1930, Isabella Lefroy presented the manuscript to King's College, Cambridge in memory both of her sister Florence (1857-1926) and Florence's husband, Augustus Austen-Leigh (1840-1905), a son of James Edward and Provost of King's from 1889 until his death.

Cassandra made a copy of the manuscript (on paper with an 1831 watermark) for her brother Francis. This is now the property of the Jane Austen Memorial Trust at Jane Austen's House, Chawton.

In the spring of 1816, the date given to *The Plan of a Novel*, the earliest symptoms of what was to be Jane Austen's final illness became evident. From details given in her letters, it is possible to identify her likely condition as Addison's disease, a form of kidney failure brought on by tubercular infection.[7] During the course of the year, her condition fluctuated. In August, she was sufficiently well to complete *Persuasion* and to take up the revision of *Susan*, published after her death as *Northanger Abbey*. At the turn of the year, she seems to have enjoyed a further period of remission, and at the end of January 1817 felt able to start work on her seventh novel, known to us as *Sanditon*. But that was for only seven weeks, until 18 March; and four months later, to the day – 18 July 1817 – she died.

Considering that Austen-Leigh allowed so little space to *Sanditon* in the 1871 *Memoir*, it is rather surprising to find that he thought highly of it. Writing to an American correspondent at the end of 1870 about the contents of the second edition, he told Miss Eliza Quincy that it had been decided not to wait longer for any new letters (specifically, those known to be in the possession of Lady Knatchbull but mislaid),

> but to procede (*sic*) to publication at once. The new Edition however will be enriched with more of my Aunts unpublished writings than I before mentioned; especially with extracts from a work which she began within six months of her death, & continued to work at as long as she could work at all. It is a rough

unfinished sketch, requiring much pruning & polishing; but I do not think that it 'smells of apoplexy' like the homilies of Gil Blas' famous Archbishop.[8]

So, although this was a work that Jane Austen was compelled to give up when illness overcame her, it was not, in Austen-Leigh's view, a piece marred by the writer's physical debility – and for this essential perception we can forgive him his urge towards 'pruning & polishing'. On the evidence of the manuscript itself, whatever the state of Jane Austen's health at this time, she was already far advanced in these processes of revision. As an unfinished working manuscript, *Sanditon* has survived in a form virtually identical to that of *The Watsons*. Both exhibit the same sequence of correction and revision, and the same attention to detail. There are concurrent changes, made along the line at the very moment of writing, such as we see on f.15^v, where 'restore' is cancelled to be immediately replaced by the following word, 'secure'; and a few lines later, 'delineated' is cancelled and replaced by 'described'. Then there are revisions that Jane Austen may have made on re-reading a passage just written or at the end of a day's work, making her corrections with the same pen. Finally, there are revisions that appear to have been made at a later re-reading. These are identifiable by a difference in the pen-strokes and inking. Overall, these corrections and revisions are exactly what we would expect. They pick up mistakes in the verb tenses, in singulars and plurals, and they strengthen the time-sequences, the logic of cause and effect, the sentence structures; and they refine the word-choice and heighten the expressive power of the language. All this points to the same conclusion: that in *Sanditon* as in *The Watsons*, the major elements of the work – its style, story-line, plotting and characterisation – were already thought through and firmly in front of Jane Austen from the outset and that few of the manuscript changes depart from what we can understand to have been her original scheme, whether that was a written plan or simply held in her mind. Broadly speaking, we can take it that her intentions are realised in the existing text; and that the present manuscript would stand relatively unchanged in a printed work, equivalent in length to the opening chapters of a three-volume novel.[9] All it awaited was a formal tidying up: introducing paragraphing, setting out the dialogue, regularising the spelling and punctuation and expanding the contractions.[10] Some of these matters of arrangement and presentation she would have left to the printers.

But these manuscript similarities between *Sanditon* and *The Watsons* pale into insignificance when we consider *Sanditon* from a literary point of view. To take an immediate example, occupying the first page of the manuscript, the awkwardness of the three long, winding sentences with which *Sanditon* begins, with their stops and starts and their ponderous unshaplíness. Read on the printed page, this could be interpreted as the clumsiness of an uncorrected trial, the gropings of a writer warming to his story, or, read biographically, evidence of someone struck down with illness and losing their grip. Yet when we turn to the first of the manuscript pages (**III**) we can see that these effects are intentional and visibly worked for. Along the course of these trailing sentences, the lines are heavily corrected and revised. The changes all work in the direction of enforcing the reader's sense of what is being described – the driver's recalcitrance, the unfitness of the road and the foundering of the coach. This dynamic start, in awkward motion, is wholly different from the way in which the other novels begin. Apart from the active dialogue that starts *Pride and Prejudice*, the opening paragraphs of the novels are relatively static and begin the process of retailing the heroines' circumstances, the information the reader needs in order to place them socially and financially. The overturning carriage of *Sanditon* is something new to the novels and it is not until we are a little way into Mr Parker's story that its significance emerges as a pre-figuring or foreshadowing of events: the futility of his wild-goose chase for a doctor[11] as he arrives at the wrong Willingden, and the threat of collapse for his Sanditon venture, perhaps a South Sea Bubble disaster in the making. In the final pages of the fragment, the first sighting of Sidney Parker is similarly prefigurative or symbolic: approaching on 'a close, misty morn^g,' his 'Carriage…appeared at different moments to be everything from the Gig to the Pheaton (*sic*), – from one horse to 4',[12] an arrival cloaked in uncertainty that seems to figure an enigmatic quality about Sidney himself and the part he has to play in the story. Is he to be in the mould of Frank Churchill, perhaps a candidate for Charlotte's hand and as much a challenge to her understanding as he may be to the reader's?

There are other ways in which *Sanditon* departs quite radically from what we recognise as the familiar pattern of an Austen courtship-marriage novel, in which the heroine is rapidly identified for us and remains at or near the focus of the narrative, and where both the plot and action of the novel take a conventional route towards resolution in marriage, following the heroine's successful negotiation of problems *en route* – traditionally a rival, a false hero, false friends, objectionable and objecting relatives, social and financial differences to be bridged, and so on. While *The Watsons* seems to be cast firmly in this mould – as Mary Lascelles puts it, seeming 'by comparison, almost to foreshadow its own fulfilment'[13] – what we have of *Sanditon* is strikingly different and largely unpredictable. At times, the narrative point of view accompanies Charlotte Heywood, seeming to mark her out as a shrewd, controlled and level-headed heroine – or is this role to be shared with Clara Brereton, so far little revealed, but whose qualities seem implied by the fact of her survival with Lady Denham? Is the hero still to appear, perhaps in the person of the local clergyman, as yet unmentioned? Or is it to be the surgeon sought by Mr Parker? Or one of the eligible professional gentlemen already staying at Sanditon, their names in Mrs Whitby's 'List of Subscribers', but so far unseen – 'Lieut: Smith R.N.' perhaps, or 'Capt: Little' or 'Mr Beard – Solicitor, Grays Inn'? And what new horizons are to open with the arrival of the 'half Mulatto' Miss Lambe, 'chilly & tender', the 'young Westindian of large Fortune'? Could she fall for Sir Edward's seductive patter and provide the solution to his financial problems? But these speculations are unprompted, they hardly arise from the story itself, since our attention is already held by the succession of eccentrics occupying the foreground, their pursuits laid out at length, from Mr Parker onwards. And the strong narrative drive of the fragment is provided by its commanding subject – financial speculation. Is it threat or promise – 'Civilzation, Civilization indeed!' – or spoilation in its effect on Sanditon, on its buildings, on its inhabitants and on the visitors it brings?

In her portrayal of Sanditon at this moment in its development, Jane Austen may have drawn on her memories of a two month stay at Worthing in 1805, four years or so into its transformation from fishing village into flourishing resort. And in planning her new work, she may have been stimulated by two recent novels. Firstly, *The Magic of Wealth* (1815), sub-titled a 'Vehicle of Opinions', a propaganda novel by Thomas Skinner Surr, knowledgeable in financial matters from his employment in the Bank of England. Essentially, this is a fictionalised satirical tract warning of the dangers of paper-money through the rise and fall of Mr Flim-Flam, a 'flim-flam' being a deception or humbug. This tradesman turned speculative banker transforms the fishing village of Thiselton – equally, an airy nothing – into the resort of Flimflampton. Secondly, Thomas Love Peacock's *Headlong Hall*, a satirical discussion novel and novel of ideas, published in 1816. At the novel's opening, Peacock has his four 'illuminati' – the so-called enlightened ones – arguing over 'improvements' as they travel toward Headlong Hall, a coach-journey with its own matching comedy of a twisted ankle and an intrusive coachman. Jane Austen's 'improver' is Mr Parker, with his plans for the development of Sanditon; and her story carries a Peacockian series of debates and disquisitions – medical, literary, economic and dietary. In the arguments between Mr Parker and Mr Heywood and between Mr Parker and Lady Denham, Jane Austen voices the opinions of contemporary Parliamentarians and political economists in the post-war debates over poverty and the Poor Law, and on the connection between spending and prices and other issues germane to the national economy; and the 'Benevolence'[14] of the Parker sisters is satirised in the light of contemporary objections to charitable subscriptions, female philanthropy and charity practised from afar. Other allusions and references are equally topical: to the Lottery, fiercely attacked in Parliament in 1816; to Tombuctoo, reached by the first English explorer in 1816, and already an easy target for suggestive sexual humour; and the 'Speculation' that is Sanditon itself – 'planned & built' by Mr Parker and Lady Denham, '& praised & puffed, & raised…to a Something of young Renown'[15] – seems only to confirm the dire 'speculation' warnings heard in the Parliamentary debates of April 1816.

Such a degree of historical immediacy is unparalleled in Jane Austen. Coupled to this, and equally unparalleled, is the sheer range and variety of language registers and jargon on display, tapping into an extraordinary range of information, literary, medical and popular scientific: Mr Parker's guide-book fluency in promoting Sanditon; Lady Denham's vulgarism; the strained and overblown literary Romanticism of Sir Edward's seductive patter; Diana Parker's hypochondriac expansiveness curbed in her passages of breathless telegraphese. And setting these off is Charlotte's cool and amused tone, a voice of balance and sanity, Jane Austen's channel for perceptive judgement and clear vision.

Chapman thought that some of the eccentrics – Mr Parker, his sisters Diana and Susan, Lady Denham and Sir Edward – were caricatured, an effect 'due in part to lack of revision; she would have smoothed these coarse strokes'.[16] This is the kind of speculation that the manuscript helps us to settle, since the written evidence points the other way. The changes are not in the direction of toning down but of enforcement – as Mary Lascelles puts it, 'the systematic deepening, in the corrections of both manuscripts [*The Watsons* and *Sanditon*], of the idiosyncrasies in the speech of almost every character'.[17] Little catch-phrases – 'you know', 'in fact'– are thrown into Mr Parker's speech, making it more colloquial.[18] Likewise, his demonstrative, emphatic manner is heightened: 'awkward Predicament' becomes 'Scrape' (f.5ʳ), 'amazing to me!' becomes 'the wonder!' (f.6ʳ), 'my Plantations astonish everybody by their Growth' is given a flourish in 'The Growth of my Plantations is a general astonishment' (f.18ʳ). An enthusiast for Sanditon, he becomes more fluent, more of an optimist. The few changes to Sir Edward's speech elevate his literary pretentiousness, his straining after 'hard words & involved sentences' (f.38ᵛ): 'unconquerable' becomes 'indomptible' (f.37ᵛ), 'sagacious' becomes 'anti-puerile'(f.37ᵛ). Lady Denham's existing vulgarisms are broadened and new vulgarisms appear: 'We lived perfectly happy together' becomes 'Nobody could live happier together than us' (f.34ᵛ). Diana's rapid fire, staccato speech pattern is accelerated: 'whom I look upon as the most desirable of the two – as the Best of two Excellent'. The sentence was to continue. But Jane Austen abandons it, alters the wording and brings it to a sharp close: 'whom I look upon as the most desirable of the two – as the Best of the Good' (f.41ᵛ). A similar truncation – 'an occasion which called for my Exertions'– is simplified and shortened to 'an occasion which called for me' (ff.42ᵛ-43ʳ). Occasionally, there are three attempts to achieve a very precise effect. This happens, for example, in Diana's account of Arthur's eating capacity. At first, she says 'he is much more likely to eat too much than too little'; neat enough but rather flat. Jane Austen then trimmed this back to 'he eats enormously'; a gain in emphasis but nothing more. At the third attempt, Arthur 'is only too much disposed for Food'. This change succeeds in catching 'the tone of Diana's crusading self-righteousness'.[19] These alterations are all in the direction of strengthening the characters' existing traits; they introduce nothing new; and in this respect they are in line with the range of other corrections and revisions in the manuscript. Altogether, they support the view that in the completed novel these opening chapters would take their place with little change.

But how was *Sanditon* to continue? Austen-Leigh could offer no suggestions. From the evidence of the manuscript, he drew a blank: 'there was scarcely any indication what the course of the story was to be, nor was any heroine yet perceptible, who, like Fanny Price, or Anne Elliot, might draw round her the sympathies of the reader'.[20] In saying this, he had the support of Anna. She was a minor author herself, having published two books for children and possibly a novella.[21] In 1814, under Jane Austen's guidance, she had started on her own novel, 'Which is the Heroine?', showing it to her aunt chapter-by-chapter.[22] When the *Sanditon* manuscript came to her after Cassandra's death she tried to continue it, but gave up after twenty thousand words,[23] commenting that 'The story was too little advanced to enable one to form any idea of the plot'.[24] She repeated this in a letter to her brother in 1862, referring back to her own 'conversations' with 'Aunt Jane…during the time that she was writing this story, 'conversations' ' wholly confined to the characters and, unfortunately, leaving the story umentioned. Aunt Jane touched on the originals – to our loss, unidentified – 'of the Parker family (except of course Sidney)…Their vagaries do by no means exceed the facts from which they were taken – but are too broadly stated for fiction…'.[25] The occasion for this letter was their anxiety that their uncle Francis's daughter Catherine Hubback (1818-77) – a prolific writer, with eight novels already published – would do with *Sanditon* what she had already done with *The Watsons* and bring out her own version.[26] This would have been based on a copy of the manuscript she had made on one of her aunt Cassandra's long visits to Francis and his family, for Cassandra was in the habit of bringing the two unfinished stories with her, to read aloud and discuss in the family circle. Anna put the problem squarely: 'The Copy which was taken, not given, is now at the mercy of Mrs. Hubback, & she will be pretty sure to make use of it as soon as she thinks she safely may'. Anna suggested a solution, 'the publishing way': that they should 'do in this case what the Authoress would certainly have done for herself – slightly alter, & very carefully correct', a revision which Anna felt unfitted to carry out.[27] Although, in the event, Mrs

Hubback made no use of *Sanditon*, the continuing threat that she might do so prompted Austen-Leigh to forestall any such possibility by including his truncated version in the 1871 *Memoir*. Possibly this was against his better judgement. As he wrote to Miss Quincy, he regarded the manuscript as no more than a 'rough unfinished sketch'.[28] Back in 1862 he had accepted his sister's view 'that the M.S. as it stands is very inferior to the published works'. Like Anna, he believed its publication could 'only gratify curiosity at the expense of the Authoresse's fame…'.[29] Returning to-day, Austen-Leigh and his sisters would be relieved and pleasantly surprised to find their anxieties groundless. Around *Sanditon* is a growing wealth of interpretative and historical scholarship together with the understanding that in this last fragment, the opening to her seventh novel, Jane Austen's art enters upon a new phase,[30] bringing with it the revelation of a 'new idiom', her 'late style', the product of 'a renewed, almost youthful creativity and power'.[31]

Notes

1   pp. 181-94.

2   p. 182. Austen-Leigh's focus on the characters rather than on the future shaping of the story was probably determined by the information he got from his sister Anna.: 'The other members of the Parker family (except of course Sidney) were certainly suggested by conversations which passed between Aunt Jane & me during the time that she was writing this story – Their vagaries do by no means exceed the facts from which they were taken' (quoted in Deirdre Le Faye, '*Sanditon*: Jane Austen's Manuscript and her Niece's Continuation' (*Review of English Studies*, n.s. 38, 1987), p. 58.

3   *Life and Letters* (1913), p. 381 n 2: 'The watering-place is called 'Sanditon', and this name has been given to the twelve chapters by the family'; Chapman explained, 'The fragment of a novel…has no name; but it has long been known to members of her family as *Sanditon*' (*Fragment of a novel* (1925), Preface, [p.i]).

4   In February 1925, Janet Sanders, a grand-daughter of Francis Austen, wrote to the Oxford University Press telling them that she had a manuscript copy of *Sanditon* made by Cassandra for Francis after Jane's death and that her own father (Francis' son Edward Austen, 1820-1908) 'had been told, his Aunt Jane intended to name her last

novel (unfinished) "The Brothers"'. Later that month – probably on Chapman's advice – Mrs. Sanders, wrote to the *Times Literary Supplement* of this family tradition ('Sanditon', 19 February 1925, p. 120). As it appears to stem from Cassandra, this tradition carries some weight, whereas *Sanditon* sounds like a title of convenience, just as James Edward Austen-Leigh named the earlier untitled manuscript *The Watsons*, 'for the sake of having a title by which to designate it' (1871 M, [p. 295]).

5   In the account of Mr Parker in ch. 2, ms f.9^v, JA wrote 'that he had 2 brothers and 2 sisters – all single & all independant – the eldest of the two ~~Brothers~~ former indeed...'.

6   A detailed account of the manuscript is given in Sutherland, pp. 168-197.

7   This diagnosis is challenged by Claire Tomalin in 'Appendix 1', *Jane Austen : A Life* (London: Viking, 1997). Her counter-suggestion is 'a lymphoma such as Hodgkin's disease – a form of cancer' (p. 287).

8   Letter to Miss Quincy, 30 December 1870, quoted by M.A.Dewolfe Howe, 'A Jane Austen Letter', *Yale Review* (1926), n.s. vol. 15, p. 335. The Archbishop of Granada's 'homilies' appear in Le Sage's *Gil Blas* (1715-35, translated by Smollett, 1749), Book 7, ch. 4. The homily that follows his stroke is 'a composition of more sound than meaning....with symptoms of apoplexy in every paragraph'.

9   Chapman judged that *Sanditon* was 'planned on the scale of *Emma*. If that is so, then we have about half of the first of three volumes' (*Facts and Problems*, p. 208).

10 A contrary view, however, was held by Mary Lascelles, who studied the text and corrections with care and sensitivity. She describes the manuscript as a 'rough draft' of which there would, normally, have been a 'final version', in which the 'laughter of farce' would have become the laughter of 'comedy', its effect less 'hilarious'; and it 'would probably have undergone, with other revision, some pruning' (*Jane Austen and her Art*, 1939, pp. 83, 181).

11 Mr Parker uses the word 'Surgeon'. This was short for surgeon-apothecary, what we would call a general practitioner.

12 *MW*, p. 425

13 *Jane Austen and her Art*, p. 39.

14 *MW*, pp. 412-13.

15 *MW*, p. 371.

16 *Facts and Problems*, p. 208.

17 *Lascelles*, p. 100.

18 See ms f.5ʳ, f.5ᵛ, f.17ʳ etc.

19 I have taken this example and quoted from Professor F.P.Lock's review of the 1975 facsimile edition of S (*Year Book of English Studies*, 1977, vol. 279, pp. 278-79).

20 *Memoir* (1871), pp. 181-82.

21 Her two books for children are *The Winter's Tale* (1841); *Springtide* (1842). Attributed to Anna is 'Mary Hamilton', published in *The Literary Souvenir* (1833), pp. 73-110; the anonymous author is described as 'A Niece of the late Miss Austen'.

22 Anna continued 'Which is the Heroine?' after JA's death. But around 1825 she lost heart with the story and destroyed it.

23 *Jane Austen's Sanditon, a continuation by her niece, together with 'Reminiscences of Aunt Jane'* by Anna Austen Lefroy, ed. Mary Gaither Marshall (Chicago: Chiron Press), 1983. The continuation is discussed by Professor Marshall in her Introduction; and further discussed by Peter Sabor and Kathleen James-Cavan, 'Anna Lefroy's Continuation of *Sanditon*: Point and Counterpoint', *Persuasions* (1997, no. 19), pp. 229-43.

24 *Jane Austen's Sanditon*, p. 153.

25 Quoted in Le Faye, *Review of English Studies*, 1987, p. 58.

26 *The Younger Sister* (1850).

27 Quoted in Le Faye, *Review of English Studies*, 1987, p. 58.

28 See note 8.

29 Quoted in Le Faye, *Review of English Studies*, 1987, p. 58.

30 See Brian Southam, '*Sanditon*: the Seventh Novel' in *Jane Austen's Achievement*, ed. Juliet McMaster (London: Macmillan, 1976), pp. 1-26.

31 I take this descriptive terminology from an essay – in which Jane Austen is not mentioned – by Edward Said, 'Thoughts on Late Style', *London Review of Books* (5 August 2004), vol. 26, no. 15, p. 3.

*

CHAPTER 1

1. Tunbridge...E.Bourne: the town of Tonbridge lay thirty miles south
of London on the main coach road which first passed through Bromley
and Sevenoaks, and on through Tonbridge a further five miles to the
spa town of Tunbridge Wells. Beyond Tonbridge, the road branched
eastwards to **Hastings**, sixty-five miles from London and westwards to
Eastbourne, sixty miles. Both were seaside towns on the Sussex coast,m
about twenty-one miles apart by road and both mentioned in *S*.

2. cut his Horses: struck them sharply with his whip.

3. overturning: overturning carriages were a feature of Gothic fiction,
the most notable instance being the carriage accident that precipitates
the first meeting of Valancourt and Emily St Aubert, the hero and
heroine of *The Mysteries of Udolpho* (1794) by Ann Radcliffe. JA alludes
to this event early in *NA*, Catherine Morland and Mr and Mrs Allen
travelling smoothly to Bath without a single 'lucky overturn to introduce
them to the hero' (vol. 1, ch. 2). JA had earlier exploited the full comic
possibilities of such accidents in Letter 13 of 'Love and Friendship', a
piece of sophisticated literary parody.

4. no wheels but cart wheels could safely proceed: The 'very rough
Lane' along which Mr Parker's coach is proceeding would be used by the
nearby farmers as a waggon road and for driving their sheep and cattle on
foot; and although it would have been used by the local people, and for
this reason be the responsibility of the parishes it passed through, it would
be beyond their means to maintain the lane in a fit state for a carriage.

5. Good out of Evil: this much-quoted saying originates with St
Augustine: 'For God judged it better to bring good out of evil than not to
permit any evil to exist'. But JA may have in mind a later source, another
carriage incident, a moment of high drama in her favourite novel,
Richardson's *Sir Charles Grandison* (1753-54): the villain, Sir Hargrave
Pollexfen is making off with the heroine, Harriet Byron, when Grandison
halts the carriage and frees Harriet, so frustrating Pollexfen's 'evil' intent.
The correspondent in the novel who reports the incident comments that
'This indeed is bringing good out of evil' (vol. 1, letter 27).

6. seen romantically...Distance: according to the theory of 'picturesque
beauty' developed by the aesthetic travel-writer William Gilpin (1724-
1804), a landscape to be admired is one which provides a composition fit
for an artist: in his basic definition, 'from some quality, capable of being

illustrated by painting' (1794, p. 3). And the 'Cottage', so **romantically** positioned, seems placed with the intention of achieving a 'picturesque' effect, situated as it is at a distance, on higher ground, and set off by the surrounding woodland. JA is echoing Gilpin's wording in *NA* when the Tilneys decide on the 'capability' of the scenery from Beechen Cliff 'of being formed into pictures' (vol. 1, ch. 14).

Henry Austen noted that 'At a very early age' his sister was 'enamoured of Gilpin on the Picturesque' ('Biographical Notice', *NA*, p. 7). Nonetheless, JA was not uncritical and her allusions to Gilpin make fun of 'picturesque' concepts, its elaborate jargon and, as here, 'picturesque' assumptions remote from the working realities of everyday life are mocked: the cottage that Mr Parker presumes to be the home of a surgeon turns out to be a dwelling of a very different kind (ch. 1).

7. Proprietor of the Place...Haymakers: this may be an instance of JA reminding her family readership of another such scene in 'Henry and Eliza', one of her juvenilia pieces. This little 'Novel' opens with 'Sir George and Lady Harcourt...superintending the Labours of their Haymakers' (*Volume the First*).

July was the traditional month for haymaking in England.

8. Goodbreeding: see *LS*, note 1 to Letter 5.

9. Surgeon's: surgeon was a short form for surgeon-apothecary, as many country doctors were known (see *W,* note 29).

10. Willingden: there was a village of this name (alternative spelling Willingdon) two miles inland from Eastbourne. The 1815 edition of *A Guide to all the Watering and Sea Bathing Places* describes it as 'very pleasant' (p. 280). One of the great families of Sussex, the Parker family, had owned the manor and estate of Willingden for over three hundred years; and JA may have borrowed the family and place names for *S*.

11. Morning Post...Gazette: 'The Morning Post and Daily Advertiser', a London daily paper, was first published in 1772. 'The Kentish Gazette', first published in 1768, came out on Tuesdays and Fridays, and advertised itself as being 'for east and west Kent, Sussex, Surrey, and Middlesex'.

12. Post-chaises: closed four-wheeled travelling carriages for two or three people, drawn by two or four horses. A postillion or postboy would normally ride the nearside horse. In a chaise, the passengers faced the driver; in a coach, the seats faced each other. 'Post' could also indicate that this was a chaise hired from a local inn or post-house.

13. double Tenement: 'Tenement' is a technical term in property law. Here, however, it merely refers to the fact that the house is divided and occupied by two separate tenant households.

14. Great Willingden…Abbots: no such places are recorded.

15. Battel: JA's spelling of Battle, a small town eight miles from Hastings on the coach road to London. It grew up around Battle Abbey, established by William the Conqueror on the site of the Battle of Hastings fought in October 1066. On account of these historic associations Battle was well-known and much-visited. The Abbey's fourteenth-century Gate-House, according to Pevsner, 'one of the finest in England' (p. 404), attracted tourists well before JA's time.

16. Weald: from the Old English 'weald' (forest), a stretch of Southern England, much of it formerly woodland, interspersed by tracts of bracken or gorse, and lying between the North and South Downs, the two ranges of hills that run east-to-west across Kent, Surrey and Sussex. By Austen's day, much of the Weald had been cleared for farmland and Mr Parker would have entered the area a few miles south of Tunbridge Wells. Its roads, with their rutted clay and mud, were notoriously difficult for coach travel. In 1813, Arthur Young, who travelled extensively along country roads in the course of his surveys, judged those of the Weald to be 'in all probability the very worst that are to be met with in any part of the island' (*Sussex*, 1813, p. 417).

17. *down*: a piece of word-play by Mr Parker, since a 'down' was an expanse of upland grassland; and the North and the South Downs referred to in note 16 are ranges of undulating chalk uplands, grassed and bare of trees.

18. Traveller: JA parodies a convention of eighteenth-century fiction in which a character was not named but, for purposes of mystification or elegant variation, described only by his or her immediate occupation, male 'travellers' and female 'wanderers' being the well-known types.

19. Town: London.

20. Turnpike road: a main road kept in repair by the tolls or fees collected at a turnpike gate for the passage of wheeled vehicles and cattle; 'turnpike' being derived from the pike-like shape of the toll bar.

21. Hailsham: a market town nine miles north of Eastbourne on the coach road to Tunbridge Wells. Hailsham was connected to Battle by cross-country roads.

22. Saline air & immersion: the medical benefits of 'Sea air & Sea Bathing'– as they are named in ch. 2 – had been promoted since the 1750's with the publication of Dr Richard Russell's *Dissertation on the Use of Sea Water* (in Latin 1750, in English 1752). During the period 1800-20, with a spurt in the growth of seaside resorts, there was a great outpouring of books and pamphlets on this subject. A typical entry for sea-water 'Baths' is to be found in *A Practical Dictionary of Domestic Medicine* (Reece, 1808) one of the standard family medical books of the period. Their benefits are recommended 'not only to the infirm and debilitated, under certain restrictions, but likewise to the healthy' (unnumbered pages). Another medical man emphasised that 'immersion' in sea water was 'not simply' to provide 'a cold bath, but a *cold medicated* bath' (Sicklemore, 1823, p. 29). The immersion ('dipping') was managed by **Bathing Women**. Otherwise known as 'dippers', they led ladies down the steps of their bathing **machine**, a cabin on wheels pulled from the beach into the water, to immerse or **dip** them in the sea. To achieve the maximum exposure to the salt water, it was thought most beneficial to go in without the covering of a costume. Hence, to preserve female decency and conceal the bather from prying eyes, the machines could be fitted with a concertina-like hood to enclose the steps and dipping area. In *P*, JA's Lyme Bay 'in the season is animated with bathing machines' (vol. 1, ch. 11).

23. well stocked...common remedies: given the scarcity of doctors in country districts, many households kept a store of basic medicines, some home-prepared, some patent medicines bought in. In addition, more prosperous country homes were likely to have commercial medicine chests. 'The Family Dispensary' of Reece, Burgess & Co., 1810, its six sizes priced between £5.18.0 and £19.8.0, was advertised as containing the medicines 'one person at least in every village ought to be provided' with as 'as an immediate resource in those sudden...contingencies of misfortune, in which it is absolutely necessary relief should be *speedy* to be *effectual*...'. Since Mr Heywood's wife and elder daughters would be seeing to the basic health care of his farm-hands, tenants, and humbler neighbours, it could be expected that a gentleman-farmer would have one of the well-stocked larger sizes in his medicine cupboard.

24. Landed Property: Mr Parker presents his credentials as a country gentleman, an important point to make to a stranger since these established his repectability. Rather than the money of outside investors and speculators, it was the enterprise of local landowners that led the way in developing a number of the late eighteenth-century and early nineteenth-century seaside resorts, including Bournemouth, Eastbourne, Folkestone, Bognor and, in the north of England, Skegness and Fleetwood.

25. Every five years…fashion: Mr Heywood would have in mind some of the fishing villages, including Seaford, Rottingdean, Littlehampton, and Hove – later engulfed by Brighton – which were establishing themselves modestly as quieter, more selective resorts. In their early days, providing only the basic facilities, with one or two lodging houses and a few bathing machines, they attracted families seeking to avoid the larger, more crowded seaside towns (Lyme, for example, is described as a 'public' place in *P*, p. 224) ; and this is precisely the 'Private' or select (ch. 9) character of Sanditon, with its own appeal to 'Families' (ch. 7).

26. Bad things for a Country…good for nothing: Mr Heywood touches on one of the arguments of contemporary political economists, while Mr Parker offers an opposing point of view a few lines later, echoing the post-war debates on poverty and the Poor Law which were coming to a head at the very time JA was writing *S*.

Her principal source for these and other socio-economic ideas and discussions that run through *S* seems to have been a very recent work, *Conversations on Political Economy; in which the Elements of that Science are Familiarly Explained* (1816, second edition 1817) by Mrs Jane Marcet. Written as a schoolroom book, it is notable as being the first sound exposition of economics for the layman. At this time, Political Economy was also seen as a 'science' which included the impact of economic laws upon society: as Marcet puts it, 'so immediately connected with the happiness and improvement of mankind' (Preface, p.v). Her discussion of prices comes in Conversation XV, 'On Value and Price'.

The arrival of free-spending visitors at small coastal villages, now budding resorts, had the direct effect of raising the price of **Provisions**, usually understood as 'the necessaries of life' (see ch. 6, note 13). This complaint was aired in a letter from Brighton as early as 1771 (quoted in Parry, p. 61). In the period of *S*, 'Provisions' was employed as a specialised term in official reports on the standard of living amongst the poor and usually included bread, meat, cheese, butter, sugar and tea, plus candles, soap and sometimes rent.

27. large, over-grown Places…East Bourne: developing from the 1750's onwards, Brighton was by far the largest and longest-established of these three Sussex resort towns, with a population of just under 7500 in 1801, rising to 16,000 by 1817; and it was generally reckoned that, with the influx of visitors, it doubled in size during the summer season. Compared to Brighton, Eastbourne (rising from about 1700 in 1801 to over 2600 in 1817) far from 'large'. On the other hand, 'overgrown' certainly suited Worthing. In 1800, little more than a fishing village, honoured by visits from younger members of the Royal family, its reputation spread and over the next twenty years its population almost quadrupled. Developers succeeded in gaining an Act of Parliament in 1805, declaring the resort a town, and by 1817, with its twelve miles of sandy beaches, it boasted billiard rooms, three libraries, two banks, a theatre, warm baths, several wine-cellars and, standing empty, an over-supply of speculative housing. According to John Evans, a contemporary historian of Worthing, between 1800 and 1814 developers invested at least £250,000 (over £15,000,000 to-day) in establishing new guest-houses (Evans, p. 44). Mrs Austen and her daughters spent a long holiday at Worthing in 1805, remaining there from mid-September until possibly after Christmas, and JA would have seen the evidence of this speculative building in its first and most active phase. With Lady Denham's comments on the 'great many empty Houses' and 'Lodging Papers staring me in the face', Sanditon itself is suffering an over-supply of accommodation (ch. 7).

28. Nursery Grounds: nursery gardens with glasshouses and hot-houses, for cultivating, transplanting and supplying ornamental and flowering shrubs, ornamental trees and exotic flowers. For the benefit of Sanditon's visitors, much of the stock is likely to have been fashionable novelties from overseas. These included wisteria, just introduced from China, dahlias from Mexico, and varieties of the petunia and lupin from South America.

JA originally wrote 'the laying out Gardens'. As gardens of this name are not known, it may be that she was referring to 'the laying out of gardens', possibly the paths, beds and lawns of new public gardens as a resort amenity or perhaps the individual gardens of the new guest houses under construction.

29. Coast is too full of them altogether: by 1817, the Sussex coast was already well-provided with seaside resorts, including (from east to west) Hastings, Eastbourne, Brighton, Hove, Worthing, and Bognor, with Brighton, under the patronage of the Prince Regent, the most flourishing, fashionable and firmly established of them all. The success of these resorts depended very considerably on their road links to London – by 1811, the fifty-one miles to Brighton, which was well-served, could be regularly covered in under seven hours – a point Mr Parker emphasises in asserting Sanditon's superiority to Eastbourne. This could place Sanditon in the vicinity of Bexhill, at this time a village attracting some visitors but not yet an established resort (see Selwyn, 1999, pp. 57-58). Bexhill lies between Hastings and Eastbourne (the stretch of coast towards which Mr Parker is travelling) and is marginally closer to London than Eastbourne. In pursuit of exactitude on this very detail, JA could have consulted one of the many road maps or gazeteers.

30. Mr Parker's eulogy of Sanditon mimics the elevated style and language of contemporary guide-books. In these, the denigration of neighbouring rivals was a common feature, mirrored exactly in Mr Parker's scornful account of 'the Celebrity of Brinshore'. In the Introduction to his *Topographical Description of Worthing* (1824), John Shearsmith, a local surgeon, described the growth of the resort with a flourish: 'in a few years a town of considerable magnitude presented itself as a new and beautiful object in the bosom of the surrounding landscape' (pp.11-12). He also gave three pages to detailing the slanders on his home town; these labelled it as unhealthy in the very terms in which Mr Parker attacks Brinshore: 'the *air* has been pronounced bad in the extreme! its situation low and marshy', criticisms to which 'some medical practitioners in London have lent themselves' (Introduction, unnumbered pages).

31. stagnant marsh…sea weed: Mr Parker is circumspect in describing what everyone would immediately recognise as the ideal conditions for malaria (from the Italian *mala aria*, bad air), the English version known to medical men as intermitting or intermittent fever and commonly known as ague. Mr Parker stops short of further blackening Brinshore by naming the disease itself. But he had already said quite enough, since information about malaria was freely available in the standard family medical guides. For example, early editions of Buchan's *Domestic*

Medicine tell us that 'Agues are occasioned by marsh-effluvia'; while the 21st edition, 1813, has it that they are caused 'by effluvia from putrid stagnating water' in 'marshy' land (p. 142).

effluvia: were understood to be minute particles, the products of putrefaction, carried by the air, which transmitted the infection; and marshy ground was regarded as a prime breeding-ground. Again, these processes were fully explained in medical books for home use; see, for example, the entry for 'Ague' in Reece's *Dictionary*.

32. insalubrious Air: according to contemporary science, the salubrious component of air was oxygen, the 'insalubrious' component azote (from the Greek, meaning the absence of life; it was the name first given to nitrogen). Azote was seen a 'fruitful source of disease' since it was 'that part of the atmosphere which is vitiated by the different processes going on in nature'. The third component was 'carbonic acid...generally the product of vegetable fermentation', such as the leaves of plants, a process heightened by damp conditions. All this was explained in layman's terms in Reece's *Dictionary*, under the entry for 'Air'.

The unspoken reminder in Mr Parker's attack on Brinshore is that, like or unlike Sanditon, its drains, sewage included, empty into the sea.

33. the Poet Cowper in his description...a mile from home: according to the family records, William Cowper (1731-1800) was JA's favourite poet. Since Cowper's verse was extremely popular, JA could expect her readers to catch the significance of Mr Parker's quotation, a single line from 'Truth' (1782), a poem of almost 600 lines. At this point, the simple cottager, happy in her faith, is contrasted with Voltaire, famous and sophisticated, yet unhappy in his vanity and worldliness:

> Just knows, and knows no more, her Bible true –
> A truth the brilliant Frenchman never knew...
> O happy peasant! Oh unhappy bard!
> His the mere tinsel, hers the rich reward;
> He prais'd perhaps for ages yet to come,
> She never heard of half a mile from home...
> *Poems* (1814, vol. 1, p. 46, ll. 327-34)

JA's use of this allusion would be seen as a daring and unexpected touch. Employed by Mr Parker, derisively, as an attack on Brinshore, the line effects a comic descent from the sententiousness of Cowper's moral reflection to attempted satire. But his half-hearted joke fails.

Mr Heywood ignores it, and, by way of a pun, rejects Mr Parker's literary 'apply' in favour of a literal, immediate and practical medical application!

CHAPTER 2

1. he was perceived to be an Enthusiast: a term originally applied in the seventeenth-century to those possessed by religious 'enthusiasm', a possession of the spirit that could be worthy and beneficent or extreme and delusive Its meaning was later extended to include those possessed by an idea, belief, or cause to the point of self-delusion and fanaticism. Johnson quotes Pope's account of Chapman as being 'of an arrogant turn, and an *enthusiast* in poetry'. In JA's time, Enthusiasts were a recognised type, often a butt of caricature and satire. JA referred to her brother Edward as 'no Enthusiast in the beauties of Nature. His Enthusiasm is for the Sports of the field only' (to Francis Austen, 25 September 1813, L, p. 230).

2. Speculation: a word carrying highly pejorative overtones from several areas of economic and political life. The classic economic account was in *The Wealth of Nations* (1776) where Adam Smith contrasted the 'great fortunes' made 'in consequence of a long life of industry, frugality, and attention' with the 'Sudden fortunes' made 'by what is called the trade of speculation' in which the 'speculative merchant' jumps from trade to trade in pursuit of 'profits' (bk. 1,ch. 10). This critique was reinforced by Edmund Burke's politically-angled account in *Reflections on the Revolution in France* (1790). Burke described revolutionary France as a regime 'founded… upon gaming' in which moral and political 'speculations' are 'as extensive as life'; he identified 'gaming' and 'speculation' as the 'vital breath' of the Republic; and in the same paragraph (pp. 279-80) 'lotteries' are mentioned (see note 9). The association with 'gaming' was readily made since there was a contemporary card game of Speculation in which the players competed in bidding for an unturned card.

For contemporary economists, the straightforward meaning of speculation was over-trading, carrying the slur of economic irresponsibility. The evidence was immediately to hand in the wave of post-war speculation, a period commencing with Napoleon's abdication in the Spring of 1814 and the opening up of trade with the Continent. The consequences were forcefully summarised in a speech by Henry

Brougham to the House of Commons in April 1816: 'a rage for exporting goods of every kind burst forth. This frenzy, I can call it nothing less… descended to persons in the humblest circumstances …the bubble soon burst, like its predecessors on the South Sea, the Mississippi, and Buenos Ayres [earlier landmarks of trading speculation]…The great speculators broke…'. Later in the speech, Brougham referred to the speculation in 'a continuance of extravagant prices' for farm-land and wheat (Brougham, 1816, pp. 22-23, 40). This was a train of thought shared by many commentators at this time and it suggests that Mr Parker's speculation in Sanditon could be heading for the same sticky end, one of JA's deliberate indirections for the story.

3. puffed: praised with inflated claims; as we would say, spun. The immediate literary associations of the word, reflected in Mr Parker's language, were with Mr Puff, the title-figure of Sheridan's comedy, *The Critic* (1779). Mr Puff holds forth 'in the style of his profession' in 'panegyrical superlatives' and 'exotic metaphors' (act 1, scene 3). JA was familiar with the play and refers to it in the opening lines of the juvenilia 'History of England' (*Volume the Second*).

4. no Profession: the following lines touch on primogeniture – the custom, legally sustained, whereby in landed families the eldest son would inherit the estate, living off its income alone and handing on the property intact and undivided to his own eldest son. Hence, Mr Parker's income enables him to take up 'no Profession'. It is the second and later sons who were be obliged to enter professions for their livelihood.

5. eldest: JA uses this superlative form for the comparative 'elder'.

6. collateral Inheritance: as distinct from a lineal inheritance (from father to son). According to the canons of civil law governing inheritance up to 1844, a collateral inheritance would be from a childless blood relative, probably an uncle. Here, JA is keeping to the strict legal terminology.

7. Liberal: the word carries no political significance; it denotes someone with the education and outlook befitting a gentleman.

8. Mine: metaphorically, Mr Parker's hoped-for source of future wealth, as in Shakespeare's *Antony and Cleopatra*: 'Thou mine of bounty' (IV. vi.34), the words of Enobarbus declaring his gratitude to the absent Antony.

9. Lottery: there were private lotteries, many of them unauthorised.

But what would come first to the reader's mind is the official Lottery (variously known as the Great, Government, State or Parliamentary Lottery), which ran almost continuously between 1694 and 1826, for most of this period organised by the Bank of England and throughout regulated by Acts of Parliament. From four to six draws were made annually, tickets cost £3 upwards and the top prizes usually ranged between £20-30,000. The profits were used to raise state loans, to reduce the national debt, for revenue and to assist public projects such as the construction of Westminster Bridge (beginning in 1737) and the building of the British Museum (beginning in 1753). Although the Lottery was very lucrative and its profits put to good use, by the mid-eighteenth century successive ministries came under attack for promoting an institution which was said to contribute to the national culture of gambling, to encourage a range of other social ills and to hit the poor most of all. An example around the time of *S* comes in a letter to the editor of the *Gentleman's Magazine* for April 1816, charging that the lotteries provided 'baneful and fascinating temptations to crime, so infinitely dangerous to the uninstructed and unreflecting vulgar' and describing the institution as 'this demoralizing System of raising Money' (vol. 86, p. 296). Soon after this, on 12 June 1816, came a notable Parliamentary debate in which a number of prominent social reformers – including William Wilberforce, Samuel Romilly and W.H.Lyttleton – took part. The government spokesman opposing them was Stephen Lushington, the Secretary to the Treasury, someone well-known to the Austens. He was the MP for Canterbury and a familiar visitor at Edward Austen's home at Godmersham. As JA wrote to Cassandra while staying there in October 1813, she was fascinated by Lushington, finding him the complete politician: 'very smiling, with an exceeding good address, & readiness of Language. – I am rather in love with him. – I dare say he is ambitious & Insincere' (*L*, p. 240). And, as a politician, successful, she might have added. For on this occasion, as on several others, the government withstood their critics and it was another ten years before it gave way, bringing the Lottery to an end in 1826.

10. **Hobby Horse**: a toy consisting of a stick with a horse's head at one end, a wheel at the other, which the child straddled and propelled as if riding. In this context, where Mr Parker's character is on show, JA's use of the word brings to mind *Tristam Shandy* (1760) in which Sterne

mentions 'Hobby Horse' more than twenty times, most significantly in the passage in volume one where he employs the word emblematically: this runs from the final words of chapter 23: 'I will draw my uncle Toby's character from his Hobby-Horse' and continues uninterrupted to open the next chapter: 'By long journies and much friction, it so happens that the body is at length fill'd as full of Hobby-Horsical matter as it can hold; – so that if you are able to give but a clear description of the nature of the one, you may form a pretty exact notion of the genius and character of the other' – just as we are meant to understand of Mr Parker.

About the time of S, the earliest form of the bicycle, known as a 'pedestrian hobby horse', was just coming in. Without chain or pedals, the rider seated in the saddled pushed it along with a walking motion. Together with the Sternian 'hobby horse', this more recent image of eccentric novelty would also fit Mr Parker's enthusiasms, slightly manic and headstrong as they are.

11. Futurity: the catalogue of Sanditon's 'claims' ends on a note of mock-grandiloquence. From Shakespeare onwards, 'futurity' carries associations of the utmost solemnity – religious, philosophical and literary – a tradition continued in the eighteenth century by Swift, Berkeley, Richardson Gibbon and others. But JA alone uses the word in this special mock-heroic sense of a nest-egg or insurance.

12. 6 weeks: the standard period for a course of medical treatment at a seaside resort, as it was at an inland spa.

13. anti-spasmodic…anti-rheumatic: in Mr Parker's spouting of medical language JA pokes fun at the ease with which new terms were routinely created simply by the addition of a prefix. A standard medical work – *A New Medical Dictionary* (1795 edn) by George Motherby – gives twenty-four such 'anti-' formations, a linguistic device JA also employs in the vocabulary of Sir Edward Denham (see ch. 8, note 16). If JA needed any prompting in this device, it could have come from a satirist whose work she enjoyed, Eaton Stannard Barrett. In the satire *All the Talents* (1807), 'Dialogue The Third' (p. 77, footnote to l. 228), Barrett refers to 'anti-bile, anti-hydrophobia, anti-head-ache – in short, the whole very numerous family of *Antis*'. A more recent attack may also have been in her mind – William Hazlitt's essay 'On Pedantry'(*The Examiner*, 3 March 1816): 'One of the most constant butts of ridicule, both in the old comedies and novels, is the professional jargon of the medical tribe…the natural language of apothecaries and physicians, the mother tongue of pharmacy!'.

anti-spasmodic: Spasmodic Medicine was a important category which included the treatment of convulsions, in-cluding hysterical attacks, spasms, cramp, asthma etc; the *antispasmodica* or anti-spasmodics included relaxants such as laudanum, ether and Peruvian balsam.

'anti-pulmonary': not recorded in the *OED*. In *E*, we see that JA associated a 'pulmonary' condition with inheritable tuberculosis. Jane Fairfax's mother (née Bates) dies of 'consumption' and when Jane herself becomes unwell while staying with her Bates relatives at Highbury, we learn that this (unspecified) 'pulmonary complaint' is, not surprisingly, 'the standing apprehension of the family' (vol. 3, ch. 9).

anti-sceptic: recorded in the *OED* as an erroneous version of 'anti-septic'. Among the most effective antiseptics were camphor, snake-root and Peruvian bark.

anti-bilious: *S* is cited in the *OED* as the earliest instance. In *E*, Mr Woodhouse diagnoses Mr Perry as being 'bilious' (vol. 1, ch. 12) and Mr Cole as 'very bilious' (vol. 2, ch. 7) . It was a condition extensively discussed in the medical literature of the time, having recently taken over from being 'nervous' as the fashionable complaint. It was thought to arise from the liver's over-production of bile (a secretion essential to the process of digestion) giving rise to jaundice or gallstones and readily identifiable by its most obvious symptom, a yellowish complexion. During 1816-17, JA's last illness affected her 'Looks' similarly, 'black & white & every wrong colour', as she joked on 23 March 1817 (*L*, p. 335), only five days after abandoning the manuscript of *S*, in which we find that Diana Parker's 'Spasmodic Bile' leaves her 'hardly able to crawl from my Bed to the Sofa' (ch. 5). If this is a wry joke that JA directs at herself, it may also communicate the climate of scepticism – something she would have been alert to – prevailing amongst doctors at this time about the very nature of the condition. For example, Reece has this to say in *The Medical Guide* (1817): 'it has been a fashion to attribute a variety of disorders, particularly of the digestive organ, and of the head, to a redundancy of bile in the stomach: an idea evidently founded in error, and first broached by designing quacks, in order the more successfully to impose their antibilious specifics on the credulous public' (pp. 202-03). His conclusion was that the symptoms were not of this order of gravity but were 'really symptoms of indigestion' (p. 204). Reece also wrote scathingly of 'hypochondriacs, and people of vacant minds, who can think of nothing else but the state of their health, instead of being *nervous*, now complain of being bilious' (p. 344).

anti-rheumatic: not recorded in the *OED* but in the *Dictionary of Domestic Medicine* (1808) Reece includes 'anti-rheumatic' mixtures, pills and decoctions within the 'Rheumatism' entry. One such mixture was composed of tincture of guaiac gum, camphorated julep and honey.

14. Dividends: interest from a bank or on a loan or, as to-day, an investor's share in the paid-out profits of a company.

15. old Coach: carrying the meaning that this was a functional country squire's coach – heavy, cumbersome and often unsprung, as distinct a well-appointed fashionable town carriage.

16. fresh lined: a re-lining of the interior of the coach, almost certainly using leather or corduroy for durability, rather than materials chosen for their appearance, such as tabinet, a watered fabric of silk and wool resembling poplin. Re-lining would cost upwards of £35, very much more if the job included re-upholstering the seats and cushions, renewing the blinds etc.

17. Tunbridge Wells...Bath: in their heyday, these places had prospered as the country's leading spa towns where both water cures and good company were to be found. But by this time their reputation for exclusivity was gone and both had been overtaken by more select resorts such as Clifton, which emerged from about 1800 onwards and Cheltenham, patronised by the royal family. Moreover, with the shift of fashion to coastal resorts, the social eminence of the older inland spas lay in the past, as JA represents the Bath of *P*, where the action of the novel is set over the Winter of 1814-15 ; and Tunbridge Wells, with its facilities unmodernised, was now regarded as rural and provincial, no longer, as it once had been, a convenient resort for fashionable Londoners.

18. Library: a circulating (or subscription) library and reading-room, considered to be an essential feature – a 'requisite' was the word normally used – of any self-respecting resort. As it was customary for visitors to subscribe on their arrival, the list of subscribers, which lay open to be consulted, provided a handy guide to the residents and newcomers, while the library itself, usually a commodious building, served as an informal gathering-ground. This was important in newly-established resorts lacking more formal meeting places such as assembly rooms. Visitors could also sit and chat and read the newspapers or just lounge. As in Sanditon, libraries often sold local mementoes and trinkets, such as the 'beautiful ornaments' that made Lydia Bennet 'quite wild' at Brighton (*P&P*, vol. 2, ch. 19). They might even run to musical entertainments and, for the gentlemen, billiards and cards. This may explain why when Fanny Burney was visiting Sandgate (on the Kent coast between Folkestone and Hythe), she wrote to her father that she had 'avoided going to the Library, the general rendezvous of the Social' (quoted in *Camilla*, edn 1972, p. 935.)

CHAPTER 3

1. Lady Denham: in JA's portrait of a shrewd and wordly-wise dowager, readers would recall an earlier Lady Denham in Hannah More's *Coelebs in Search of a Wife* (1809), first encountered at the opening to Chapter 10 as 'a dowager of fashion, who had grown old in the trammels of the world'.

2. Manor & Mansion House: these technical terms carry legal and historical significance and serve to emphasise Mr Hollis's prominence in the Parish. The Manor refers to his ownership, occupation and use of the property as Lord of the Manor and to certain property rights to which he was thereby entitled. Formally, the title of Manor could only be used for those in existence in or before the reign of Edward I (1274-1307). The Mansion House points to its dignity as his principal residence.

3. all at her Disposal: JA emphasises the point that the Hollis property was not, as was usual among land-owners, entailed down the male line but was held on to by Lady Denham as his widow, a retentiveness which (as we see in the passage that follows) she successfully maintains within her second marriage. Readers would appreciate her shrewdness in achieving this. By the common law of England, as marriage meant that the legal personality of the wife was merged with that of her husband, whatever she owned was transferred to him and as a married woman she was not normally capable of holding or acquiring property. However, during the course of the seventeenth and eighteenth centuries, an increasing number of women, most commonly widows, found legal devices, including settlements and trusts, to secure their property from their husbands; 'too wary to put anything out of her own Power', Lady Denham is able to 'boast' that she had '*given* nothing' in her marriage to Sir Edward Denham (ch. 3).

4. his own Domains: a lightly figurative legal reference, conveying the concept that the rights Sir Harry held in his property were the fullest, most complete and inheritable.

5. her Original Thirty Thousand Pounds: the sum of money, known as her marriage portion (or, to use the older term, dowry), that Lady Denham brought with her as a bride on her marriage to Mr Hollis.

6. his rank in Society: Sir Edward Denham is a Baronet, the lowest of the hereditary titles, with precedence over all other knights save for the highest of the orders of knighthood, the Knights of the Garter. In terms of their formal rights and privileges and their social standing, Baronets were classified as commoners, not nobility.

7. a noble Coadjutor: a strongly literary word for a fellow-helper. Much used by novelists since the time of Richardson and Smollett.

8. Cottage Ornée: the stylish name for (literally) an ornamented (properly 'orné') cottage, a mock-rustic gentleman's rural retreat or, on a larger scale, a family house, designed to be picturesquely and quaintly charming, and providing a place of quietude and retirement from the pressures of urban life. Contemporary architects provided many designs but typically they came with Elizabethan and Tudor touches, and were built of traditional materials, with a thatched roof, overhanging eaves, half-timbering and weatherboarding, trellised walls, stained glass in leaded panes, and tall ornamented chimney stacks. All this was calculated (in the words a contemporary architect) to throw 'an air of romance over a rural residence' (Bartell, 1804, p. 5), sometimes heightened by a fashionable Gothic styling to the windows and doors. Yet there would be no shortage of mod cons, including French windows, awnings, verandas, servants' quarters, stables and a succession of other gentlemanly outbuildings, including coach-, cart-, brew- and wash-houses, and so on. Seaside or 'marine' cottages ornés, as this one is, were designed for holiday use.

Nonetheless, by their critics these buildings were regarded as vulgar and pretentious, playthings for the *nouveaux riches*. Somewhat in this spirit JA jokes at this style of building in *S&S*: Barton Cottage is 'defective' in its very unrusticality (vol. 1, ch. 6). Later, we are treated to Robert Ferrars' views on the 'elegance' and 'comfort' of cottages and to his admiring account of Lady Elliott's so-called cottage, a building sufficiently commodious to seat eighteen couples in the 'dining parlour' with further accommodation in the 'drawing-room', the 'library' and the 'saloon' (vol. 2, ch. 16).

9. Waste Ground: in legal terms, this was land that had never been cultivated nor used for pasture or arable purposes.

10. Companion: providing company and service to a widow or single woman, companions were among the familiar distressed victim-figures of eighteenth-century fiction. It was regarded by educated women as a domestic position of last resort, even more repugnant than serving as a teacher or governess. An object of compassion, Clara Brereton has been driven to this by 'Poverty & Dependance' (ch. 3). At worst, as JA has it, a companion was only one-up from a nursery maid (see note 17). A credible witness is Mary Wollstonecraft who worked as a companion at the age of nineteen: 'It is impossible to enumerate the many hours of anguish such a person must spend. Above the servants, yet considered by them as a spy, and ever reminded of her inferiority when in conversation with the superiors. If she cannot condescend to mean flattery, she has not a chance of being a favourite….She is alone, shut out from equality and confidence…she must wear a chearful face, or be dismissed' (*Thoughts on the Education of Daughters* (1787, pp. 69-71).

11. Sanditon House: JA originally wrote 'Hall', understood to be the residence of a considerable landowner, with the feudal associations of status and tradition belonging to an ancient baronial or manorial hall. Presumably JA judged that 'Hall' conjured up too grand an origin for the Denham residence, described in ch. 12 in terms that indicate a mid- or late-eighteenth-century building.

12. Michaelmas: 29 September, the feast day of St Michael. It was one of the quarter-days in the English business year when accounts were settled, rents and dividends paid and other legal and financial transactions were dated to take place. This suggests that Lady Denham's visit to London was, at least in part, to look after her financial affairs. Possibly this was to be a minor strand in the plot arising from speculation.

13. the interest of his story…Character: a pastiche of the language and method of the contemporary novel, continued in Mr Parker's description of Clara Brereton as a model heroine; also in the wording of the final comment, 'She was as thoroughly amiable as she was lovely' (ch. 3).

14. an Hotel…expensiveness: not exactly hotels as we know them to-day but generally the word denoted a new style of large inn providing a level of cleanliness, accommodation, comfort and service above that found in ordinary inns and with pretensions and prices correspondingly higher, so attracting a better class of guest. Yet at the seaside, very humble establishments called themselves hotels and Sanditon's 'Hotel' (mentioned in Chapter 4 onwards) is an unknown quantity. JA may have intended to describe it in more detail later in the story, telling us of its size and amenities, and whether, in particular, it possessed an assembly room for dancing, and smaller rooms for cards, coffee and private receptions, features essential to any budding resort seeking to attract fashionable visitors. That it had such ambitions is suggested by the fact that the hotel imitates a gentleman's house in featuring a **Billiard Room** (ch. 4). Billiards was a gentlemanly pursuit, providing entertainment with moderate exercise and attracted the ladies as onlookers. In *S&S*, a billiard room is regarded by Mr Palmer as necessary to the 'comfort' of a house (vol. 1 ch. 20). Bingley has one at Netherfield Hall, while at Mansfield Park the 'billiard-room' enjoys some status, adjacent, as it is, to Sir Thomas Bertram's study, just as in *NA* the billiard-room leads to General Tilney's 'private apartment' (vol 2, ch 7).

But billiards had its sleazy side too. Like cards, it was a focus for gambling and a hunting-ground for 'gamesters' ready to fleece the unwary. This explains the emphatic wording employed in a guidebook for Eastbourne: 'an excellent Billiard Table, kept quite select for the use of gentlemen only' (Heatherley, p.13).

15. at all hazards: a standard phrase meaning whatever, or despite, the risk or bother.

16. politic: 'We say, "a politic man," for an artful fellow' (Campbell, 1776, vol. 2, bk. 2, ch. 2).

17. Nursery Maid: a menial position: 'generally a girl who does the household work of the nursery, and attends the children when they go out for the air, &c. carrying such of them as may be required' (Adams,

The Complete Servant, p. 271). With wages from six to ten guineas a year, the nursery maid was the lowest paid of the woman servants. JA's readers would remember the menially-employed nursery maid in Burney's *The Wanderer* (1814).

18. She was as thoroughly amiable…that Loveliness was complete: the language and structure of the sentence are a mimicking pastiche of the cliché descriptions of the heroines of popular romantic fiction.

CHAPTER 4

1. the best embellishments: 'rural embellishments' was the standard term for the cultivated domestic surroundings of a house in the country and the collective term 'garden' would be understood to include the separate areas of the pleasure, kitchen, nursery and fruit gardens.

2. modern Sanditon: what Mr Parker describes to Charlotte in this passage and to the end of Chapter 4 is the rather disjointed lay-out and piecemeal development typical of resorts, since many of them grew out of fishing villages: the old village, its church and one or two shops a mile or two inland; a line of fisherman's cottages immediately facing the sea; and work in progress on the resort – Sanditon's 'unfinished Buildings' – continuing along the front and filling in the open land back towards the old village.

3. South foreland …end: the extent of England's Channel coast from Dover in the east to the western extremity of Land's End.

4. Trafalgar…Waterloo: Mr Parker's patriotic reflections on house-naming recall Britain's two greatest victories of the Napoleonic wars: the first, Admiral Nelson's defeat of the combined French and Spanish fleets off Cape Trafalgar in October 1805; the latter, in June 1815, the Battle of Waterloo (south of Brussels), the final and decisive meeting between the Allied troops, led by their Commander-in-Chief, the Duke of Wellington, and the Army of France, led by the Emperor Napoleon. In considering a change of names, Mr Parker is following a national trend. London's Strand Bridge – so-named because it led off the Strand to cross the Thames – its construction started in the Autumn of 1811, was renamed Waterloo Bridge in June 1816 by Act of Parliament, so providing the capital with 'a lasting Record of the brilliant and decisive Victory' (Local Acts of Parliament 53, George III, cap.184, and 56, cap.63). Along the coast, Brighton too could provide its own quota of patriotic naming with its Nelson Street and Trafalgar Place; and further east, on the Kentish coast, was Ramsgate, its terraces celebrating Nelson, Wellington and Albion.

5. a little Crescent: first used in the name of the Royal Crescent at Bath in the 1760's for a stately row of linked houses forming a crescent shape. The name became the generic term for fashionable developments designed to attract occupiers from the higher classes, a point that JA spells out a few lines later. Brighton, for example, was one of the towns that copied Bath in having a Royal Crescent – built in 1798-1807, it was described in an 1815 *Guide* as 'one of the principal ornaments of the place' (pp. 115-16). Resort crescents could also be thoroughly commerical, as in the Crescent at Buxton Spa (finished in 1784), complete with lodgings, hotels, shops, post office and other facilities.

6. of its formalities: the term usually employed to include the robes and insignia of a high official such as a Mayor or an Archbishop. Austen brings the word down to earth, attaching it here to such items as the manure heap, the bean poles, the greenhouse etc. This is a mild joke on the landscape-gardening debate: Humphry Repton (1752-1818), the fashionable landscape gardener of the day, mentioned by name in *MP*, was a radical re-shaper, moderniser and 'improver' of country estates, removing or concealing such old-fashioned 'formalities' as avenues, fences, formal gardens, and out-buildings and working towards a tidied-up landscape of broad, uncluttered views, even to the point of removing cottages and hamlets that might interfere with otherwise open prospects. One his most vocal critics was Richard Payne Knight (1750-1824) whose theories are set out in his didactic poem *The Landscape* (1794) and in his discursive *Analytical Enquiry into the Principles of Taste* (1805). Always seeking for dramatic contrasts between light and shade and capturing the appeal of the rugged picturesque, Knight allowed for cottages, ruins and other rough and rustic irregularities as features proper to the country scene.

7. a Parasol at Whitby's...Bonnet: whereas – as in the following lines – sunshine was considered beneficial for boys, girls were to be protected to preserve a fashionably pale complexion. And beyond its utilitarian function as a sunshade, in summer a parasol was also regarded as a necessary item in a lady's walking-out ensemble, so enabling Mary to 'fancy herself quite a little Woman' (as Mrs. Parker comments a few lines later). Lascelles connects the discussion on 'shade' between Mr and Mrs Parker – natural shade contrasted with the man-made, portable shade of the 'Parasol' – with a similar passage in Cowper, *The Task*:

> We bear our shades about us; self-depriv'd
> Of other screen, the thin umbrella spread
>
> Book I, lines 259-60

8. Grandeur of the Storm: in eighteenth and early nineteenth-century philosophical aesthetics, 'Grandeur', as a source of the sublime is most fully discussed in Burke's *A Philosophical Enquiry into the Origin of our Ideas of the Sublime and Beautiful* (1757). Deriving from Burke's *Enquiry* was *Lectures on Rhetoric and Belles Lettres* (1783) by Hugh Blair (1718-1800). In the *Lectures*, Blair writes of the 'the pleasure which arises from Sublimity or Grandeur…'; and he finds 'grandeur' in 'the vast and boundless prospects presented to us' in 'the boundless expanse of the Ocean' (vol. 1, Lecture 3). Elsewhere Blair speaks of grandeur arising 'from the violence of the elements' (1771). The *Lectures* were in print throughout JA's lifetime and in 1817 had reached a 13th edition. Blair is alluded to in *NA*, vol. 1, ch. 14.

9. I encouraged him to set up: as a market gardener.

10. being a Hospital: hospitals, or infirmaries, were charitable foundations first established at resorts to provide accommodation for the poor and give them the benefit of seaside air and a seawater cure.

11. Improvements: 'improvement' was a central term in landscape gardening, which is how we meet it in JA's novels, slightly widened to include the up-dating and modernising of old buildings and their grounds. Alongside this particular meaning is the historical sense of 'improvement' in value and Sidney's joke holds the suggestion of speculation and profiteering inherent in such resort developments.

12. neat equipage: primarily his horses and carriage.

13. Many a respectable Family…E. Bourne & Hastings: whereas Brighton was regarded as fast and somewhat raffish, the smaller and more recent seaside place promoted themselves as family resorts, free from any raffish element. This was the claim made for Eastbourne in Heatherly's guide of 1819, where an advertisement describes the resort as 'having for many years been a Watering-place of great respectability'.

14. enclosures of Sanditon House: land, formerly waste-land or common-land, subsequently fenced off and legally taken into private ownership for cultivation. A system with its beginnings in the thirteenth-century, its heyday was between 1760 and 1820 when enclosure was effected either privately 'by agreement' (which often meant 'by pressure') or by private Act of Parliament. The General Enclosure Act 1801 largely removed the need for private Enclosure Acts, which could be lengthy and costly to obtain. Throughout, the landowning gentry were the beneficiaries and the common people the losers, since they no longer enjoyed the benefit of grazing their sheep or cattle, of gathering wood, or growing a few vegetables on land now privatised and fenced off from their use. Hence, the later reference to **Enclosure** (ch. 12) throws an equivocal light is across the heritage of the Sanditon House estate.

15. the sound of a Harp: 'highly blissful to Mr.P.' because it signified the arrival of metropolitan taste and 'increasing fashion'. Harp-playing heroines figured prominently in contemporary novels, most notably in the person of Glorvina in *The Wild Irish Girl* (1806) by Sydney Owenson (Lady Morgan), in Madame de Staël's *Corinne* (1807) and in Scott's *Waverley* (1814). The instrument carried a multitude of associations – classical, romantic and bardic-mediaeval. And in the hands of society women it also carried a hint of artful sophistication, a modern touch that JA exploited in chapters six and seven of *MP*: the transport of Mary Crawford's instrument from London into the countryside is an intrusion upon the rural world, since all the local waggons and carts are busy with the harvest; and harps, with recent developments, were weighty instruments, running to a height or six feet and more, with ornamental frames and pedal mechanisms. Nonetheless, 'as elegant as herself', Mary Crawford's arrives to complete the very scene 'to catch' Edmund Bertram's 'heart' (vol. 1, ch. 7), this last possibly a faint and playful counter-allusion to the high and sensuous romance of Owenson's novel: drawn by the harp's mellifluous chords, the hero scales a castle wall to discover the harpist's beauty, 'her fine form…her attitude! her air!' (2000, p. 50), a train of ideas continued in *S* in the description of the Misses Beaufort and the elder sister's hired harp (ch. 11). Of all musical instruments, the harp was the one best calculated to show off the charms of the performer. Scott's harp-playing Lady Heron, in *Marmion*, is able to display her 'rounded arm' and 'her bosom's rise and fall' (Canto Fifth, Section xi). As 'A Lady of Distinction' explains in *The Mirror of Graces* (1811), 'the shape of the instrument is calculated, in every respect, to show a fine figure to advantage. The contour of the whole form, the turn and polish of a beautiful hand and arm, the richly-slippered and well-made foot on the pedal stops, the gentle motion of a lovely neck...these are shown at one glance, when the fair performer is seated unaffectedly, yet gracefully, at the harp' (p. 193). Moreover, while Miss Beaufort performs in pursuit of 'praise & celebrity' (ch. 11), readers of *MP*, *E* and *P* would already know that proficiency on the harp was not necessarily a praiseworthy accomplishment: beyond its connection with Mary Crawford there is also Mrs Elton's commendation of this 'accomplishment' to Jane Fairfax for strengthening her prospects as a governess; and the fact, too, that Anne Elliot has 'no knowledge of the harp' (*P,* vol. 1, ch. 6) is a matter of evident if unspoken approval on JA's part.

16. He anticipated an amazing Season: the formal London social season ran from May to July while the season for seaside resorts was from August until October.

17. Blue Shoes: black was the serviceable colour for ladies' walking shoes, whereas from the 1790's onwards, for stylish shoes blue in various shades, including Prussian and cerulean, was a favourite colour. For day wear, these were usually pumps, flat or very low-heeled and made of silk, cloth or decorated kid. They were light and slipper-like in design, tied with ribbons and had rounded toes. For evening wear indoors or, as we see in fashion plates, for gentle strolling in a 'Promenade Dress', they were made of silk or satin. JA may be reminding her family readers of a detail in 'A Tour through Wales': 'a young Lady' reports to a friend that when all their walking shoes were worn out 'Mama was so kind as to lend us a pair of blue Sattin Slippers' which she shares with a companion and 'hopped home from Hereford delightfully' (*Volume the Second*, MW, p. 177).

18. nankin Boots: ladies' light half-boots with uppers made of nankeen, a distinctive, naturally yellow Chinese cotton named after Nanking, its place of origin. Close-textured, the material was durable and hard-wearing and from about 1811 such boots were commonly worn by women of fashion for walking and riding

19. just the time of day...dinner: in the country, dinner was served as early as 3 pm and up to about 6.30 pm. During the London season and in spa towns such as Bath and Tunbridge Wells, dinner was served later, up to about 8 pm. We can suppose that Mr Parker's ambition is for Sanditon's visitors to be following this more fashionable time.

20. aspiring to be the Mall of the place: a covered, tree-shaded, or otherwise sheltered pathway serving as Sanditon's promenade, the social gathering-ground where visitors walked to be seen and to see others. The English prototype, setting the tone in the seventeenth and eighteenth-centuries for such features, was The Mall, then a tree-lined walk in St James's Park, which became London's most fashionable promenade.

21. Milliner's shop: selling hats, ribbons for trimming, lace and other small items of ladies' clothing.

22. her ample, Venetian window: a central arched window flanked on either side by a square-headed window. Described here as **ample** on account of its width. With the relaxation in the classical styles of architecture at the end of the eighteenth-century, and the growth of gothic and other decorative styles, both French and Venetian window styles became fashionable.

23. miscellaneous: this is JA's only use of the word.

CHAPTER 5

1. Spasmodic Bile: in its serious form this could be biliousness accompanied by a haemorrhage; or, less acutely, and more likely in Diana Parker's case, given her energy and activeness, bouts of constipation. But see ch. 2, note 13 quoting Reece's reservations on the diagnosis of biliousness.

2. Friction: a standard medical treatment for the relief of sprains, rheumatism and other kinds of inflammation. 'Dry' friction was rubbing by hand or with a cloth; 'moist' was with the addition of opium mixed in with olive oil, lard or camphor. Normally, friction was given morning and evening for fifteen or twenty minutes. So Diana's administration of dry friction with her 'own hand' 'for six Hours [increased in revision from '4'] without Intermission' (ch. 5) needs no comment.

3. Apothecary: strictly speaking, a pharmaceutical chemist. But, in the absence of a trained doctor, country apothecaries would often act as general practitioners. Apothecary could also be short for apothecary-surgeon, a fully-trained doctor.

4. Medical Tribe: a derisive term commonly met with in eighteenth and early nineteenth-century comedy.

5. Physician: this would refer not to doctors in general but only to a Fellow of the Royal College of Physicians. About two hundred in number and graduates of Oxford and Cambridge, they were at the top of the English medical establishment. Giving no actual treatment themselves, they restricted their practice to consultation, the diagnosis of internal disease and prescription, and they were only to be found in London, Bath and other provincial centres. Also practising in England were Fellows of the Royal College of Physicians of Edinburgh, products of the far superior (but socially inferior) Scottish system of medical education.

6. Headache...for 10 days together: blood-sucking leeches were used as a means both of prevention and treatment, notably for fevers, pleurisy, and inflammations, especially those around the eyes, nose and mouth and other places where it was awkward to use a lancet or where there were no veins to lance. For headaches, leeches were applied to the temples. Six to twelve was a standard application, with up to two or three dozen for dangerous fevers. But their safety was in question at this time: the quantity of blood they extracted could not be measured; the after-bleeding could be difficult to stop; and the wounds did not always heal easily.

7. the Evil lay in her Gum: dentistry was regarded as a branch of surgery and the gums featured prominently in medical literature as a prime site for the symptoms of scurvy (caused by an excessive intake of salt and a shortage of vitamins from fresh fruit and vegetables). The symptoms included sponginess, ulceration, bad breath and the loosening and loss of teeth. Amongst other gum afflictions Susan's complaint could also have been a gum-boil or abcess, or a callous thickening of the gums; and caries of the teeth and sockets could bring about gum tumours and what were called 'excrescences'. Infected and suppurating gums were another affliction stemming from the widespread practice of inserting artificial teeth in old sockets. Diseased teeth were regarded as a possible source of headaches.

For all these conditions the various treatments – which included cutting back the gums, scarification (making small incisions) and cauterisation with a heated instrument or using concentrated acids and caustic alkalis – could be as painful as the complaint itself, if not more so. And as the methods of anasthaesia were barely effective, there was little relief.

The anodynes included opium pills to deaden the pain in cavities and the surrounding gums, sniffing powerful scents such as oil of lavender, laudanum applied externally, and even blistering behind the ears or at the nape of the neck, a procedure thought by one authority, John Hunter, Surgeon Extraordinary to the King, to 'divert the pain', just as he recommended 'hot brandy, to divert the mind' (*A Practical Treatise on Diseases of the Teeth* (1778, edn 1810, p. 151).

8. 3 Teeth drawn: another leading authority, the Surgeon-Dentist Leonard Koecker (qualified as a Doctor in both Medicine and Surgery), explained in *Principles of Dental Surgery* (1826) that drawing or extraction was regarded with 'fear and horror' (p. 301) because many dentists used the key, an instrument calling for brute force in its operation. Clumsily used, it was nothing less than 'a dangerous weapon' (pp. 307-08). Like the other 'exceedingly imperfect' instruments currently used for extractions, it worked by direct leverage on the gums, and all of them were liable to cause 'great suffering' (p. 307). Koecker himself favoured forceps (also known as pincers). But at this time their design was unsophisticated and it was only later in the nineteenth century that a range of forceps was developed with beaks anatomically designed to fit the specific shape of the tooth.

9. more languid...fear for his Liver: 'languid' was used as medical term denoting a lack of vigour or vitality; and the liver, along with the heart and the brain, was traditionally regarded as one of the vital organs, a source of energy both physical and emotional. In contemporary medicine, it was understood to be the principal organ involved in purifying the blood. Thus malfunction of the liver could transform it into a source of disease.

10. your Beau Monde: adopted into English in the eighteenth-century as the smart phrase for 'the fashionable world' or 'fashionable society'. Although by JA's time, the term often carried an ironic or contemptuous tone, this does not seem to be present in Diana's use of the phrase.

11. a rich West Indian: this term was usually used for members of planter families resident in the British West Indies, almost all of them of English or Scottish origin. Their wealth – from the highly profitable business of running slave-worked sugar plantations – was proverbial. Equally proverbial was the lavishness of their spending when they returned to England on an extended visit or to establish themselves permanently and socially by the purchase of landed estates. Their presence at a seaside resort would be understood as another step towards establishing themselves in polite society.

12. from Camberwell: a Surrey village set in farmland three miles south of the Thames. It was popular amongst the well-to-do as a quiet, convenient and healthy retreat from the dirt and noise of the capital. With these benefits, it was also home to a number of almshouses, asylums, hospitals and, as in this case, schools.

CHAPTER 6

1. the Straw Hats & pendant Lace: we are to visualise a simple style of window display – aping fashionable milliners' shops in London, Bath, and Brighton – with the lace draped over a coloured silk ribbon. The arrival of machine-made lace in 1808 made it widely available and it was soon came into use for trimming and decorating bonnets and straw hats.

2. Mrs. Whitby: as both spellings appear in the ms, JA seems not to have fixed on whether the name was to be 'Whitby' or 'Whilby'. The Austens knew a Whitby family at Bath and JA could be using the name as an in-joke for her family and friends.

3. The Lady Denham: there is an uncertainty about the prefixed 'The'. Is it JA's device to place a lightly ironic emphasis on the fact that Lady Denham is Sanditon's one and only titled lady, its prize exhibit, as it were? Or is it to signify that she is widowed, a dowager – although, strictly speaking, 'The' would only be correct for the widow of a peer (other than a Duke), whereas her late husband was no more than a Baronet? If Sir Edward, the current Baronet, marries, his wife would be Lady Denham, and the present Lady Denham, his aunt, would then be known as Dowager Lady Denham.

4. her Toilette: Miss Whitby's Toilette is the process of making herself ready to appear in public to attend to her customers.

5. smart Trinkets: JA originally wrote 'ornamented Combs'. These could be of tortoiseshell or ivory set with glass or semi-precious stones, or studded with silver or gold. Presumably they would have formed an ornament in Miss Whitby's 'glossy Curls'.

6. She had not Camilla's Youth...Distress: *Camilla, or, a Picture of Youth* (1796) by Fanny Burney, originally published in five volumes. At the novel's opening, the heroine is a girl of nine. JA could anticipate that members of her family would catch the self-referential joke in this, since she was known to have enjoyed the novel and her name is listed as a subscriber in the first edition. In Burney's own account of the novel, the subsequent 'distress' is economic, arriving when the 'Sudden affluence' of Camilla's family, the Tyrolds, suffers an equally rapid reverse: 'Suddenly all is lost'; they are 'Reduced to poverty', with its consequent 'shifts & cramping' (*Camilla,* edn 1972, pp. x-xi). Camilla's personal distress arises at Tunbridge Wells where she is persuaded to live beyond her means, overspends on expensive knicknacks, clothes and entertainment, ending up seventeen pounds over her budget. This allusion explains the references to Mr Parker encouraging 'Expenditure' and to Charlotte's contrary decision to practice economy and pay on the spot 'for what she bought'.

7. **Interesting young Woman**: JA plays with one of the most heavily-used terms of contemporary gothic and romantic fiction; it hints at some intriguing or enigmatic quality in the heroine's past. Very often this relates to a mystery or uncertainty around the her origins, name or parentage – factors which often lead to twists and complications in the novel's plot as identities are concealed, confused or come to light circuitously. JA had satirised this device in her juvenilia, and later in Emma's fantasies about Harriet Smith and in General Tilney's taking Catherine Morland for an heiress. In S, the wider literary associations are now elaborated succinctly in the 'Heroine'-characterisation of Charlotte Brereton that follows. Her attributes of beauty, modesty and charm etc are conveyed in the stock phrasing found in the fiction of the time.

This playful burlesque may have been suggested to JA by one of the most entertaining and widely-read novels of the day, Eaton Stannard Barrett's *The Heroine, or Adventures of a Fair Romance Reader* (1813); a second edition, 'with considerable additions and alterations' came out in 1814 with a new sub-title: *or Adventures of Cherubina*; followed by a third edition in 1815. JA may be signalling an allusion in the repetition of 'Heroine', the main title-word. Barrett's heroine – 'extremely interesting' and 'regularly handsome' etc etc – is described in much the same cliché terms as Charlotte Brereton. JA was reading the novel in March 1814, was 'very much amused by it' and found it 'a delightful burlesque' (L, p.

255-56). We can see why JA enjoyed it. As the 1814 sub-title indicates, the 'heroine' – plain Cherry Wilkinson romanticised into Cherubina De Willoughby – is a figure whose trail of Quixotic 'adventures' takes the story through a world of gothic, sentimental and romantic parody. Possibly this is one of the lines of development Austen had in mind for S beyond chapter 12.

8. graceful Address: manner of speaking and bearing towards other people.

9. barbarous conduct: JA uses 'barbarous' here, as in the major novels, as a term of comic hyperbole or satirically (*MP*, vol. 2, ch. 10; *P&P*, vol. 3, ch. 13; *S&S*, vol. 2, ch. 7), just as Barrett does in *The Heroine* (1813). Both were laughing at the extent to which the word was over-used by contemporary novelists, including Fanny Burney, Anne Radcliffe, Charlotte Smith, Mary Brunton and Maria Edgeworth.

10. number of Visitants: visitors. Although the word was still widely employed, nonetheless by then it was an eighteenth-century usage, literary and archaic, and it conveys an impression of Lady Denham's 'oldfashioned formality'.

11. A West Indy family...West-ingines: there were many slang or colloquial ways of referring to Europeans who had settled in the West Indies. The closest recorded as current at this time is 'West Injee'. 'Indy' was a common way of referring to India and in the seventeenth century the West India Company was referred to formally as the 'West-Indy Company'. So although the forms JA uses here are not recorded in literary use they may well have been current in the spoken language and familiar to her, as many of the families known to her in Hampshire had a younger son seeking his fortune out there. If from no other source, she could have heard them from her brothers Francis and Charles, both of them serving naval officers for the period of the French wars and beyond; Charles, in particular, served for five years on the North America and West India station, with a patrolling area which took him into the Caribbean

12. spend more freely: the debate that opens here between Lady Denham and Mr Parker on the pros and cons of spending money and raising prices, stems directly from the public debate on the state of the national economy, a controversy at its height in the years 1815-16. This was a period of serious depression, with price levels falling rapidly in the last quarter of 1815 and throughout the following year. A solution was proposed by Thomas Attwood, a London and Birmingham banker, in *The Remedy, or, Thoughts on the Present Distress* (1816). He called for the Bank of England to issue more notes, so increasing the money supply and its circulation, leading to higher prices, higher wages and increased production. This is rendered in homely terms in the exchange between Mr Parker and Lady Denham and JA could have picked up the threads of Attwood's argument from her brother Henry. The failure of Henry's London and country bank in the Spring of 1816 was in part due to the state of the national economy.

Elements of the case can also be traced to Marcet's *Conversations on Political Economy*, Conversation XV, 'On Value and Price'. Mr Parker's reference to 'Bakers' echoes an example given by Marcet, p. 298.

JA may also have had in mind the views of Dr Johnson, who had much to say on the economics of everyday life (see Mathias, 1979, ch. 16 'Dr Johnson and the Business World'). In Boswell's *Life* (1791) a recurrent topic is Johnson's dogmatic contention that spending money on luxuries brings benefits to the poor.

13. necessaries of Life: Marcet discusses these in Conversation VIII, 'On Wages and Population', and includes 'food, clothing…Fuel…Houses with glazed windows and a chimney' (p.121). The phrase was something of a literary cliché and appealed to contemporary writers of all kinds, minor poets, dramatists and novelists as well as political economists. Readers of *MP* would remember the discussion between Mrs Norris and Sir Thomas Bertram about what can be done for Fanny Price, with her aunt's ringing declaration that she would rather deny herself the 'necessaries of life…than do an ungenerous thing' (vol. 1, ch. 1).

14. consumeable Articles: food; JA's pastiche of the jargon of the political economists, as in the following note.

15. diffusion of Money: JA could have met this term in the work of the philosopher and historian David Hume (1711-76). He writes of the 'universal diffusion and circulation' of money in his *Essays* (1741-42, 1963, 'Of Money', p. 301); and there is a discussion of the circulation of money, the 'increase or diminution of money in a country' (p. 328), including the 'diffusion' of gold and silver (p. 339), in Marcet's *Conversations* XVI and XVII, 'On Money'.

16. Butchers & Bakers: these characters also feature in the homely illustrations of economic theory in Marcet's *Conversations*.

17. Asses milk: provided by the 'Milch asses'(literally, asses giving milk) of the next line. Considered superior to the milk of cows, goats, ewes and mares, it was thought to most closely resemble human milk. Easily digestible, it was regarded as particularly suitable for invalids and was often prescribed for obstinate coughs, especially the 'consumptive' coughs symptomatic of tuberculosis.

18. Chamber-House: JA's spelling is clear in the manuscript. But such a compound is not recorded in the *OED*. However, she used the term again two lines below, later correcting this second 'House' to 'Horse'. A 'Chamber-Horse' was an early exercise-machine for use indoors, a highly-sprung bouncy chair simulating the up-and-down movement of a rider trotting or galloping.

CHAPTER 7

1. Gig: the common name for a range of small, light two-wheeled open carriages usually drawn by a single horse, for two passengers. The word was derived from 'whirligig', something twisting, turning and whirling about and constantly on the move.

2. a tone of great Taste & Feeling: these are aesthetic qualities that the writers of contemporary guide-books, especially those for seaside resorts, also strove for both in their own heightened rhetoric and the wealth of quotation from literary sources, usually poetry, with which they ornamented their otherwise prosaic texts. The outpouring of quotation that meets us in Sir Edward's discourse in this chapter suggests that JA intended her readers to recognise such guide-books as one of the likely sources for his own literary knowledge, such as it is. Typical of the genre is a guidebook to Eastbourne – *East-Bourne*, 1787. Having brought the visitor to the beach, 'it may not be disagreeable to insert the following panegyric on that noble object the sea: "Hail! thou inexhaustible source of wonder and contemplation! – Hail! thou multitudinous ocean! whose waves chase one another down, like the generations of men; and, after a momentary space, are immerged [sic] for ever in oblivion!…How glorious! how aweful are the scenes thou displayed…" ' (p. 10) and so on, for another page.

3. in praise of their Sublimity: a quality central to any eighteenth-century discussion of 'taste'. Sir Edward's ideas are taken from the masterworks on this subject, Edmund Burke's *Philosophical Enquiry into the Origin of our Ideas of the Sublime and Beautiful* (1757, 2nd edn 1759); Campbell's *The Philosophy of Rhetoric* (1776), where the 'sublime' is treated at the outset; and Blair's *Lectures on Rhetoric and Belles Lettres* (1783) (see ch. 4, note 8). In *The Heroine* (1813), Eaton Stannard Barret includes the 'sublime' in a sequence of satirical oxymorons describing Cherubina: 'mildly sublime, sweetly stern...' (vol. 3, letter 33).

4. undescribable: a variant of 'indescribable'. JA's use of italics indicates that this is a direct quotation from Sir Edward's over-charged rhetoric of 'Taste', 'Feeling' and 'Sensibility'. In turn, JA would expect her readers to recognise Sir Edward's source, Sterne's *A Sentimental Journey Through France and Italy* (1768): 'I felt such undescribable emotions within me' (vol. 2, section Maria. Moulines). JA also uses 'undescribable' in *MP* (vol. 3, ch. 10).

5. Mind of Sensibility: characterised by an acuteness of feeling and emotion and intensity of experience. According to its devotees, the cultivation of 'sensibility' rather than reliance on the faculty of 'sense' provided the path to truth, virtue, judgement, choice and action. See *LS*, Letter 5, note 5.

6. terrific: Johnson: 'Dreadful; causing terrour'. This lay at the heart of the concept of the sublime: 'whatever is in any sort terrible, or is conversant about terrible objects, or operates in a manner analogous to terror, is a source of the *sublime...*' (Burke, *Philosophical Enquiry*, Part I, Sect. vii). Similarly connected to Burke's ideas is the passage following, **quick vicissitudes...sudden Tempest**, touching upon a set of related Burkean concepts: 'the great and sublime in nature' arousing 'Astonishment' (Part II, Sect. i), with the 'ocean' as a prime 'object of terror' (Part II, Sect. ii); 'Suddenness' in the form of 'the sudden Tempest' (Part II, Sect. xviii) and the sublimity of 'visual objects of great dimensions' (Part IV, Sect. ix). All this is indeed **rather commonplace** since the *Philosophical Enquiry* was regarded as a source book of aesthetic ideas which anyone with pretensions to **Taste & Feeling** was expected to have at his fingertips. However, there were sceptics who cast doubt on the Burkean scheme. Prominent among these was the satirist Richard Payne Knight. His *Analytical Inquiry into the Principles of Taste* (1805) provides an entertaining critique of specific ideas in the *Philosophical Enquiry*. For example, Knight ridicules Burke's notions on terror as the sources of the sublime: 'If…he had…walked up St.James's street without his breeches, it would have occasioned great and universal *astonishment*; and if he had, at the same time, carried a loaded blunderbuss in his hands, the astonishment would have been mixed with no small portion of *terror*: but I do not believe that the united effects of these two powerful passions would have produced any sentiment or sensation approaching to sublime, even in the breast of those, who had the strongest sense of self preservation, and the quickest sensibility of danger' (pp. 374-75).

These ideas were also 'rather commonplace' because they formed part of the standard vocabulary of tourist guidebooks, following the lead given by the authoritative aesthetic travel writer William Gilpin. The opening pages of his *Observations on the Coasts of Hampshire, Sussex, and Kent, Relative chiefly to Picturesque Beauty* (1804) include such remarks as 'In *coast scenery*…the ideas of grandeur rise very high' (p. 3), 'the sublimity of storms' (p. 4) and the 'picturesque grandeur' of the coasts (p. 6). : 'Grandeur': in eighteenth and early nineteenth-century philosophical aesthetics, a source of the sublime and most fully discussed in Burke's *A Philosophical Enquiry into the Origin of our Ideas of the Sublime and Beautiful* (1757). Deriving from Burke's *Enquiry* was *Lectures on Rhetoric and Belles Lettres* (1783) by Hugh Blair (1718-1800). In the *Lectures*, Blair writes of the 'the pleasure which arises from Sublimity or Grandeur…'; and he finds 'grandeur' in 'the vast and boundless prospects presented to us' in 'the boundless expanse of the Ocean' (vol. 1, Lecture 3). Elsewhere Blair speaks of grandeur arising 'from the violence of the elements' (1771). The *Lectures* were in print throughout JA's lifetime and in 1817 had reached a 13th edition. Blair is alluded to in *NA*, vol. 1, ch. 14.

7. Ocean: 'the ocean is an object of no small terror' (Burke, *Enquiry*, Part II, Sect. ii).

8. Samphire: a strongly aromatic plant found among seaside rock and shingle. Its leaves were used in salads, cooked dishes and pickles. Its association with 'terror' in the Burkean sublime is established in Edgar's famous image in *King Lear*, the passage in which he conjures up a high cliff-face and, on it, 'half way down/Hangs one that gathers samphire, dreadful trade!' (IV.iv.15-16).

9. Man of Feeling: sentimental and sensitive, he is a familiar literary type in Richardson, Sterne, Goldsmith and features as the title of *The Man of Feeling*, the novel by Henry Mackenzie, published in 1771. This figure also features in later Romantic fiction, notably in Fanny Burney's *Camilla* (1796) and Maria Edgeworth's *Belinda* (1801) and *Patronage* (1814). In *Patronage*, which JA was reading in 1814, the phrase is used several times.

10. the number of his quotations: in their moments of heightened emotion it was fashionable for characters of fiction to turn to quotation, a trait that JA laughed at gently in drawing Anne Elliot's response to 'the last smiles of the year' and 'The sweet scenes of autumn' in *P* (vol. 1, ch. 10) and her recommendation to the tremulously quoting Captain Benwick that he take a 'a larger allowance of prose in his daily study' (vol. 1, ch. 11).

11. the nerves of an Assassin: assassins were abundant in gothic fiction and drama.

12. in either of Scott's Poems: Walter Scott's commanding contemporary reputation was first as a poet and only later as a novelist. A prolific writer, by 1817 Scott had at least half-a-dozen volumes of verse to his name. The works likely to have been in Charlotte's mind are the two by which he was then best known, *Marmion* (1808) and *The Lady of the Lake* (1810) the two poems from which Sir Edward quotes in the passage following. However, given their enormous popularity, this is not evidence that Sir Edward possesses poetic taste: there were four editions of *Marmion* in its year of publication and a further five editions by 1815; similarly, *The Lady of the Lake* went into eight editions in its year of publication, and another three editions by 1816. So by 1817 both poems would have been regarded as war-horses of the literary scene. As to *Marmion*, JA had her reservations: on first hearing the poem, in June 1808, at the time of its publication, she commented, 'Ought I to be very much pleased with Marmion? – as yet I am not' (20-22 June 1808, *L*, p. 131). But she thought sufficiently well of the poem to send her own copy out to her brother Charles, then on naval service in Bermuda. Both poems are mentioned in *P* where the poetically-minded Benwick wonders which 'were to be preferred' (vol. 1, ch. 11).

13. Nor can I exactly recall: the difficulty that Charlotte and Edward have in recalling Scott's 'lines on the sea' is due to the fact that, strictly speaking, he wrote none. The closest we get are two unmemorable lines in the account of the nuns' voyage in *Marmion*: 'The whitening breakers sound so near/Where, boiling through the rocks they roar' (ii.8).

14. "Oh!…Ease: *Marmion*, vi.30.

15. "Some feelings…&c: *The Lady of the Lake*, ii.22.

16. Burns Lines…to madden one!: There is no poem with this precise title and JA is pointing to the woolliness of Sir Edward's literary enthusiasms. Nonetheless, JA's readers would have had no difficulty in calling 'Mary' poems to mind. Burns was exceedingly popular at this time, the volumes of his poetry were constantly reprinted and he was heavily represented in anthologies. One poem, redolent with melodramatic 'Pathos' (see below), is 'A Song' in *Poems* (1789): this Mary is dead and in the concluding lines Burns cries out to her 'Seest thou thy Lover lowly laid!/ Hearest thou the groans that rend his breast!'. Another candidate is 'Highland Mary', first published in 1799: the lover recalls his last 'fareweel' before 'fell Death's untimely frest…nipt my flower sae early!'. However, the renowned 'Mary' poem is 'Mary Morison', *Poems* (1800), where 'Pathos' is contained until the final stanza: 'Or canst thou break that heart of his,/ Whase only faute is loving thee!'. A dependable contemporary witness is Hazlitt. In *Lectures on the English Poets* (London:Taylor, 1818) he named 'the pathetic and glorious love-songs' as those poems of all Burns' work 'which take the deepest and most lasting hold of the mind….Such are the lines to Mary Morison' (Lecture 7). However, there was a rival – 'To Mary in Heaven'(1790), the most heavily anthologised of all the 'Mary' poems. A histrionic piece, heavy with 'Pathos', with a noisy climax in the last four lines, it might well appeal to Sir Edward's declamatory taste: 'My Mary, dear, departed Shade!/ Where is thy place of blissful rest!/ Seest thou thy Lover lowly laid!/ Hearest thou the groans that rend his breast!' (Burns, 1968, vol. 1, p. 493).

Pathos: at this period, a literary quality to be prized; and 'true pathos' was the term that Burns himself used of poetry that moved him greatly (Burns, 1968, vol. 3, p. 1023).

17. Montgomery has all the fire of Poetry: James Montgomery (1771-1854), a minor poet of the Romantic period, now best remembered for *The Abolition of the Slave Trade* (1814). JA, an abolition sympathiser herself, may have mentioned him on account of this poem. As to his having 'all the Fire of Poetry', he was most productive as a writer of moral and religious verse, hymns and epics cast in a sub-Miltonic style. Alongside Burns, he was one of the most heavily-anthologised poets of the day.

18. Wordsworth: JA does not mention Wordsworth in her letters, nor is there any indication in the family memoirs to suggest which, if any, poem she had in mind. *Lyrical Ballads* (1798, enlarged 1800), *Poems in Two Volumes* (1807) and *The Excursion* (1814) were among his major publications by this time.

19. Campbell...few & far between: as this is the most memorable line from the *Pleasures of Hope* (1799), Pt.II, l. 378, by Thomas Campbell (1777-1844), Sir Edward's enthusing reveals no special discernment on his part. Hugely popular, the poem was reprinted in every year up to 1817 and *The Oxford Companion to English Literature* (Oxford: Oxford University Press, 1932, 2nd edn 1936) cites it as one of those 'single lines that have become proverbial' (p. 133). As to the 'Sublime', Sir Edward is at fault: its essence is power and grandeur; it does not melt.

20. But Burns... his Pre-eminence: Sir Edward's championing of Burns and Charlotte's tart rejoinder, a few lines later, that she was 'not poetic enough to separate' his 'Poetry entirely from his Character' echoes a debate returned to again and again by the reviewers: was it possible to judge Burns's poetry without regard to his troubled and troubling life, with all its 'known Irregularities' of womanising and drink? Or is 'Genius' (to quote Sir Edward) 'perhaps incompatible with some of the prosaic Decencies of Life'? James Montgomery, a regular contributor to the *Eclectic Review*, was one of those who turned from Burns's works, 'glowing with enthusiastic admiration', to discover a life 'wantonly dissolved in the cup of pleasure, and quaffed by its possessor at one intemperate draught' (quoted in John Holland & James Everett, *Memoirs of the Life and Writings of James Montgomery* (London:Longman, 1854, vol. 2, pp. 236-37). Since this judgement was the common currency of the monthly and quarterly reviews, and many editions of Burns carried biographical material equally weighted, Charlotte's awareness of the debate is not to be taken as a mark of any special alertness on her part. We might wonder why Sir Edward makes no reference to Byron, who was not unlike Burns in the passionate and sometimes scandalous character of his life and poetry. He was highly productive (no fewer than fifteen works were published by 1816), very popular and widely discussed in the reviews and quarterlies; and it is entirely plausible that a poetry-lover such as Benwick in *P* should discuss with Anne Elliot the comparative merits of Byron and Scott; and that – Denham-like – he should repeat 'with such tremulous feeling, the various lines which imaged a broken heart, or a mind destroyed by wretchedness' (vol. 1, ch. 11). Was it that JA judged Byron's hard satirical strain and subversive wit to be at odds with the vaporousness of Sir Edward's romantic gesturings and yearnings?

21. It were Hyper-criticism: a learned-sounding compound. However, JA may be wanting to make the point that Sir Edward has picked up his exotic vocabulary not from highbrow reading-matter, but, in this instance, from a popular contemporary burlesque, Stannard's *The Heroine* (see ch. 6, note 7). The word occurs in a passage whose elaborate, mildly exotic and malapropistic phrasing would suit Sir Edward very well: 'He, therefore, who presents his own memoirs to the public, may surely merit the reasonable applause of all whose minds are emancipated from the petulance of envy, the fastidiousness of hypercriticism, and the exacerbation of party' (vol. 1, p. 138). JA may have also had in mind a novel she read in 1814, Fanny Burney's *The Wanderer* (1814): 'all severities of hypercriticism' (vol. 2, bk. 3, ch. 24).

Or JA may have been alluding to another source, equally appropriate to Sir Edward. In an 1811 edition of Burns' *Poems*, the word 'hypercriticism' occurs within a lengthy discussion (by an unnamed 'Friend' of the 'Editor') of the poet's 'genius', the conflict between his 'great talents and ungovernable passions', and the writer's own 'ungrateful task of hypercriticism' (vol. 2, pp. 265-67) in responding to two recent reviews of *Reliques of Burns* (1808), edited by R.H. Cromek. These unsigned reviews were by Francis Jeffrey in the *Edinburgh Review* (January 1809) and Walter Scott in the first issue of the *Quarterly Review* (February 1809). Both reviewers discussed weaknesses they found in his poetry yet both acknowledged his 'genius' unstintingly: 'a great and original genius' (Jeffrey, p. 185), 'this wonderful and self-taught genius'(Scott, p. 209), are only two examples.

22. Pseudo-philosophy: this was a well-established compound, used to designate false or misleading philosophy.

23. high toned Genius: a key term in literary and artistic discussions and debates of the period and carefully distinguished, in Blair's *Lectures* from 'Taste', 'frequently…by inaccurate thinkers, confounded. They signify, however, two quite different things. The difference between them can be clearly pointed out; and it is of importance to remember it. Taste consists in the power of judging; genius in the power of executing' (1784, edn 1817, vol. 1, p. 46). Richard Payne Knight, ever contrary, advanced a counter-view, appealing to usage rather than semantics. In a section entitled 'Abuse of Words' he wrote, 'The words genius and taste are, like the words beauty and virtue, mere terms of general approbation, which men apply to whatever they approve, without annexing any specific ideas to them. They are, therefore, as often employed to signify extravagant novelty as genuine merit' (*Analytical Enquiry*, 1805, pp. 428-29).

24. illimitable: a term much used by poets of the period, usually applied to 'oceans', 'powers', 'space', 'eternity' and such-like grand and expansive notions. In *Waverley* (1814), Scott played with the word, writing of 'illimitable correspondents' (vol. 1, ch. 25).

25. Poor dear Sir Harry...thought at first to have got more: at the time of his marriage to the widowed Mrs Hollis, Sir Harry assumed that, according to the normal workings of the laws of property in marriage, he would gain possession of his bride's inheritance from her late husband. However, by means of trusts and other legal devices, she had so arranged her affairs that this inheritance remained beyond his reach.

26. For though I am only the Dowager...It is I that help him: Lady Denham is making the point that, in the normal way, as the widow of the previous Baronet, she would only be entitled to a one-third share of her late husband's estate for the duration of her life, whereas Sir Edward, as 'Heir', would be in possession of the remainder, to which her one-third would be re-united on her death. However, in circumstances which are not explained, the Denham estate is impoverished; and according to Lady Denham, far from Sir Edward supporting her, she is helping him.

27. or even a Co: a co-, as we would say, joint-heiress.

28. Landed or Funded: money invested in the Government stocks, otherwise known as the public funds.

29. Half pay officers: naval officers between ships and awaiting their next posting, or older officers no longer on active service and who remained in the navy until death, were all on so-called 'half pay' (the actual rate was slightly higher).

30. Widows with only a Jointure: this legal term originally referred to the holding of property for the joint use of husband and wife. By extension, it came to mean the specific share of a husband's estate, negociated before marriage, that was assigned to support his widow for the remaining period of her life or until her re-marriage. If the jointure was negociated after the marriage, then the widow had the right to choose either the existing jointure or a dower, this being, on the same conditions, a one-third share of her husband's estate

31. when Rich People are Sordid: along with its other meanings, in this context the word carried a specialised meaning of mercenary, materially-minded, as in Johnson (1799): 'covetous; niggardly'. This is JA's only use of the word.

CHAPTER 8

1. 5 vols. under his arm: judging from Sir Edward's subsequent conversation with Charlotte, these '5 vols' are likely to be the set of volumes for a novel and by specifying the number – the usual number was three – JA could be indicating a novel by Fanny Burney: *Cecilia* (1782), *Camilla* (1796) or, most recently, *The Wanderer* (1814), all of which came out in five volumes.

2. Trash of the common Circulating Library: 'Trash' takes us directly to *Northanger Abbey*, which JA was revising in the second half of 1816. In her famous statement on the novel she speaks scornfully of 'the Reviewers', leaving it to them 'over every new novel to talk in threadbare strains of the trash with which the press now groans'(vol. 1, ch. 5). This may be an allusion to an earlier statement made by a sister-novelist, Anna Laetitia Barbauld, in the Introduction –'On the Origin and Progress of Novel Writing' – which headed a fifty-volume edition of *The British Novelists*: 'a great deal of trash is every year poured out upon the public from the English presses' (1810, vol. 1).

3. those puerile Emanations: 'puerile' from the Latin 'puer' (child), first carried the straightforward meaning of childish or childlike, often signifying innocence. But from the late seventeenth-century it took on the meaning of immature or trivial, and its conjunction with such a dignified word as 'Emanations' is another example of Sir Edward's malapropistic leanings. Of the five citations given in Johnson, including quotations from the seventeenth-century theologian Jeremy Taylor, and from Dryden and Pope, 'emanations' are from the 'sun', the 'heart', the 'soul' and 'God'; and in Fanny Burney's *Camilla* (1796), the two sets of 'emanations' are those 'of a truly elevated mind' and of the heroine's 'virtues'.

4. discordant Principles: could these 'discordant principles' include sense and sensibility, and pride and prejudice? According to Mary Brunton's *Self-Control* (1810), a novel that JA read more than once, marriage is not intended to sanction the union of 'those whose principles are discordant' (vol. 2, ch. 17).

5. incapable of Amalgamation: a very modern usage, since 'amalgamation' was a process in metallurgy and the word had only recently been applied, metaphorically, to other ideas of combination or union. The word had entered fiction recently in a novel familiar to JA, Hannah More's *Coelebs in Search of a Wife* (1809). It comes in a comment referring to More's Lady Denham: 'she has a moral chemistry which excels in the amalgamation of contradictory ingredients' (vol. 1, ch. 12). This scientific train of thought is continued in Sir Edward's vocabulary a few lines later.

6. those vapid tissues: 'vapid', meaning empty or worthless, was an overworked epithet in minor verse of the period and in novels too, including some read by JA. Hannah More uses the word five times in *Coelebs in Search of a Wife* (1809) and Fanny Burney three times in *The Wanderer* (1814). 'tissues', as in 'a tissue of lies', normally refers to a web of obscurities or deceit. Here, Sir Edward appears to be talking about something much more mundane, namely the apparent cross-connections in the events of everyday life that are no more than meaningless coincidences, wholly fortuitous and without any significance whatsoever.

7. ordinary Occurrences: is this meant to call to mind Johnson's account of Edward Young (best known for his poetical *Night-Thoughts*, 1746) in *Lives of the Poets* (1781): 'The prose of ordinary occurrences is beneath the dignity of poetry'? Walter Scott was perhaps offering an oblique response to Johnson in his 1815 review of *E*: in the passage where he uses the word 'occurrence', Scott speaks of 'the common walks of life', and praises the 'style of novel' which 'has arisen, within the last ten or fifteen years... presenting to the reader...a correct and striking representation of that which is daily taking place around him' (quoted in Southam, 1968, p. 63).

8. Alembic: the apparatus formerly in common use in the process of distillation. Following technical advances in the years 1770-1800, it was largely replaced by the still. As a consequence, by 1817 its lingering associations were largely with alchemy, the so-called chemistry of the middle ages, whose principal aim had been the transmutation of base metal into silver or gold, a seemingly magical change in which the alembic featured as the essential vessel, emblematic of the alchemical art. Scott also used the word metaphorically in the second chapter of *Waverley* (1814).

This play upon quasi-scientific language comes up again in *S*: Arthur Parker's 'enjoyments in Invalidism' were 'by no means so spiritualized' as his sisters' and that 'A good deal of Earthy Dross hung about him' (ch. 10) – a mingling of terms from distillation and metallurgy.

In introducing these scientific ideas and imagery, it may be that JA – and perhaps like Hannah More (see notes 5,6) – was drawing upon a widely-known educational work, Jane Marcet's *Conversations on Chemistry*. First published in 1806, by 1813 it had reached a 'considerably enlarged' fourth edition, in which the alembic is illustrated and described as 'highly useful in all kinds of distillation' (vol. 1, p. 237).

9. Science: originally 'knowledge' of all kinds. In the *OED*, the earliest example in its modern, more specialized sense is dated 1865. However, in this instance JA seems to be combining both meanings.

10. You understand me I am sure?…that I do: JA reminds her readers of Sir Sedley Clarendel in Fanny Burney's *Camilla* (1796). Very like Sir Edward Denham, Clarendel is a figure of fun with his 'quaint conceits and remarks' and is 'the least comprehensible person' the heroine 'had ever known' (vol. 2, bk. 4, ch. 7).

11. Fair Questioner: another such figure appears in *Camilla*, where Indiana Lynmere, the heroine's cousin, 'began a negociation with the fair questioner' (vol. 1, bk. 2, ch. 13).

12. Human Nature: a familiar concept to readers of JA, appearing in all the novels except *E* and no less than four times each in *NA* and *P*, the two novels Austen was working on immediately before *S*.

13. some Aberration: Scott's use of the word in *Waverley* (1814) – in the opening paragraph of book one, chapter five – seems to connect his portrait of the romantic Edward Waverley with Sir Edward Denham. Scott declares his intention 'not to follow the steps' of Cervantes 'in describing' a Don Quixote-like imagination, 'such a total perversion of intellect as misconstrues the objects actually presented to the senses, but that more common aberration from sound judgement, which apprehends occurrences indeed in their reality, but communicates to them a tincture of its own romantic tone and colouring'.

14. strict line of Primitive Obligations: primary and basic 'obligations' such as the duty to family, to religion, to King and Country etc. In law, 'obligations' implied the existence of a bond carrying a penalty for non-performance.

15. indomptible Decision: presumably this is JA's personal spelling of 'indomptable', listed in the *OED* as rare and obsolete and thus at home in the exotica of Sir Edward's vocabulary, whereas in the ms JA originally gave him 'unconquerable', a word uncharacteristically tame and commonplace. At the end of the paragraph, JA makes a similar change, from the ms 'sagacious' to **anti-puerile**: with this curious compound, JA emphases Sir Edward's addiction 'to all the newest-fashioned hard words' (ch. 7).

16. anti-prosperous: a nonce-compound, recorded only in S.

17. high-toned Machinations: it may be that Sir Edward's repetition of 'high-toned', already used in the previous chapter in his description of Burns's 'Genius', is merely a stylistic fault that JA would have corrected in further revising S. Otherwise, we can take it that the repetition is intended by JA to signal the limitations of Sir Edward's vocabulary – also its inappropriateness, since contemporary writers were customarily attaching 'high-toned' to 'spirits', 'minds', 'poetry', 'feelings', and – just as Sir Edward has done – to 'genius' rather than to 'machinations'. These belong to the world of melodramatic villainy, as we see early in chapter two of *NA*, the passage in which JA enlarges on the 'alarming presentiments of evil' that might have afflicted Mrs Morland as she contemplates Catherine's departure for Bath: that she might have cautioned Catherine 'against the violence of such noblemen and baronets as delight in forcing young ladies away to some remote farm-house...', an allusion to *Richardson's Sir Charles Grandison* where such 'machinations' occur and the word itself is used five times. However, knowing 'so little of lords and baronets' Mrs Morland 'was wholly unsuspicious of danger to her daughter from their machinations.' Now we have Sir Edward's 'machinations', his exotic seduction fantasy of spiriting Clara Brereton away to 'some solitary House' in 'the Neighbourhood of Tombuctoo', a line of amusing Gothic extravagance that Austen seems to have carried over from the earlier novel.

18. T'were Pseudo-Philosophy: Sir Edward repeats himself, see ch. 7, note 20.

19. Eleemosynary: Johnson gives the meaning 'Living upon alms; depending upon charity' and comments 'Not used'. However, the word was being used in 1811: Bath's General Hospital, Almshouses, Dispensary and Charitable Schools are listed as 'Eleemosynary Institutions'. The word also appears in poems and novels of JA's period, including Barrett's *The Heroine* (1813) and Scott's *Guy Mannering* (1815).

20. sentimental Novels: by this time, a term of amused contempt for a school of fiction characterised by extravagance of feeling and emotional posturing. Sentimental fiction became the dominant mode c1760-1800 and was extensively satirised by JA in the juvenilia. The term was used twice, derisively, by Barrett in *The Heroine* (1813).

21. the impassioned, & most exceptionable parts of Richardsons: Samuel Richardson, author of *Pamela* (1740), *Clarissa* (1747-48) and *Sir Charles Grandison* (1753-54), was one of JA's favourite novelists. 'the most exceptionable parts' refer to what many critics have described as an ambivalent and prurient element in his treatment of sexuality. This is most evident in *Clarissa*, the tragedy of Clarissa Harlowe: attracted by Lovelace, an unscrupulous rake, she runs away with him but resisting his overtures of seduction is drugged and raped by him.

22. Knowledge of modern Literature: literature from the eighteenth-century onwards.

23. Essays, Letters, Tours & Criticisms: these types of writing formed the staple contents of the *Gentleman's Magazine*, the *Edinburgh* and *Quarterly Reviews* and other such monthly and quarterly publications, together with the collected editions of the essay-periodicals of Richard Steele and Joseph Addison, including the *Tatler* (1709-11) and its continuation, including the *Spectator* – both of which remained continually in print. Such collections, and the *Spectator* is mentioned by name, come under fire in JA's defence of the novel in *NA* (vol. 1, ch. 5). 'Tours' were travel writing including accounts of the European Grand Tour undertaken by wealthy young Englishmen as a journey combining the benefits of cultural education and life-experience.

24. the line of the Lovelaces: the type of the seductive and ruthless womaniser, descended from Robert Lovelace, the charming, deceiving and unscrupulous rake of Richardson's novel *Clarissa, or, The History of* *a Young Lady* (1747-48). Clarissa's cousin Belford avenges her, killing Lovelace in a duel.

25. the Neighbourhood of Tombuctoo: modern Timbuctoo. A city fabled for its remoteness and riches, located on the Niger in what is now the West African state of Mali. There was widespread interest in Tombuctoo at the very time JA was working on S, following the account that appeared in *The Narrative of Robert Adams* (1816), thought to have been the first white man to reach the city. *The Narrative* was widely discussed in the papers and reviews. Adams' comments on the sexual habits and skimpy dress of the inhabitants were quoted, giving rise to further suggestive comment, such as 'The African Expedition', a poem which appeared in the *Morning Post* for 1 January 1817. It advised the sons of Albion to cease their 'schemes of prurient enterprise'. Did this, or something like it, inspire JA to set down Sir Edward's musings on a similarly 'prurient enterprise' involving 'Clara's reception' in 'the Neighbourhood of Tombuctoo'?

CHAPTER 9

1. Chichester: the ancient county town of West Sussex, sixty-two miles south-west of London and thirty miles due west of Brighton.

2. no Hysterics of consequence: in contemporary medicine hysterics was taken seriously as a woman's disease arising from a disorder of 'the nervous system' and leading to fits and convulsions – the 'violent' 'attack' of Susan's mentioned in the following lines. These could leave sufferers in a swoon, a state of unconsciousness, from which they generally returned with no recollection of the episode. According to the entry on 'Hysterics' in Richard Reece's *Dictionary of Domestic Medicine* (1808) (from which the quotations here are taken), the vulnerable period was around mensuration, the vulnerable years from puberty to 35, and its prime trigger was 'the passions of the mind'. The favoured treatment was laudanum.

3. Lumbago: rheumatism of the lower back and legs, thought to be caused by strong winds from the north and east. Visitors to the seaside were considered to be especially prone to this affliction and resort guides of this period carried due warning.

4. Seminary: from the late eighteenth-century, a synonym for school, often, as here, a private school for young ladies. JA characterises such establishments in *E* as being places which 'professed, in long sentences of refined nonsense, to combine liberal acquirements with elegant morality upon new principles and new systems – and where young ladies for enormous pay might be screwed out of health and into vanity…' (vol. 1, ch. 3).

5. I have been taking some Bitters of my own decocting: a homemade astringent tonic for stomach upsets, stimulating the appetite, aiding the digestion and as a general pick-me-up. Its principal ingredient was usually wormwood (from the plant *artemisia absinthium*) typically mixed with orange-peel, cardomon and other flavoursome ingredients.

6. lessons on Eloquence and Belles Lettres: as distinct from carrying one's audience by the force of argument, **Eloquence** or public speaking, as it was often called, was the art of persuasion employing the devices of oratory. It was regarded as an important asset and 'Lessons' would touch upon the many devices of expressive speaking identified at this time, including pace, pronunciation, intonation, modulation, articulation, accentuation, harmony, pauses, tone and force. Lessons would also give practice in the non-vocal devices: posture, deportment, facial expression and gestures of the hands and arms. For all these aspects of eloquence there were exercises to be followed. The importance of the subject in contemporary educational thinking is signified in the space given to it in the 1817 edition of the *Encyclopaedia Britannica*, no less than fifty pages (vol. 15, pp. 341-90).

Alongside eloquence, and within the broad subject-area of rhetoric, some educationalists included **Belles Lettres** (Johnson: 'polite literature' or fine writing). The master-work in this area was *Lectures on Rhetoric and Belles Lettres* (1783) by Hugh Blair (1718-1800). Among the principal topics of Belles Lettres were the history of English literature and language; the study of style; figures of speech; epistolary writing; types of poetry, including pastoral, didactic, descriptive, epic, dramatic; and types of prose, including judicial, deliberative, forensic, pulpit, periodical essays and fiction.

CHAPTER 10

1. Projector: Johnson: 'One who forms wild impracticable schemes'; a far-fetched visionary, often in pursuit of highly speculative enterprises; commonly satirised as a figure of fun, deriving from the 'Academy of

Projectors' depicted by Swift in Part III of *Gulliver's Travels* (1726) and by Johnson in *The Adventurer* (no. 99, 19 October 1753).

2. quack Medecine: a term of abuse, the word 'quack' is thought to derive from the Dutch 'kwakzalver', someone who boasts about his 'salve' or medicinal ointment. The English form, 'quacksalver', commonly used in the seventeenth century, was superceded by the abbreviated form, referring to tricksters untrained in medicine who profited from the sale of their own widely-promoted patent pills, potions and other nostrums, concoctions or treatments for which miraculous cures were claimed. Many of these quack remedies were patent medicines (see ch.11, note 10), some of them harmless placebos, some with such lethal ingredients as mercury, antimony and arsenic.

In JA's time, quacks continued to flourish despite dire warning in reputable medical books, including those for home use. There was also a self-interested outcry from medical practitioners against druggists – apothecaries or dispensing chemists – and other shopkeepers, including grocers, who supplied medicines to the public at much lower prices than the doctors, so depriving them of a valuable source of income.

The term also carried the sense, as here, of ignorant and often injurious self-medication: a term for self-dosing was to 'quack' oneself. Moreover, Reece's *Dictionary of Domestic Medicine* (1808) provides a connection between quackery and two of the medical themes of S, namely nervous complaints (see note 11) and hypochondria: 'Quack doctors, however, artfully refer all diseases of the body to a morbid state of the nervous system, in order to impose their nervous cordials on the credulous and ignorant...hence the hypochondriac...falls an easy prey to the allurement; and unfortunately this class of people are but too numerous in this country...'.

3. a spirit of restless activity: at this point on the ms, JA made a change worth noting: 'the disease of activity' into this memorable phrase. Another such ms change comes in the description, later in this chapter, of Arthur Parker : the mundane 'Earth' that 'hung about him' becomes resonant 'Earthy Dross' (see note 19).

4. posting over the Down: hurrying.

5. the Establishment in general: in the specialised sense of the household, its component furniture, furnishings and people.

6. salts in her hand: smelling salts, usually of sodium carbonate, often used as a restorative to combat faintness or sickness, as were **drops**: a medicine, commonly a patent medicine, to be taken in drops or small doses, and kept in a small medical bottle or **Phial**.

7. Broad made & Lusty: lusty, not with the modern sense of lively and energetic but large, with the suggestion of corpulence.

8. two Post chaises…two Hack-Chaises: the chaise was a four-wheeled closed carriage for two or three passengers, with two or four horses, and a postillion or postboy, the 'Post' indicating that it was hired from a local inn. 'Hack' was an abbreviation of 'hackney', meaning either the vehicle or the horses or both were hired. 'Post' and 'hack' were broadly synonymous.

9. as a screen: fire-screens, either held in the hand or standing on the floor, were necessary around an open fire; and, as next lines tell us, the larger the better.

10. heavy in Eye: (possibly, as there is no other recorded use of the phrase) with sleepy-looking, heavy, drooping eyes. Or is this JA's facetious circumlocution, a polite re-phrasing of 'heavy-arsed', current slang for lethargic, sluggardly?

11. perhaps you are nervous…Nerves: some medical writers treated this area seriously and at length; others, more sceptically; and since early in the eighteenth-century, it had been known in Europe as 'the English malady'. In his *Dictionary of Domestic Medicine* (1808), Reece mocked 'Nervous Disorders' as 'a species of modern disease which entail upon the unhappy sufferer much misery, with all the dread of death without much danger of its taking place' (unnumbered pages). Among these 'disorders' were the vapours (sometimes defined as lowness of spirits or melancholia), hysterics and hypochondria. Reece was equally forthright in *The Medical Guide* (1817). Here, he linked 'Nervous Diseases' (his section heading) directly with bilious hypochondria: 'within these few years, it has become fashionable to attribute complaints to the bile; and hypochondriacs, and people of vacant minds, who can think of nothing else but the state of their health, instead of being *nervous*, now complain of being bilious' (p. 344). Another long-established medical guide, William Buchan's *Domestic Medicine* (21st edn 1813) was equally dismissive. It spoke of 'That class of diseases, which, for want of a better name, we call nervous ' as having 'made almost a complete conquest of the one sex, and is making hasty strides towards vanquishing the other'

(p. 638). According to Buchan, nervous diseases could sometimes lead to 'an uncommon craving for food' (p. 419), the symptom JA displays a few pages later in Arthur Parker's appetite for strong cocoa and butter soaked toast. Some authorities, sceptical of 'Nerves' as a medical complaint, prescribed a regime of healthy living for its cure, just as Reece recommended 'firm persuasion' and 'physical activity' as the antidote to 'Hypochondriasis' (see that section in the *Dictionary of Domestic Medicine*), an approach JA echoes here in Charlotte Heywood's confidence in 'the efficacy of air & exercise'.

12. such a Perspiration: a central topic in medicine of the time. According to Reece's *Dictionary* (1808), 'The health of man chiefly depends on the proper state of this function'; and Buchan (1813) tells us, 'It is of great importance to health, that few diseases attack us while it goes properly on; but when it is obstructed, the whole frame is soon disordered' (p. 115). Obstructed perspiration was considered to be fatal and there were patent medicines, such as 'Cook's Rheumatic Pills', addressed to this problem. In *Conversations on Chemistry* (1813), Marcet discusses perspiration, pointing out that it 'acts a most important part in the animal economy' (vol. 2, p. 327).

13. his own Cocoa: this is not cocoa as we know it but old-fashioned drinking chocolate made from the cacao (cocoa) bean, sweetened and flavoured with vanilla, cinnamon and other spices and mixed with flour or arrowroot to counteract the richness of the cocoa-fat (modern cocoa being the residue remaining after the fat has been extracted, a process invented by Van Houten in 1828). Although chocolate was predominantly a social drink in the seventeenth and eighteenth centuries, when it first came to England c1657 it was promoted as medicinal, an anti-dysenteric well-suited to the stomach and bowels of invalids and the elderly. Later, it came to be regarded as a stimulant, which explains the Parker sisters' concern at the increasing strength of Arthur's evening drink.

14. one sort of Herb-Tea & Miss Diana another: there were many varieties, made from leaves, flowers, roots, bark and seeds, and in many different combinations and strengths. *The English Physitian* (1652) by Nicholas Culpeper, established herb-tea in the *materia medica*. Culpeper's book, the key compendium in the medicinal use of herbs, was many times reprinted and adapted down to JA's time. Under Royal Patronage was the Rev J.Gamble's 'British Medicinal Tea', advertised as containing only homeland herbs – these could include rosemary, sage, hyssop, balm and veronica – and claiming to be a remedy for 'Nervous, Hysteric, or Hypochondriac Disorders' and 'Windy and Bilious Complaints'. At this very moment, in view of her recent dental experiences, Susan Parker could be drinking cowslip tea, a sedative, and the hyperactive Diana a tranquiliser such as catnip or lavender or even the sedative valerian.

15. sat coddling: this combines the culinary process of boiling gently and the figurative sense of nursing. We meet this latter sense in *E* when John Knightley responds brusquely to his wife's concern for his health: 'Be satisfied with doctoring and coddling yourself and the children, and let me look as I chuse' (vol. 1, ch. 12).

16. A large Dish: early forms of the cup were without a handle and came with a matching 'dish', a shallow saucer, into which the tea, coffee or chocolate was poured and drunk.

17. dry Toast…With a reasonable quantity of Butter: since the 1740's it had been customary to serve buttered toast with tea, a point that establishes Charlotte's normality in this local comedy of dietary eccentricity.

18. the Coats of the Stomach: this anatomical-medical term referring to the four protective membrane layers lining the stomach. JA may have expected her readers to be reminded of a comic episode in Smollett's *Peregrine Pickle* (1751) in which Mrs Trunnion, suffering agonies in her bowels from doctored brandy, is treated with 'oily draughts and lubricating injections to defend the coats of the stomach and intestines…' (vol. 1, ch. 14). Another reference – equally, if unconsciously comic – linking the 'coats of the stomach' with 'the pernicious effects of drinking tea' (see note 20) comes in Knight's *Analytical Inquiry into the Principles of Taste* (1805, 4th edn 1810). He recalls having read that 'a single ounce of that deleterious drug, having been steeped for only five minutes in a quart of boiling spring water, rendered it so corrosive, that it immediately took all the hairs off a raw pig's tail…What havock must it then make with the tender coats of the stomach!' (footnote to p. 382).

19. A good deal of Earthy Dross: Earthy carries strong poetic associations from its use by Sidney, Shakespeare, Milton and Dryden and became a cliché in verse contemporary with JA. Dross, too, was a highly literary word and JA may be invoking Scott's description of the Bailie in *Waverley* (1814) as 'a man of earthly mould, after all; a good deal of dirt and dross about him' (vol. 2, ch. 13). Dross was the scum forming on the surface of melted metal; more generally, any waste residue; here, Arthur Parker's fat. Both words were also commonly met with in contemporary scientific writing.

20. strong Green Tea: green tea was made from fresh leaves dried immediately after picking. (Black tea – sometimes known as bohea – was differently prepared: the leaves were spread for two to four hours in a highly humid atmosphere, rendering them fermented or oxidised). Green tea was introduced to Britain in the mid-seventeenth century as a medicinal drink and although tea-drinking later became a social occasion in JA's time, tea was still recommended by some medical writers as a stimulant for the appetite and as an after-dinner aid to digestion and sleep. Other doctors, however, warned that it should be drunk in moderate quantities only, not too strong, nor too hot. On account of its heavy tannin content green tea was said to be habit-forming and lead to sleeplessness, tremors and spasms and the problems Arthur soon describes. According to Buchan (1814), it brought a multitude of ills: it was bad for the nerves, 'preventing sleep, occasioning giddiness, dimness of the sight, sickness, &c' (p. 390). To ameliorate the effect of the tannin, green tea was often diluted with cream or milk and sweetened with sugar. That its benefits and ill-effects were under debate at this time can be seen in the 5th edition of the *Encyclopaedia Britannica* (1817, vol. 20, p. 229). And beyond the medical issue there remained the vestiges of an eighteenth-century moral debate: the Nonconformists, led by John Wesley, regarded tea-drinking as a pernicious, habit-forming indulgence while such vocal tea-drinkers as Dr Johnson sang its praises.

21. studied right sides & Green Tea scientifically: JA's satire has an identifiable target since there was an abundant quasi-scientific literature devoted to the study of green tea and its effects. Among the many *Treatises and Observations*, she would have had in mind such formidable studies as *A Dissertation upon Tea, Explaining its Nature and Properties By many New Experiments; And demonstrating From Philosophical Principles, the various Effects it has upon different Constitutions* (1730), by Thomas Short MD and *The Natural History of the Tea-Tree, with Observations on the Medical Qualities of Tea, and on the Effects of Tea Drinking* (1772, 1799) by John Oakley Lettsom MD. Another of those who had studied the 'frequent use' of green tea 'scientifically' was William Cullen in *Lectures on Materia Medica* (1773). He found that its tannin content led to 'a weakening of the tone of the stomach, weakening the system in consequence, inducing tremors and spasmodic affections' (p. 305).

The notable satirical use of 'scientifically' is in Sheridan's *The Critic* (1781) where Mr Puff (the critic) admits that his profession has never been 'scientifically treated' (Act 1, Sc. 2). JA had known the play since childhood and the word may well have lodged in her mind. A recent reminder was Scott's *The Antiquary* (1815). Oldbuck (the antiquary), delighted to have Lord Glenallan's 'patient attention', holds forth pedantically (somewhat in the manner of Sir Edward lecturing Charlotte Heywood) on the etymology of 'Bog' and the names of various bog grasses, including 'the couch-grass or dog-grass, or, to speak scientifically, the *triticum repens* of Linnaeus' (vol. 2, ch. 14).

22. some private hand: a letter delivered by private carrier or stage coach in breach of the 'General' or official Post Office monopoly.

CHAPTER 11

1. a happier catastrophe: JA plays with the two meanings of catastrophe. First, a dramatic conclusion, often, as here, accompanied by a laughable coincidence, or dénouement, a swift unravelling of the plot – possibly expecting her readers to pick up the obvious Shakespearian allusion, the words of Edgar in *King Lear* : 'and pat he comes, like the catastrophe of the old comedy' (I.ii.150-51). Equally, they might recall Blair's account: 'The Fifth act is, the seat of the catastrophe, or the unravelling of the plot' (1783, vol. 2, p. 493). Second, the more recent sense of a (minor) disaster.

2. genteel kind of Woman: in her description of the Heywood daughters as 'two or three genteel looking young Women' (ch. 1), JA uses the word in the straightforward sense of 'polite', 'elegant', as a gentlewoman would be; and this is precisely the meaning we find in the novels. But in this account of Mrs Griffiths there is the faintest suggestion of adopted gentility, a faintly mocking tone that had began to shade 'genteel' following the assumption of gentry manners by the aspiring ladies of the rising trading and commercial classes. Also see W, note 156.

3. their Displays: occasions for these 'great girls & young Ladies' to show off their talents, known as their 'accomplishments' ('ornamental' and 'practical') in music, dancing, eloquence, painting, drawing etc (see *LS*, Letter 1, note 7) and the social graces.

4. half Mulatto: a mulatto was the child of a white – usually the owner or manager of a West Indian plantation – and a black or coloured slave. To designate each successive generation there was a precise term specifying the exact degree of relationship, from mulatto (having one-half black ancestry), to quadroon (one-quarter) and octoroon (one-eighth). Miss Lambe was a quadroon, the child of a mulatto, probably a freed slave, and a rich plantation-owner, and readers could suppose her to have been educated in England to be launched in English society with the aid of her great wealth. The term mulatto is used in the literature of this period but JA provides the only recorded example of half mulatto.

5. every body must now "move in a Circle...": pointing to the social necessity of having a 'circle' or group of acquaintances in which to 'move' and of having an accepted place within that circle – that is, a circle in which, after having first been formally introduced, a young lady can make and receive social calls or visits, and can accept invitations to other social occasions. This was a particularly sensitive point in budding resorts, anxious to maintain their social standing and to attract the superior sort of visitor. Aping the spas, the resorts employed Masters of Ceremonies to lay down the forms and rituals of polite social behaviour; and the elites preserved their privacy, with a strict line drawn between public and private events. As we see at the opening of Chapter 12, Charlotte Heywood has so far been frustrated in her attempts to call on Lady Denham, the undisputed leader of Sanditon society. This is a necessary 'attention' to be paid, one of the steps essential to complete Charlotte's moving in a circle. JA's sardonic view of this process can be glimpsed in *E*, in Mrs Elton's advice to Jane Fairfax to avoid employment 'in a family not moving in a certain circle' since, with 'superior talents', 'you have a right to move in the first circle' (vol. 2, ch. 17).

6. rototary Motion: JA's spelling for 'rotatory'. The phrase is found in the literature of science, especially astronomy. But at the front of Austen's mind may have been a moment of farcical comedy in Barrett's *The Heroine* (1813): Cherubina De Willoughby on the dance floor, caught up in a 'rotatory motion', having already lost half her dress is about to lose the other half too (vol. 2, letter 26).

7. her Milch Asses: see ch. 6, n. 17.

8. a Decline: not simply failing health but a specific illness such as consumption.

9. Physician...Prescriptions: see ch. 5, note 5.

10. some Tonic pills...a Property in: tonic pills were to strengthen and invigorate, commonly made from rhatania powder (the root of a South American shrub) together with extract of madder and mistletoe powder. In this case, the pills were a patent medicine, commercially manufactured and sold, with investors in the business, such as Mrs Griffiths' cousin.

11. never deviate from the strict Medecinal page: literally, as well as metaphorically, since the pills, as patent medicines invariably were, would come with a sheet stating how many and when the pills were to be taken, plus publicity material and testimonials to their effectiveness.

12. commanded in front: overlooked.

13. the favourite Lounge: a place where visitors would congregate, exchange gossip, and relax.

14. at the low Windows upstairs: in Regency houses it was usual for the living-rooms to be on the first floor and for the windows to be full-length, in effect glass doors ending at floor level, hence 'low', and opening onto a balcony, as here.

15. Telescope: we are to visualise the Misses Beaufort gazing out to sea or even along the beach. But the telescope may also mark them out as 'amateurs of astronomy'. The discoveries of William Herschel (1738-1822), the leading astronomer of the day, knighted in 1816, led astronomy to become a very fashionable field of science, with an abundance of introductory books and lecture courses. Following the success of Herschel's sister, Caroline – with her discovery of nebulae and comets and her revision and extension of Flamsteed's catalogue of stars – the amateur pastime of observational astronomy was regarded as a scientific hobby which ladies could follow.

CHAPTER 12

1. charitable subscriptions: a specialised form of philanthropy which flourished at this time as a form of conspicuous charity. It afforded social recognition for one's good works and combined Christian duty with the virtue of benevolence. The success of these schemes depended on persuading the local big-wigs to head the list of subscribers. In the countryside, these would include the Lord of the Manor, the county MP, the parish clergyman, and any other local people of prominence. Then the remaining gentry and the well-to-do tradesmen and farmers would feel obliged to follow as a matter of pride. Eventually, the full list was printed for everyone to see. First came the nobility, church prelates and anyone else of eminence, in the strict order of their social standing, then followed the body of donors, listed with their donation and ranked according to its size. Typically, these might run between twenty guineas and half-a-guinea. In the case of Sanditon, Mr Parker is willing to 'promote' the scheme providing that it has Lady Denham's approval. With her name at the head of the list, the residents and visitors could be expected to fall in line.

However, in the post-war years there was such a proliferation of these schemes that weariness set in and others besides JA began to make fun of them. Just before S, for example, there appeared a satirical pamphlet, *The Art of Evading a Charitable Subscription* (1815); and a play on this idea, or something like it, may point to a continuing strand in S's scheme of subversive social comedy.

2. a poor woman in Worcestershire: the county town is Worcester, 111 miles north west of London. Its staple occupation was the manufacture of gloves

3. establishment of a Charitable Repository at Burton onTrent: an ancient town in Staffordshire about 125 miles north of London, famed for its ale: Bass and Worthington were among its nine major breweries. JA mentions in her letters that a Repository opened in a lodging house in Bath in 1797 (*L*, p. 74). According to town guides of the period, there was a 'Repository for the Works of the Poor'(or 'for Works of Industry'), at 8 Bath Street. Its purpose is described in *The Improved Bath Guide* [1809?] as being for 'the Encouragement of Industry...of persons reduced to distress, by affording them a ready sale for the articles of their industry' (p. 80). The distressed persons fixed the price at which their products were sold and the receipts came to them in full.

As to the choice of Burton, in 1806 JA visited her cousin Edward Cooper, Rector of the Staffordshire parish of Hamstall Ridware. During her five-week stay, she is likely to have travelled the ten or twelve miles into Burton. Although there is no record of a charitable repository there, it was particularly well-endowed with charitable foundations and a repository would not have been out of place.

4. the family of the poor Man who was hung last assizes at York: York was an ancient city 210 miles north of London. The assizes were judicial sessions at which major criminal cases were heard by a judge travelling on circuit.

In chapter ten of *E*, JA presents a leisurely scene of charitable visiting 'to a poor sick family' – whereas the account of Diana's strenuous scheme of charity-in-prospect seems to be JA's comment on the contemporary encouragement of individual *female* philanthropy as a voguish activity (promoted, for example, in such fashionable publications as the *Lady's Magazine* between 1810 and 1820). JA may also be reflecting on the idea that women needed to occupy themselves with estimable projects as an escape from boredom and the waste of their 'time and money' on 'vain and frivolous purposes' – to quote Hannah More (1745-1833), a voice of the time, in *Moral Sketches of Prevailing Opinions and Manners* (1819, p. 214).

Mrs Marcet has much to say critical of Diana's style of long-distance, arm's-length charity. In Conversation X, 'On the Condition of the Poor' (1816), she applies strict economic tests, pointing to the need for 'compassion' to 'be regulated by good sense' and enlarging on the consequences of 'undistinguished benevolence' in encouraging 'indolence, prodigality, and vice' among the poor (p. 176).

5. her first Dip...go in the Machine: see ch.1, n. 22.

6. when the Leaches have done: see ch. 5, n. 6.

7. a close, misty morn[g]: the effect of this atmosphere and the 'great thickness of air', soon experienced, is to confuse Charlotte's perception of objects and people; and in this striking visual effect JA may be reminding her readers of a passage in *S&S* where Edward Ferrars, intent on parodying Gilpin's theories, speaks of the picturesque quality of 'objects...indistinct through the soft medium of a hazy atmosphere' (vol. 1, ch. 18).

8. from the Gig to the Pheaton: normally, a gig and a phaeton [JA has her own spelling] would be easy to tell apart. Drawn by a single horse, a gig was a light, two-wheeled vehicle. The phaeton, far smarter, was a four-wheeled, one or two-seater open carriage, owner-driven, usually drawn by a pair of horses. The sporty model was the 'high flyer' or 'perch-high', so-called on account of its large wheels (up to eight feet) and high suspension. It was built for speed and was thought to combine swiftness, dignity and a gentlemanly degree of risk. First popularised by the Prince Regent and his circle, the high-flyer signified that the owner was a stylish buck, a man of fashion and means, a frequenter of racing and other sporting functions. The two horses harnessed in line, one behind the other, were in **tandem**, considered to be a rather dashing arrangement favoured by gentlemen drivers.

9. a broad, handsome, planted approach: the drive or approach-road leading to a country-house between an established avenue of trees.

10. Beauty & Respectability…Timber could give: in this context, 'timber' is not a straightforward synonym for woodland or trees. Here, it carries a specialised legal meaning, whereby the oak, ash and elm alone are so defined. Of these, the trees aged twenty years and above form part of the freehold inheritance of Sanditon House. The concept of freehold was that an estate would pass down intact and undivided from father to eldest son and that neither the estate, which included the house, nor parts of it, including the 'timber', would be sold off for profit (while, of course, mature 'timber' could be cut down in the interests of good forestry, or it might be sold off to provide a 'portion' for the support of younger sons, or, in war-time, provided patriotically for the construction of fighting ships). Thus the 'abundance of very fine Timber', testifying to the lineal heritage, the cherishing and integrity of the Sanditon House estate, confers 'Respectability' ie worthiness of respect upon its owner. The phrase can be glossed from *E* where Donwell Abbey's 'abundance of timber in rows and avenues, which neither fashion nor extravagance had rooted up' (vol. 3, ch. 6) testifies slightly more fully to the character of its lineal ownership.

11. Paddock: an enclosed area in which deer or other animals were kept.

12. proper Park paling: a solidly constructed fence with vertical stakes supporting horizontal beams to which were fixed vertical planks or 'pales'. The legal definition of a 'Park' was that it should be enclosed by a pale (a fence so constructed), a wall or a hedge, and contain wild deer permitted either by royal Grant or by Prescription (ancient custom). In any event, a park fenced in this way was a mark of both social and financial status, and the Denham claim to these is signified in the paling's 'excellent condition'.

13. the usual sitting-room: ordinary or everyday, as distinct from the sitting room kept for special occasions and receiving honoured guests.

———

Poems

Jane Austen was not a born poet and her verses, relatively few in number – including the items of juvenilia, about thirty over as many years – are best understood as occasional pieces written for the entertainment of her relatives and friends, and with no thought of publication. The writing of light verse, including charades, riddles and other rhyming games, was a pastime for many families in the second half of the eighteenth-century, and the Austens, led by Mrs Austen, were no exception. As a child of six, she entertained her uncle, the Master of Balliol, with several 'Smart pieces promising great Genius' and was praised by him as 'the Poet of the family.'[1] Many years later her grand-daughter, Anna Lefroy, remembered Mrs Austen as 'a quickwitted woman with plenty of sparkle and spirit in her talk who could write an excellent letter either in prose or verse, the latter making no pretence to poetry, but being simply playful common sense in rhyme'.[2] Anna had her own experience of this in her grandmother's poem of congratulation on her marriage to Ben Lefroy in 1814. The gift carried a PS: 'what I then said in Verse I now repeat in plain prose – May you both be very, very happy in this world, and perfectly so in the next'.[3] This easy talent for versifying Mrs Austen used for occasions of all kinds. One such event was a ball at the assembly rooms in Basingstoke. For the benefit of either Jane or Cassandra (we are not sure which), she made a versified list of the 'six and thirty folk' present.[4] A very different occasion, in March 1804, was her own recovery from illness, inspiring her to a half-humorous, half-serious 'Dialogue' with 'Death' in which she tells her adversary that his 'ill success' is owing 'To the prayers of my husband…the care of my daughters' and her physician's 'skill and attention'.[5] Three years later, she joined with Cassandra, Jane and her daughter-in-law Elizabeth – Edward's wife – in a verse word-game where every line had to rhyme with 'rose'; and she led the family in the writing of riddles and charades

How widely this poetic talent was shared among the Austens can be judged from David Selwyn's *Collected Poems and Verse of the Austen Family*: twelve members of the Austen and Leigh families are represented there; added to this is the single volume given to the considerable output of Jane's brother James.[6] As a young girl, she would have been familiar with the lengthy verse-Prologues and Epilogues that James added to the plays performed at Steventon during the 1780's. A follower of Cowper and James Thomson, James also wrote reflective nature verse and lighter pieces. Some of this would have been read in the family circle and played its part in shaping Jane Austen's taste. Henry Austen's 'Biographical Notice' tells us that 'Her favourite moral writers were Johnson in prose, and Cowper in verse'.[7] The 1870 *Memoir* mentions the influence of Cowper and also her enjoyment of 'Scott's poetry', and Crabbe, 'perhaps on account of a certain resemblance to herself in minute and finished detail'.[8] The later family biography, the *Life and Letters* (1913), tells us that she was attracted 'by the return to nature in Cowper and the introduction of romance in Scott.'[9] Much of this can be confirmed in the novels and letters, which also reveal her knowledge of Shakespeare, Milton, Pope and Byron, and a number of minor poets. And she would also have come across the women poets of the age, many in number and prolific in output. Young ladies were encouraged to develop their skills in verse by the teachers of rhetoric, elecution and belles lettres: it was recommended as a desirable accomplishment. Even Mary Wollstonecraft added her voice of encouragement, providing a Preface to *The Female Reader* (1789), an anthology of prose and verse designed 'For the Improvement of Young Women'. The fruit of example and encouragement can be seen in the mass of women's poetry published in the books, magazines and journals of the time.

It would be misleading, however, to judge Jane Austen's output alongside these traditions. The story of her life as a writer is that of a woman set on succeeding as a novelist, a published novelist, and there is no evidence that she had the least desire to see any of her verse in print. Some of it is the lightest of light verse, thrown off on the spur of the moment, triggered perhaps by no more than her whimsical delight at a pair of names and the opportunities they offered for word-play. Marriages were irresistible: the middle-aged Miss Wallop to the elderly Mr Wake, Miss Gill to Mr Gell. Exactly as her niece Caroline Austen relates: 'her description of the pursuits of Miss Mills and Miss Yates –

two young ladies of whom she knew next to nothing – they were only on a visit to a near neighbour but their names tempted her into rhyme...'.[10] Mr Best, too, was a gift, with 'Oh! Mr Best, you're very bad' as the *donnée* of an opening line. This leads us to a very particular and extra-literary significance to the poems – the insights they give us on Jane Austen's life and the lives of her friends and others of the Austen circle. In this instance, as much as being a joke on Mr Best, the poem was motivated by Jane Austen's affection and concern for the well-being of Martha Lloyd. Her mother had died the previous year and Martha had been offered a home by Mrs Austen and her daughters. Likewise, 'This little bag', trivial and even banal as it is, carries a touching message of friendship and farewell to Martha's sister, Mary, when the Lloyd family was moving away from their neighbourhood at Steventon.

In some poems we meet a genuinely poetic charge, even if this quality is intermittent and local, as it is in the mock panegyric, 'In Measured Verse', a 'character' poem composed with her niece Anna in mind. The verses gain in interest with the progression of the American imagery; and there is an intriguing complexity and challenge to stanza four: in the analogy with 'transatlantic groves', Anna's 'judgement' is characterised as 'thick, black, profound'. And the final stanza, in its expansiveness and the delicate hesitation of its cadences, is quite Marvellian in its wonderfully poised suggestion that before Anna's 'charms' can be described 'Another world must be unfurled,/Another language known'. Likewise, 'To the Memory of Mrs Lefroy' is also remarkable for its ending. A somewhat stilted and conventional *in memoriam* piece, it is cast in eighteenth-century elegiac form, with all the expected furnishings of elegy, the sentiments of the bereaved and tributes to the deceased; and it maintains a measured elegiac pace, interrupted by the customary quasi-dramatic apostrophes – until suddenly halted in the last line, as the poet-mourner's voice breaks though the formal surface with an anguished cry, an unadorned appeal to 'Reason': to forgive the self-indulgence of this poem, brought into being to celebrate the supposedly mystical union implicit in the coincidence of dates in Jane Austen's birthday, the death of Mrs Lefroy, and this fourth anniversary.

Two very different poems are totally successful, each its own way. The first is the welcoming-epithalameum, written to celebrate Francis Austen's marriage in 1806. It catches the moment of the newly-weds' arrival at Godmersham in a wonderfully conceived dramatic form which combines simplicity, intimacy and human presence. The other poem – 'On Sir Home Popham's sentence' – is altogether different. A ferocious little squib, it stands in the tradition of Dryden, Swift and Pope, and would look perfectly at home in any anthology of Augustan political verse. However, these poems have been little discussed in biographies of Jane Austen. Quite understandably, the one that has attracted most attention is her final work, the fantasy on St Swithin and the Winchester races, a work which caused such embarrassment to the Austen-Leighs for the seeming incongruity between the solemnity they thought proper to their aunt's death-bed and the grotesque hilarity of the poem itself. For modern readers, the poem is of intense biographical interest, remembering that the verses must have been composed in Jane Austen's head and dictated, probably to Cassandra; and it testifies to her unflagging wit and her readiness, as in *Sanditon*, to find a source of comic inspiration in her own decline.

Notes

1   Family papers, quoted in *FR*, p. 10.
2   Ibid.
3   Ibid., p. 218.
4   Ibid., pp. 115-16.
5   Ibid., p. 141.
6   David Selwyn, ed. *Jane Austen: Collected Poems and Verse of the Austen Family* (Manchester: Carcanet & Jane Austen Society), 1996; *The Complete Poems of James Austen* (Chawton: Jane Austen Society), 2003.
7   *NA&P*, p 7.
8   *1870 M*, p. 111
9   *Life and Letters*, p. 237.
10 *My Aunt Jane Austen: A Memoir* (1952), p. 8. The Mills/Yates poem seems not to have survived.

*

'This little bag'   1792

Autograph manuscript   In family possession

First published   1870 *Memoir* (p. 124).

In January 1792, the Lloyd family left Deane Parsonage, in the next parish to Steventon, to move sixteen miles away to the hamlet of Ibthorpe. To mark the occasion, Jane wrote these verses for her friend Mary, sending them in a housewife, a small, cotton holdall of her own making, for pins, needles, thread etc, contained in a cotton bag decorated with the same zig-zag needle-work pattern as on the housewife itself. A secret compartment holding the poem – on a slip of paper 2 x 3in. – is just behind the pin-cushion of red velvet in the shape of a mouth.

Title: In 1797 Mary Lloyd became the second wife of James Austen. The bag and its contents remained in the family and is described by his son, James Edward Austen-Leigh, in chapter five of the *1870 M*, as 'a curious [neat and elegant] specimen of her [JA's] needlework....In a very small bag is deposited a little rolled up housewife, furnished with minikin needles and fine thread. In the housewife is a tiny pocket, and in the pocket is enclosed a slip of paper, on which, written as with a crow quill, are these lines [he then quotes the poem, altered slightly to Victorian taste: its punctuation tidied up and with an 'improved' line 3: 'For should you thread and needles want,']....The whole is of flowered silk, and having never been used and carefully preserved, it is as fresh and bright as when it was first made seventy years ago; and shows that same hand which painted so exquisitely with the pen could work as delicately with the needle' (pp. 123-24). In turn, James Edward's great-grand-daughter, Joan Austen-Leigh, provided more details of the bag: 'made of white cotton with gold and black zigzag stripes'; and the poem was on a folded paper (2 x 3in.) in a 'tiny pocket' hidden under a red flannel needle-holder (*Country Life*, vol. 172, 28 October 1982, p. 1323). There is a strange discrepancy in the descriptions, between the M's 'flowered silk' and the 'white cotton'; but 'white cotton' certainly appears to be the material illustrated in *Country Life*. Was the 'silk' a Victorian 'improvement', perhaps made in the same spirit as the corrected punctuation (with its added commas, semi-colon and colon) on show in the M text of the poem?

The poem, the bag and housewife remain together in family possession.

ll.7-8: Such a decorated bag was valued as a particularly meaningful keepsake between girls and young ladies since it provided the opportunity for the donor to show off her 'accomplishment' in needlework, making it a very personal memento.

*

Lines *supposed* to have been sent to an uncivil Dress maker 1805

Manuscript copy   Lefroy manuscript

First published   *Times Literary Supplement*, 20 February 1987, p. 185: Deirdre Le Faye, 'Jane Austen's Verses'.

At the end of March 1805 Cassandra went from Bath to Ibthorpe to help Martha Lloyd in nursing her mother through her last illness, which ended with her death on 16 April. Cassandra remained at Ibthorpe a week or so longer to keep Martha company. Throughout this time, she was in regular correspondence with JA and must have reported that the dressmaker was slow in making up Martha's mourning wear. In response, it may be that JA sent Cassandra these verses, together with some lines from her mother, 'Miss Green's reply', to gently lighten the mood of the grieving household at Ibthorpe. If these verses were seen by Martha they seem to have caused no lasting offence, judging by the fact that she was soon to join the Austens, remaining with them as a companion for many years.

Title: probably supplied by Anna Lefroy when copying the verses into the Lefroy manuscript.

l.1. In women's clothing, little beyond cloaks was ready-made, and the usual course was for materials chosen and purchased by the customer to be sent to a professional dressmaker, often known as a mantua-maker (a mantua being a style of loosely flowing gown), to make up.

l.3 black Ploughman's Gauze: a fine gauze with satin spots, fashionable at this time and used for ladies' evening dresses. In black, the decorative element provided by the satin spots would set off the deep mourning with a subdued decorative element.

l.8 The playful idea that the mourning wear is essential, providing the authorisation for Martha's display of grief.

l.10 Presumably to avoid provoking an 'uncivil' reply on the spot.

*

Lines written for the amusement of a Niece 1806

Manuscript copy   Lefroy manuscript

First published   *Times Literary Supplement*, 20 February 1987, p. 185:
                    Deirdre Le Faye, 'Jane Austen's Verses'.

Francis Austen was married at St Lawrence's, Ramsgate to a local girl, Mary Gibson, on 24 July 1806. For the honeymoon, they drove to his brother Edward's estate at Godmersham Park. At the time, JA was with Cassandra and Mrs Austen on their way to stay with cousins in Staffordshire and she sent this poem to her thirteen-year-old niece Fanny, the eldest of Edward's family, who recorded in her diary that on 29 July 'I had a bit of a letter from Aunt Jane with some verses of hers'. Here, Jane Austen adopts Fanny's voice as the girl excitedly watches the approach and arrival of her uncle and his bride.

This feat of ventriloquism, conveying the girl's undiluted expectation and delight, is particularly notable since the Austen family was not enthusiastic about Francis's marriage to Mary Gibson and had hoped that he would marry Martha Lloyd, as indeed he did in 1828, following Mary Gibson's death five years earlier, following the birth of her eleventh child.

Title: probably supplied by Anna Lefroy when copying the poem into the Lefroy manuscript. Fanny Knight became Lady Knatchbull on her marriage in 1820 to Sir Edward Knatchbull Bt.

l.1 post haste: at great speed. According to Johnson, 'Haste like that of a courier', ie 'A messenger sent in haste'.

  Thanet: Ramsgate is on the Eastern extremity of Kent, an outcrop of land known as the Isle of Thanet.

l.3 Richard Kennet: probably a groom at Godmersham; a family living in the small town of Wye (about two miles from Godmersham) had this name.

l.4 Parents of the Bride: Mr and Mrs John Gibson, of the High Street, Ramsgate.

ll.5-7 Canterbury…village: places along the route of the couple's thirty-five mile journey westwards from Ramsgate to Godmersham.

l.8 yonder ridge: we are to visualise Fanny pointing across the park to the high ground to the north of the house, from which the driveway descended in a long curve.

l.10 Park: in full, the Deer Park.

l.11 Cattle: these would be sheep, not cows.

l.13 Brothers: addressed to the four eldest of Fanny's brothers, then aged between seven and twelve.

  Pier gate: the main gate to the house with piers or pillars on either side.

l.17 chaise: see S, ch. 1, note 12.

*

'Oh! Mr Best, your're very bad' 1806

Autograph manuscript   In family possession

First published   Verses 1-3, *Life and Letters* (1913), p. 70
                         Complete text, *Ninteenth Century Fiction*
                         (1975), vol. 30, pp. 257-60, Donald Green,
                         'New Verses by Jane Austen'.

On the verso of the manuscript: 'To Martha'.

JA signs the poem 'Clifton', the town to which Mrs Austen and her
daughters moved from Bath on 2 July 1806 accompanied by Martha
Lloyd, a close family friend, who had made her home with the Austens
since her mother's death the previous year. According to the poem,
Martha is about to leave them for the spa town of Harrogate, expecting
to be escorted by a regular visitor, a Mr Best, who is reluctant to make
the journey. JA scolds, encourages and threatens him in verses of ballad-
like doggerel. As there is no historical record of these circumstances,
nor a known identity for Mr Best, the poem may be purely a joke created
by JA out of some similar set of events at Clifton involving her friend.

1.1 Mr Best: the only Best known in JA's circle is a George Best of
Chilston Park, Kent (ten miles south-east of Maidstone) and his
daughter Dorothy, whose expected marriage is mentioned in a letter of
November 1813 (*L*, p. 250).
1.5 Harrowgate: Harrogate was a Northern spa town about 200 miles
from London. The medicinal qualities of its spring waters – sulphur
and iron – were well-established by the seventeenth century. By JA's
time the town had developed all the facilities expected of a fashionable
resort – a theatre, library, crescent, race-track, balls twice-weekly etc
and attractive countryside to provide for day excursions.
1.10 Posting: the cost of hiring horses from the posting houses, inns,
along the route.
1.11 stouter: robuster, in better health.
1.13 waters...use: the curative properties of the spa waters.
1.14 All's...below: this sentiment, a commonplace in classical literature,

sounds like a quotation, as yet unidentified, not dissimilar to 'All flesh is grass' (*The Task*, 1785, bk. 3, l. 261), Cowper's metrical versification of the Biblical 'For all flesh is as grass' (I Peter, ch. 1, verse 24).

l.19 Richard's pills: probably a patent medicine, so far unidentified.

ll.21-28 These two stanzas expand on the stylistic joke of line 20 with the larger image of Mr Best as a man 'ennobled' – his act of gallantry formally recognised and rewarded with a title – for being a 'friend', in its special sense of 'protector' and 'patron', whereas the expression 'friend of all' (l. 28), applied to Martha Lloyd, refers to her activity in charitable good works.

l.36 From...Hill: the market town of Newbury, Berkshire, was one mile from Speen Hill, the home of Martha Lloyd's widowed aunt, Catherine Craven, whom the Austens knew well.

l.37 Morton's wife: in a letter to Martha Lloyd, 29 November 1812, JA asks for a Mr Morton's address in order to send him a Christmas turkey on Martha's behalf. But nothing is known of him or anyone else of that name.

*

On Sir Home Popham's Sentence – April 1807   1807

Autograph manuscript   Fondation Martin Bodmer

First published   Brabourne, *Letters* (1884), vol. 2, p. 344, with the heading 'In Jane Austen's handwriting, enclosed in the same Letter of 1807' (this being the 'same Letter' in which the 'Verses to rhyme with 'Rose' were enclosed).

On 6 March 1807, Captain Sir Home Riggs Popham RN appeared before a Court Martial held at Portsmouth. He was charged with having withdrawn his Squadron from the Cape of Good Hope in April 1806 without orders, leaving the Colony unprotected, in order to transport a military expedition to Buenos Aires. After a trial lasting five days, Popham was found guilty. Although there is no record that JA knew

Popham personally, she would certainly have known of him, since the trial itself was widely reported. An effective self-publicist, Popham had trumpeted the achievements of his naval career extending over twenty years. Beyond championing Popham, JA intended the poem as a political squib aimed by a Tory Austen at the Whig Ministry then in office.

l.1 Ministry: the collective term used for the various ministers who together constituted the government. This specific Whig Ministry, headed by Lord Grenville, entered office in January 1806, resigning on 18 March 1807. It was known as the Ministry of All the Talents – from Grenville's much repeated claim that in his choice of ministers he brought together all the talents of the country. JA's string of epithets can be read as a satirical comment on Grenville's boast.

1.2 Gallant: from 1793 onwards, this was the standard epithet applied to soldiers and sailors distinguished in action during the Napoleonic wars.

victim...seen: Popham's opportunism in taking a military force across to Argentina was regarded as a venture opening up great trading prospects and access to Spanish treasure, and to the silver and gold mines of Mexico and Peru. His expedition was very popular with the public at large, his trial was sympathetically reported, and Popham was indeed widely seen as a 'victim' of the Grenville Ministry.

1.3 Success: the material evidence of this came with the hoard of gold coin, over a million dollars, which Popham seized from the Royal Treasury at Buenos Aires and shipped back to England, making a great parade of its journey from Portsmouth to the Bank of England in September 1806.

1.4 severe reprimand: the sentence of the Court Martial was that Popham be severely reprimanded – the heaviest of the lenient sentences available. However, being found guilty was no setback to his career. Only a month after the trial, Popham was given command of a small Squadron; and three months later, in July, he was appointed Captain of the Fleet to Admiral Gambier, Commander of the expedition to Copenhagen.

1.7 warrant: JA plays on at least two meanings of 'warrant': 'authorise' and 'deserve'.

*

Verses to Rhyme with 'Rose'   1807

Autograph manuscript   Fondation Martin Bodmer

First published   Brabourne *Letters* (1884), vol. 2, pp. 341-43.

There are also copies by Fanny Lefroy (daughter of Anna) of the verses by Jane and Cassandra Austen in the Hampshire Record Office, Winchester.
See Gilson (1984, 1998), p. 49.

Word-games and verse-writing were linked as family traditions and since childhood Mrs Austen had been regarded as 'the poet of the family', skilled at 'riddles, charades, bouts-rimés' among other forms (David Selwyn, 2005, pp. 59, 61). A good example is found in this verse word-game in which every line is required to end with a word or syllable rhyming with 'rose'. The four participants were Mrs Austen, Cassandra, JA and Elizabeth, Edward Austen's wife, who died in October 1808, eleven days after the birth of her eleventh child. The poems could have written when all four happened to be staying together in August and September 1807 when Edward organised family gatherings at Chawton House and at the Austens' house in Southampton. Such a dating corresponds with the heading given – presumably by Brabourne himself – to the set of four verses printed in his edition of the *Letters* (1884): 'Enclosed in one of the Letters of 1807' (vol. 2, p. 341).

l.1 Happy the Lab'rer: a version of the classical turn of phrase 'Beatus ille', familiar in English through the many seventeenth and eighteenth-century translations and imitations, the closest being Dryden's version of Horace, Ode xxix, 'To Maecenas', verse 8: 'Happy the man, and happy he alone,/ He, who can call to-day his own…'.
l.2 light-drab: a light or yellowish brown.
    well-darn'd hose: this seems take its lead from line 6 of Mrs Austen's contribution: 'I employ'd myself next in repairing my hose'.
l.5 Cabbage rose: this is the eye-catching *rosa centifolia*, 'a double red rose, with a large round compact flower' (*OED*).

l.7 London Beaux: the fashionable, leisured, smart and eligible young-men-about-town.

l.8 among the rows: in the ordinary pews for the *hoi polloi* as distinct from the high box-pews occupied by the gentry of the parish.

*

To Miss Bigg 1808

Autograph manuscript	Fondation Martin Bodmer
	There is also a manuscript of the first poem at the Jane Austen Memorial Trust, Chawton. See Gilson (1984, 1998), pp. 50-51, 58.
First published	Brabourne, *Letters* (1884), vol. 2, p. 344.

This and the following poem were written to accompany the gift of handkerchiefs to Catherine Bigg, although only the first was sent. This was on the occasion of her marriage in October 1808 to the Revd Herbert Hill, an uncle of Robert Southey. Born in 1775, the same year as JA, she was a close friend of the Austen sisters. Until her marriage she lived at Manydown Park, six miles from Steventon.

l.1 Cambrick!: a particularly fine white linen; its name is derived from Cambray in Flanders where the material was originally made. We are to understand the exclamation mark rhetorically, as signalling that the lines are addressed to the handkerchiefs themselves.

l.2 employ: the occupation of hemming referred to in JA's continuation of the title: 'previous to her marriage, with some pocket handfs. I had hemmed for her. –'.

l.4 There was some underplay to this line since Catherine Bigg was thirty-five at the time of her marriage, Mr Hill fifty-nine, an issue both JA and her friend would have at the back of their minds. Given the normal order of things, at some point in the future Catherine could expect to have a widow's 'tears to wipe'.

*

On the same occasion

Autograph manuscript   Fondation Martin Bodmer

First published   Brabourne, *Letters* (1884), vol. 2, p. 344.

1.4 small in compass: the fineness of the material allowed it to be folded many times.
1.6 To…name: this suggests that JA had embroidered Catherine Bigg's new initials, CH.

*

To the Memory of Mrs Lefroy 1808

Autograph manuscript   Winchester Cathedral Library

Facsimile   Frontispiece and endpiece, Frederick Bussby,
                                   Jane Austen in Winchester Cathedral (1969).

First published   With slight variants in John Henry Lefroy,
                                   *Notes and Documents Relating to the Family of
                                   Laffroy* (1868), pp. 117-18.

A version, lacking stanzas 4 and 5, was published in the 1870 *Memoir*, pp. 76-78.
A second manuscript – thought to be JA's original, of which the Winchester manuscript would be a fair copy – was sold at Sotheby's in May 1948. The location of this manuscript is now unknown (Gilson,1998, pp. 43-44).

For a full account of the four manuscripts of this poem – two of them copies of the Winchester manuscript – and its appearances in print, see Gilson (1998), pp. 42-45.

Mrs Anne Lefroy, née Brydges (b.1749), known locally as 'Madame

Lefroy', died on 16 December 1804 following a fall from her horse the previous day. The date was of particular significance to JA as 16 December was her own birthday. This coincidence provides both the starting point and the closure for this elegaic, *in memoriam* poem, written four years later. Mrs Lefroy was married to the Rector of Ashe, the next parish to Steventon. Twenty-five years JA's senior, she became one of JA's closest friends and her trusted confidante and mentor from childhood onwards. One of Mrs Lefroy's brothers recalled that as 'a little child' JA looked on her as 'a perfect model of gracefulness and goodness', 'was very intimate with Mrs Lefroy and much encouraged by her' – encouragement which may well have taken a literary turn, since the older woman was extremely well read and 'composed easy verses herself with great facility'(FR, p. 59) . Three of her poems were published in *The Poetical Register* for 1802. In the 1870 M, Austen-Leigh writes of Mrs Lefroy as 'a remarkable person' of 'rare… talents', 'while her enthusiastic eagerness of disposition rendered her especially attractive to a clever and lively girl'; and Austen-Leigh included this poem not for it 'merits as poetry' but in order 'to show how deep and lasting was the impression made by the elder friend on the mind of the younger' (p. 48).

l.1 my natal day: JA was born 16 December 1775.

l.8 torturing Memory!: JA would have learnt the circumstances of Mrs Lefroy's death from her brother James. When he met Mrs Lefroy in the small town of Overton, she remarked to him 'that the horse was so stupid and lazy she could scarcely make him canter'; '…next morning the news of her death reached Steventon. After getting to the top of Overton Hill, the horse seemed to be running away – it was not known if anything had frightened him – the servant, unwisely, rode up to catch the bridle rein – missed his hold and the animal darted off faster. He could not give any clear account, but it was supposed that Mrs Lefroy in her terror, threw herself off, and fell heavily on the hard ground. She never spoke afterwards, and she died in a few hours…'. (FR, p. 145). The opening words of this quotation are Deirdre Le Faye's, the remainder a direct quotation from the *Reminiscences* of Caroline Austen, a daughter of James. Born in 1805, she heard the details of the accident from her mother. In any event, the full story, in its painful detail, would certainly have been known to JA.

l.9 Angelic Woman!: an obituary in a Reading newspaper described Mrs Lefroy as a 'good angel' (Honan, p. 210). JA may have had in mind Mrs Lefroy's reputation for good works. Her brother reported that she taught 'the village children to read and write and make straw plait for bonnets and hats – then a profitable village industry' and that 'she personally vaccinated all her husband's parishioners' (FR, p. 47).

ll.13-16: this stanza versifies a tribute recorded in the closing pages of James Boswell's biography of Johnson: ' "Johnson is dead. – Let us go to the next best. – There is nobody. – No man can be said to put you in mind of Johnson" '. Boswell is reporting the words of Johnson's friend – whom he does not identify by name – William Gerard Hamilton (*The Life of Samuel Johnson L.L.D.*, 1791, London: Dilly, vol. 2, p. 581).

l.10 Talents: we can take this, together with the 'Genius', 'Taste' and 'Eloquence' mentioned later in the poem, to refer, if only in part, to Mrs Lefroy's writing of verse.

l.13 In the copy of the manuscript thought to be JA's original, 'Burke t'was finely' is deleted and replaced by 'Hamilton t'was'.

l.20 The rather grandiloquent terms of stanzas 4 and 5 may be explained by JA's sense of the public commemoration of Mrs Lefroy's death in an obituary in the *Gentleman's Magazine*, 1805 (vol. 74, p. 1178) and in 'Elegaic Lines' by her brother Samuel Egerton Brydges in the fourth edition of his *Poems*, 1807 (pp. 208-12).

In the supposed original is the reading 'shall' for the Winchester manuscript's 'may'.

l.21 fond...Power: 'fond' carries the meaning of 'indulgent' and 'Fancy', the imagination, is semi-personified as a 'Power', a divinity with superhuman abilities.

l.22 desponding: despairing.

l.28 Expression, Harmony: the first, a quality of her 'Looks' and 'Countenance'; the second, a quality of her 'accents' and 'voice'.

l.34 palliate Vice: a stock term in sermons and devotional literature throughout the eighteenth-century and beyond.

    deck: Johnson: 'To adorn; to embellish'.

l.37 sincere: we are probably to understand this word in one of Johnson's definitions: 'pure'.

l.51 connection...date: that the day and month of JA's birth is the same as that on which Mrs Lefroy died.

l.52 A bleak, unadorned appeal to 'Reason' to allow this exercise in wishful thinking and emotional self-indulgence.

*

"Alas! poor Brag" 1809

Autograph manuscript	Pierpont Morgan Library
First published	Brabourne, *Letters* (1884), vol. 1, pp. 63-64.
Facsimile	Modert, F-187.

The card game speculation commiserates with another card game, brag, as they have been ousted by yet other games as the Christmas entertainments at Godmersham. Speculation is described in the *OED* as 'A round game of cards, the chief feature of which is the buying and selling of trump cards, the player who possesses the highest trump in a round winning the pool'. It was a simple game to play, a favourite with children for its noisiness. Brag: 'The name is taken from the "brag" or challenge given by one of the players to the rest to turn up cards equal in value to his own' (*OED*). In *MP*, Henry Crawford teaches Lady Bertram and Fanny Price to play speculation (vol. 2, ch. 7).

The poem comes in JA's letter to Cassandra dated 17 January 1809 (*L*, p. 167). Cassandra was staying with Edward Austen's family at Godmersham and in earlier letters had told her sister about the card games being played there. Having heard from Cassandra that her nephew, Edward jnr, was playing more brag than speculation, JA wrote back on 10 January: 'The preference of Brag over Speculation does not greatly surprise me I believe, because I feel the same myself; but it mortifies me deeply, because Speculation was under my patronage' (*L*, pp. 163-64) – here JA is referring to her own visits to Godmersham, the most recent in June the previous year, and to her involvement in the children's games, for which she was especially remembered . Then, in the body of her next letter, a week later, JA introduces the 'Brag' poem under the pretence that it comes from elsewhere: 'I have just received some verses in an unknown hand, & am desired to forward them to my nephew Edwd at Godmersham'. In her following letter, 24 January, JA continues the joke, supposing, as before, that Cassandra would share this part of it with the Godmersham family: 'I am sorry my verses did not bring any return from Edward, I was in hopes they might – but I suppose he does not rate them high enough. – It might be partiality, but they seemed to me purely classical – just like Homer & Virgil, Ovid & Propria que Maribus' (L, p. 170). In this linking of names, Jane Austen moves from the sublime to the ridiculous, connecting three of the great poets of the classical world with some Latin words familiar to all schoolboys – these come from the very opening of the section treating 'the Gender of Nouns' in the widely-used schoolroom textbook, *An Introduction to the Latin Tongue*, a primer commonly known as the *Eton Latin Grammar*, and probably familiar to young Edward and his brothers. In the 4th Edition, 1808, the words 'Propria Quae Maribus'[JA's 'que' is wrong] are unmissable; they are printed in block capitals at the head of page 128.

l.1 "Alas…fame?: the opening words are a play on 'Alas! poor Yorick', the first words of Hamlet's soliloquy in the graveyard scene, as he contemplates the skull of his old playfellow, a man 'of infinite jest'. This pastiche continues in the rhetorical questions of the poem's next two lines, echoing Hamlet's 'Where be your gibes now? your gambols? your songs?' etc (*Hamlet*, V.i . 201-11).

    boastful: a play on 'brag' understood both as a boast and, in terms of the game, a call or challenge.

    empty name: carrying the idea of an 'empty boast', one which is unfulfilled.

l.5 Ejaculation: a brief, extemporare poem. Could 'Alas! poor Brag' be an instant composition on JA's part? This question is relevant because the lines are written without correction or alteration of any kind, as if JA had formed them in her head in the very act of writing (as can be seen in the manuscript of the letter of 17 January, Modert facsimile F-187). If this is the case, then the poem is a fine example of an 'ejaculation' 'darted out'. The likelihood of this is suggested in the 1870 *Memoir*, where Austen-Leigh, gives his belief that the twenty-eight line poem

'In measured verse' was 'nearly extempore' (p. 76), a view which is supported, without the 'nearly' qualification, in *Life and Letters* (p. 241) and likely to have been based upon family papers.

*

'My dearest Frank' 1809

Autograph manuscript   British Library

Facsimile   Modert, F-199-201, with variants F-203-04.

First published   Chapman, *Letters* (1932), vol. 2, pp. 264-66.

Jane Austen retained a copy of the letter, inscribed by her 'Copy of letter to Frank, July 26. 1809.' Jane Austen Memorial Trust.

This verse-letter from JA to her brother Francis William Austen is dated 26 July 1809 and sent to congratulate him on the birth on 12 July of his second child and eldest son, Francis William jnr, at Rose Cottage, Alton. JA uses the occasion to recollect her brother's own qualities in infancy and childhood with the hope that his son will inherit them. As a coda, she tells him how she, her mother, her sister Cassandra and their friend Martha Lloyd are settling into their new home at Chawton – they had arrived on 7 July. The domesticity of this letter is carefully judged, given that Francis was at this moment at sea, in command of the *St Albans* protecting a convoy on its long journey to China, and away for eighteen months.
The metrical form of the verse is the same as that Walter Scott employed for much of the historical verse-romance *Marmion* (1808). As JA had already sent Francis a copy of Scott's poem in January 1809, she may have expected him to recognise, be amused and perhaps flattered by the similarity in the verse form.

l.2 Mary's: his wife, Mary (née Gibson).
l.4 Mary Jane: Mary's first child, born 27 April 1807.

l.7 Good: a strong term, see Johnson's definition: 'Moral qualities, such as are desirable…'.

l.12 insolence: pride.

l.18 "Bet…bide": young Francis speaks to the nurserymaid in Hampshire accented baby-talk: 'I haven't come to stay'.

l.22 engine: Johnson: 'Any means to bring to pass, or to effect'.

l.24 aweful: Johnson: 'That strikes with awe, or fills with reverence'.

l.43 Chawton home: known in the family as 'the Cottage', it was provided by Edward Austen – who owned Chawton village as part of his Hampshire estate – for the use of his mother and sisters, who arrived there on 7 July 1809. Originally a late seventeenth-century roadside inn, it had six bedrooms with garrets above for the servants, outbuildings, a kitchen garden, shrubbery and orchard. It was later described by James's daughter, Caroline, as 'altogether a comfortable and ladylike establishment', although her elder sister, Anna, considered the Cottage as 'small & not very good' (FR, p. 175).

l.45 when complete: structural alterations and plumbing works were still being carried out.

l.50 Charles & Fanny: since late 1804, JA's sailor brother Charles had been serving in Bermuda, where he met his wife Fanny (née Palmer), marrying her in 1807. Although there must have been some suggestion that they would be coming back to England in the near future, their return was not for another two years and they made their home in a naval guardship, the *Namur*, moored at the mouth of the Thames off Sheerness.

l.53 over-right: a Hampshire dialect word meaning 'right opposite'. JA may have had in mind Chawton House, situated a few hundred yards southwards along the Gosport road, which Edward lent to his sailor brothers during their time on shore.

*

'In measured verse' ?1810

No manuscript known

First published   1870 *Memoir* (pp. 117-18).

According to the 1870 *Memoir*, JA 'took it into her head to write the
following mock panegyric on a young friend, who really was clever and
handsome' (p. 117); and *Life and Letters* (pp. 240-41) makes it clear that
'the young friend' was her niece Anna, the eldest daughter of James
Austen, born in 1793, and that Anna was with JA during the composition
of the poem. This circumstance supports the conjectural dating of 1810
since in the summer of that year Anna was sent to Chawton for three
months following an unhappy and unsuitable engagement with the Rev
Michael Terry, a man twice her age. The *Life and Letters* describes Anna
as 'mercurial and excitable', with the 'giddiness' of youth (p. 241), and
JA's concern at the broken engagement with Mr Terry is reflected in
her anxiety three years later at Anna's second unlikely engagement, to
Ben Lefroy, whom she was to marry in November 1814. JA discerned
'an unfortunate dissimilarity of Taste between them...he hates company
& she is very fond of it; – This, with some queerness of Temper on his
side & much unsteadiness on hers, is untoward' (to Francis Austen, 25
September 1813; *L*, pp. 231-32).

JA's frank and critical view of Anna helps us to understand the
joking tone to the extravagant 'transatlantic' metaphors in which her
'charms' are described. On this matter, Austen-Leigh is dismissive,
presuming that the American imagery simply follows on from the initial
rhyming of 'Anna' with 'savannah', an aural association characteristic of
extempore verse: 'the fancy of drawing the images from America arose
at the moment from the obvious rhyme which presented itself in the first
stanza' (*1870 M*, p. 118). But this ignores the literary context in which
JA was writing – that in the later eighteenth century, the wildness and
vastness of the North American scene, together with its associations
of strangeness, remoteness and danger, were taken up by poets and
novelists, beginning with Frances Brooke in an authentic Canadian
novel, *The History of Emily Montague* (1769) and including Charlotte
Smith in *The Old Manor House* (1793) and Mary Brunton in *Self-Control*

(1810). Moreover, the lightly mocking, ultimately subversive, twist given to JA's American imagery seems to be developed from *The Landscape, A Didactic Poem* (1794) by Richard Payne Knight, in which he argues that landowners do not necessarily need the 'vast and unconfin'd' to achieve their 'landscape' effects of the 'sublime' etc ; they can succeed even working on a small scale, employing the resources of 'genius', 'art' and 'taste' (Bk. 2, ll. 155, 160-61), a line of argument very much to JA's own taste, given her enterprise in *NA* in formally rejecting Gothic extravagance – its shocks, horrors and foreignness – and finding material of engaging interest in the sobriety of day-to-day social and domestic life in England. (Knight's specific American references are given in the notes below.)

A letter from Caroline Austen (a younger sister of Anna) to her brother James Edward Austen-Leigh, when he was preparing the *Memoir* for publication, mentions this poem as one of the 'light nonsensical verses' that might contribute 'to the *stuffing* of the projected volume' ie fill out the book without detracting from their aunt's literary reputation or revealing anything personally embarrassing to the family, issues of importance to Caroline and her generation and mentioned later in the letter (dated 'April 1st.' [?1869], M, p. 185).

l.1 measured verse: verse 'Consisting of "measures" or metrical groups' (OED). The term 'measured verse' was first used in *The Defence of Poesie/An Apologie for Poetrie* (1595) by Philip Sidney.

rehearse: Johnson: 'To relate; to tell'.

l.2 charms: in describing the poem, Austen-Leigh is able to use the term 'panegyric' in its technical sense, as referring to a formal and elaborate eulogy, since each of stanzas one to four celebrates a specific 'charm' or 'virtue': her 'mind', 'fancy', 'wit', 'judgment', while stanza five returns to Anna's 'mind' and stanzas six and seven treat her 'face' and body.

l.4 vast savannah: Johnson quotes from the poet James Thomson (1700-48) : 'Plains immense,/And vast savannas, where the wand'ring eye,/Unfix'd, is in a verdant ocean lost'. Knight: 'So the rude gazer ever thinks to find/ The view sublime, where vast and unconfin'd' (*The Landscape*: Bk. 2, ll. 154-55).

l.5 Ontario's lake: *The Times* spoke of 'Lake Ontario', mistakenly, as 'one of the largest lakes in the world, being 300 miles long, and 100

miles broad' (7 March 1791, p. 2); and Isaac Weld described the Lake
as being 220 miles in length and at its widest point, 70 miles (*Travels
Through the States of North America and the Provinces of Lower Canada*,
1799, p. 288). When referring to such natural features, it was customary
to give their dimensions. Knight made a joke of this: 'Oft have I heard
the silly trav'ller boast/ The grandeur of Ontario's endless coast;/...[its]
boundless water' (*The Landscape*: Bk. 2, ll. 129-31). (In fact, Lake
Ontario is the smallest of the five so-called Great Lakes).

l.7 strict: accurate.

l.10-11 Niagara's...all: see Oliver Goldsmith, 'And Niagara stuns with
thund'ring sound' (*The Traveller, or, A Prospect of Society*, 1764, l. 412).
The Falls were regarded as one of the wonders of the natural world.
The Landscape: 'Nor yet expect, where Niagara roars,/ And stuns the
Nations round Ontario's shores,/To find such true sublimity display'd'
(Bk. 2, ll. 124-26).

amaze: although the word fits neatly into the metre and rhyme
scheme here, it is not a poetic shortening but a word only just out of
common currency in JA's time; defined by Johnson as 'Astonishment;
confusion, either of fear or wonder'.

ll.14-15 thick...groves: In the *The Landscape*, Knight compares the
'gloomy' 'American or horse chesnut' with the 'elm' tree, the leaves of
the elm providing little shade whereas the chestnut, 'in Atlantic forests
born', 'with embow'ring leaves' 'extends its shade/ Excludes the sun, and
deep embrowns the glade:' (Bk. 2, ll.159, note to 174, 167,150, 161-62).
The exotic character of North America was often emphasised, eg: 'bold,
picturesque, romantic, nature reigns here in all her wanton luxuriance,
adorned by a thousand wild graces which mock the cultivated beauties
of Europe' (Frances Brooke, *The History of Emily Montague*, Letter 10,
1777 and several times reprinted).

*

" I've a pain in my head "   1811

Autograph manuscript   Winchester City Museum
There are two other manuscripts, see Selwyn (1996), p. 67.

First printed   *Minor Works* (1954), pp. 448-49.

In February 1811, Jane Austen took Maria Beckford – the sister-in-
law of John Charles Middleton, Edward Austen's tenant at Chawton
House – into Alton to see Charles Newnham about an 'old complaint'.
Newnham was a qualified apothecary-surgeon or general practitioner; in
addition, he acted as an apothecary, a dispensing chemist. JA overheard
their 'conversation, as it actually took place' (quoted in *FR*, p. 199) and
set it down in verse, amused by the role-reversal in which the patient
ends up by prescribing both for herself and the doctor.

1.2 suffering: possibly, in part, a consequence of being unmarried and
having to act as hostess at Chawton House and help look after her
widower brother-in-law's six children aged between five and sixteen.
l.12 Calomel: a drastic purgative, mercury based. Widely prescribed, it
was nonetheless regarded as injurious by some physicians.

*

On reading in the Newspaper, the Marriage of "Mr Gell of Eastbourne to Miss Gill" 1811

Autograph manuscript	Bath and North East Somerset Council
Facsimile	1870 *Memoir* (facing p. 123), is reproduced a lithograph facsimile of a manuscript with a variant text. It is unclear whether Austen-Leigh had two different manuscripts or whether the textual variants on p. 115 are simply the consequence of faulty transcription.
First published	1870 *Memoir* (p. 115), printed as four lines.

A third copy of the manuscript is in private possession.
For an account of the manuscripts, see Gilson (1984, 1998), pp. 45-47.

This poem and 'When stretch'd on one's bed' are written on a folded half-sheet of paper, giving four sides. On one of these sides is written in pencil 'For Capt. Austen R.N.' in a hand, not JA's; this could be Cassandra's instruction. This poem occupies one side and 'When stretch'd on one's bed' the remaining two.

The marriage was announced in the *Hampshire Telegraph and Sussex Chronicle* for 25 February 1811: 'Sussex, Saturday, February 23, 1811. On Saturday was married, Mr.Gell, of Eastbourn, to Miss Gill, of Well-street, Hackney'. No connection is known between the Austens and this couple; presumably, JA's attention was simply caught by the amusing consonance of their names and the word-play it could give rise to. The 1870 *Memoir* comments that this poem, together with 'On the Marriage of Miss Camilla Wallop' and 'In measured verse', are 'specimens' which 'may be given of the liveliness of mind which imparted an agreeable flavour both to her correspondence and her conversation' (p. 115).

Title: Eastbourne: originally a small fishing village, this developed into a fashionable seaside resort on the Sussex coast. See S ch. 1, notes 1, 27 and 28.

Hackney: on the outskirts of London, about three miles north of St Paul's, it was a suburb favoured by prosperous families.

l.7 restore: restore me to my former state, with a hint of Johnson's definition: 'To recover passages in books from corruption'.

*

"I am in a Dilemma"   1811

Autograph manuscript   Pierpont Morgan Library

Facsimile   Modert, F-214.

First published   Brabourne, *Letters* (1884), vol. 2, p. 99.

On 30 April 1811, JA wrote from Henry Austen's house in Sloane Street to Cassandra at Godmersham. Commenting on news that Cassandra had sent her, probably also including news from her eighteen year-old niece Fanny Knight, JA responded 'Oh! yes, I remember Miss Emma Plumbtree's *Local* consequence perfectly. – '. Her '*Local* consequence' is explained in Fanny's diary entries during April about the presence of the Local Militia – raised to meet the threat of a French invasion or of civil disturbance – in Canterbury and finding dancing partners among the young officers of the Militia's East Kent 1ˢᵗ Regiment. Presumably, Fanny had also reported on Emma Plumtre's presence on these occasions. In her entry for April 26, Fanny noted: 'Papa went to the ¼ sessions at C'bury & dined there…Heard that E P is talked of for H Gipps' – this was Henry Gipps, a Captain in the Local Militia.

In the letter of 30ᵗʰ April, JA then launched directly into the double couplet that forms this little poem. She then continued her letter in the same vein: 'But really, I was never much more put to it, than in contriving an answer to Fanny's former message. What is there to be said on the subject? – Pery pell – or pare pay? or po. – or at the most, Pi pope pey pike pit.' JA's 'answer' is given in the childish code that she and Fanny used intermittently in writing to each other: the initial letter or letters of each word are replaced by a 'p', or a 'p' is added, and a following vowel can be changed, giving us: 'Very well – or are they? or no. – or at the most, I hope they like it.' Possibly this was an answer to Fanny's enquiry: what did her Aunt think of the match? were the couple really in love? or not? – a subject close to Fanny's heart at this time, since not only was she a close friend of Emma but a romantic friendship was growing between herself and Emma's brother John Plumptre, one of her dancing partners at the Local Militia balls. (In this letter, JA jokes with the spelling of their family name).

We can suppose the setting for the poem is a Local Militia ball or a Canterbury assembly. Emma Plumtre has promised Henry Gipps the first dance but is late. Does he sit out the dance in the expectation of her arriving or does he take the risk and find himself another partner?

Dilemma: a term in logic, for which Johnson provides a neat definition: 'An argument equally conclusive by contrary Suppositions'. Colloquially, a 'fix'.

Emma: a younger daughter of the Plumtre family, East Kent neighbours and friends of Edward Knight.

Henry Gipps: his father was Rector of Ringwould, near Dover, not far from the Plumtre home at Nonington. Henry and Emma's brother John overlapped as students at St John's College, Cambridge and they were both officers in the East Kent 1st Regiment of Local Militia. Henry became formally engaged to Emma in September 1811 and they were married at Nonington in June 1812.

*

"Between Session & Session"   1811

Autograph manuscript   Pierpont Morgan Library

Facsimile   Modert, F-214.

First published   Brabourne, *Letters* (1884), vol. 2, p. 99.

On 30 April 1811, JA wrote from Henry Austen's house in Sloane Street to Cassandra at Godmersham to congratulate her brother Edward, having just read in a newspaper of the postponement of Parliamentary consideration of a Private Bill designed to allow the construction of a navigable canal to link the River Medway near East Peckham with the Royal Military Canal near Appledore: 'I congratulate Edward on the Weald of Kent-Canal-Bill being put off till another Session, as I have just had the pleasure of reading. There is always something to be hoped from Delay. – ' This sentence is followed by the poem itself – which expresses JA's hope that right thinking will prevail and that the Bill be abandoned. Immediately after the poem and continuing the letter, JA writes: 'There is poetry for Edward & his daughter. I am afraid I shall not have any for you' (L, p. 186).

Although the politics and financing of canal-building may seem to be an arcane subject, they were procedures of which JA would probably have some knowledge from the building of a canal not far from Steventon. The Basingstoke Canal Navigation Company was launched in 1788 and the construction of the Canal took place between 1788 and 1794. Many friends and neighbours of the Austens were shareholders.

Title: Session: Parliamentary Sessions were the periods during which the business of Parliament was conducted. The current session ended on 24 July 1811 and the next began on 7 January 1812.

l.2 just: hitherto, all editors (following the Brabourne text) have read this word as 'first', which makes no sense in this context. JA also wrote 'just' in her letter, three lines above, and this word in the poem is calligraphically identical. See Modert, F-214.

Prepossession: Johnson: '…preconceived opinion'.

l.4 villainous: JA's violence of language reflects the strength of Edward's objection, shared by other landowners whose property was affected and who petitioned Parliament against the Bill.

A branch of the canal was planned to follow a route Ashford-Wye-Canterbury, continuing northwards to the sea. The Wye-Canterbury section would take it through Edward's Godmersham estate.

l.5 forced…still: as it turned out, the Bill made progress in the following session, receiving the Royal Assent. Yet the canal's financial viability came in question and the scheme was finally abandoned in 1816.

l.6 Wicked Men's: JA would have in mind the members of the

Committee formed in support of the project, and the Subscribers who put down deposits towards its financing. These included such notabilities as the Earls of Romney and Camden, Sir William Geary, an MP for Kent, and a prime enthusiast, the civil engineer John Rennie who was largely responsible for choosing the route, supervising its surveying and proposing the offending branch via Ashford which would have carried it past Godmersham Park.

*

'When stretch'd on one's bed'   1811

Autograph manuscript   Bath and North East Somerset
                                  Council

There is a copy in the Lefroy manuscript. At the time this was made, the poem was confused with 'Written at Winchester' (1817) and was headed 'Lines written at Winchester by Jane Austen during her last illness'.

First published   *Minor Works* (1954), pp. 447-48.

The date JA puts at the end of the poem shows that it was written only a few days before the appearance of *S&S*, her first novel, originally planned for May. David Selwyn suggests that this long delay, coupled with her expectation of financial loss, since publication was at her own expense, may have contributed to headaches such as these.

l.8 Waltzes: at this time, the waltz was still seen as an unwelcome import from the Continent (it was sometimes called the German waltz), *risqué* on account of the bodily proximity of the partners, and only considered permissible for married couples. There is no waltzing in the novels – the reference to Mrs Weston's 'waltz' in *E* (vol. 2, ch. 8) is not to the dance itself but to the tune and time signature of a slow-paced country dance.

    reels: Scottish or Irish were energetic dances, usually performed by two couples facing each other and tracing an interweaving pattern. As opposed to waltzes, reels were regarded as entirely proper: even Mr

Darcy feels able to unbend sufficiently to invite Elizabeth Bennet to 'dance a reel' when Miss Bingley plays 'a lively Scotch air' (*P&P*, vol. 1, ch. 10).

ll.10-12: JA had second thoughts about her vivid outspokenness in these lines. The original wording is heavily cancelled and over-written. But it seems to have read: 'How little one thinks / Of the Steps or the Stinks / Which pervade the Assemblies all '. These lines were cancelled and the new lines 10-12 squeezed in above them.

l.12 flounces: a flounce is an ornamental strip of decorative material sewn along its top edge to the bottom of the skirt, its bottom edge left unattached and free to move and float gracefully with the movement of the skirt. Flounces could be double or elaborately multilayered to form graduated steps. 'What…may befall' is that flounces trodden on could become detached or ripped off during the progress of a ball.

l.16 muse: thinking about, concern.

ll.19-24 Like lines 10-12, the original stanza 5 was heavily cancelled. It seems to have read: 'For ourselves & our pains / Ev'ry faculty chains. / We can feel on no subject beside. / 'Tis for Health & for Ease / The Time present to seize / For their Friends & their Souls to Provide.'

l.20 Peels: the pealing of bells to celebrate a marriage.

    Knells: the pealing of a funeral bell.

l.23 Corse: Johnson: 'a poetical word' for a corpse.

l.26: compels all our attention.

*

On the marriage of Miss Camilla Wallop 1812

Manuscript copy   Lefroy manuscript.

First published   1870 *Memoir* (p. 116), with a different title and the changes specified below.

For details of transmission and variants, see *L*, p. 409, note 7; and Gilson (1984, 1998), pp. 47-48.

JA had read of the engagement of Miss Urania Katharine Camilla Wallop, a middle-aged niece of the 2nd Earl of Portsmouth, to the elderly Rev Henry Wake. (Subsequently, they were married at All Saints, Southampton, 26 March 1813). The names of the couple caught her attention as they offered the opportunity for a neat pun on the groom's name and other verbal humour; and as the Wallops lived in Southampton, it may have been that JA had met Camilla during the Austens own residence in the town between 1806 and 1809.

On 29 November 1812, JA wrote to Martha Lloyd, 'The 4 lines on Miss W. which I sent you were all my own, but James afterwards suggested what I thought a great improvement & as it stands in the Steventon Edition' – the Steventon Edition being the version James Austen wrote out at Steventon Rectory, his home since 1801. It may be that his 'suggested…great improvement' was to make the changes found in the 1870 *Memoir*: to lengthen the title, to 'On the Marriage of a Middle-Aged Flirt with a Mr.Wake, whom, it was supposed, she would scarcely have accepted in her youth'; to substitute 'Maria' for 'Camilla'; and to transform JA's 'merry, & small' Miss Wallop into someone 'handsome, and tall'. These alterations may have been made to disguise the identity of the bride so that the poem could be circulated without causing offence. In addition, the poem's last four words, 'jump at a Wake', were italicised, perhaps to draw attention to the pun. This was the version first printed in the 1870 *Memoir*.

A slightly variant text exists in the diary of Stephen Terry of Dummer. He was a Hampshire neighbour and friend of the Austens, once a dancing partner of JA's and father-in-law to Anna Lefroy's daughter, Geogiana. The entry is for 13 April 1860: 'Camilla good humoured & merry & small / For a Husband it happend was at her last stake; / & having in vain danced at many a ball / Is now very happy to Jump at a Wake.' He notes: 'These lines given to me this day by Mrs Ben Lefroy here, Georgies mother; they were written by her very clever Relation Miss Jane Austen, the celebrated Novelist, about the beginning [of] the Century' (quoted in *L*, p. 409).

Title: probably supplied by Anna Lefroy when copying the verses into the Lefroy manuscript. She left a space in the expectation of being able to insert Mr Wake's christian name.

l.2 Miss Wallop was middle-aged and this was her last chance of marriage.

l.4 jump at: seize the opportunity eagerly; currently a slang term for 'to seize and rob'.

Wake: Mr Wake was elderly and a 'wake' could refer both to the watching over a dead body and to the drinking and feasting that sometimes accompanied this custom.

*

Riddles	Dates unknown.
Autograph manuscripts	Untraced.
First published	*Charades &c. written a hundred years ago by Jane Austen and her family* (London: Spottiswoode & Co., undated. Preface, June 1895), nos. 18-20.

A manuscript in the possession of David Gilson, containing the twenty-two published in *Charades &c* plus an additional twenty-two, is supposed by him to be a transcript by a member of the Austen-Leigh family (1984, 1998, p. 54).

The second and third riddles are also found in the Lefroy manuscript, where the second is headed 'A Riddle'. David Selwyn suggests that as the attributions are to 'Jane', it is possible that they were added 'by either Cassandra or one of her brothers' (1996, p. 18).

Together with others in the family, JA had a lifelong attachment to riddles, charades and other kinds of word games. The earliest we know comes in 'The history of England' (1791) at the end of the entry for James I where the King's favourite is referred to in a somewhat daring joke: JA quotes 'an excellent Sharade on a Carpet...as I think it may afford my Readers some amusement to *find it out*' (MW, pp. 147-48). JA had to admit herself defeated when Cassandra sent her several in October 1813: 'We admire your Charades excessively, but as yet have guessed only the 1st. The others seem very difficult. There is so much beauty in the Versification however, that the finding them out is but a secondary pleasure' (*L*, p. 202). Three months later, JA began *E* with all its joking about riddles and charades at the opening of chapter 9, in particular the 'courtship' charade. Doubtless with a special meaning for the Austens, this touched on in Mr Woodhouse's fond recollection of his wife's cleverness 'at all those things' and his own failings of memory (vol. 1, ch. 9). The mention of Harriet's 'riddle-book' (ch. 10) raises the possibility that such a record of the family riddles and charades was maintained by JA herself or someone close to her; this would be a 'private collection' as opposed to the abundance of published charades available since the 1770's.

In the Gilson manuscript of the second charade, the third line, the words 'Man who oft' are underlined in pencil and the words 'Monster who' written above the line, also in pencil.

Solutions given in *Charades &c.* Whether or not they are Jane Austen's is unknown.

1. Hemlock: the familiar name for the wild flowering plant *conium maculatum*, used medicinally as a powerful sedative and a notoriously fatal poison.

2. Agent: agents acted as stewards or managers of property or as business agents; in whatever capacity, agents could be expected to fleece their employers, or so at least they were depicted on stage, from Ben Jonson onwards.

3. Bank Note.

*

Written at Winchester 1817

Manuscript copy   by Cassandra Austen   Jane Austen Memorial
                         Trust

First published   *Jane Austen's Sailor Brothers* (1906), pp. 272-73.

A second manuscript, in an unidentified hand, in the Berg Collection,
New York Public Library. Seemingly a rough and inaccurate copy, it has
cancellations and misspellings.

For an account of the mss, see Gilson (1984, 1998), pp. 54-55.

In *Minor Works* (p. 451), Chapman entitles the poem 'Venta', a word
taken from line 13. It may be that in Chapman's mind was an untitled
poem James Austen wrote on his sister's death in which 'Venta!' is the
opening word: James's poem is listed by Chapman as item 21(a) in
his record of the sale and dispersal of JA manuscripts and associated
materials ('A Jane Austen Collection', *Times Literary Supplement*, 14
January 1926, p. 27).

In May 1817, as her final illness became more severe, JA was brought
the sixteen miles from Chawton to Winchester to be under the care of
a doctor at the County Hospital. When precisely she composed – and
probably dictated – this poem is uncertain. The text in *Jane Austen's Sailor
Brothers* is untitled and, towards the right margin, headed 'Winchester,
July 15, 1817' (p. 272). This seems to be corroborated by a statement
at the bottom verso of the Berg manuscript: 'written July 15:th 1817: by
Jane Austen who died early in the morning (½ past 4) of July 18.th 1817
aged 41y:rs'. This dating conflicts with that given by Henry Austen in his
'Biographical Notice of the Author', 1818. Henry made the point that
although his sister was struck with 'bodily weakness', nonetheless, 'The
day preceding her death she composed some stanzas replete with vigour'
(*NA & P*, p. 4), ie on 17th July.

The 1833 version of the 'Biographical Notice' omits any mention of
the poem, as do both the first and second editions of the *Memoir*. These
omissions were evidently in response to the family embarrassment

that Aunt Jane should disturb the solemnity of her final days on earth by composing comic verse in which the miracle-working powers of a revered saint are incongruously brought to bear on a race meeting. The fifth Earl Stanhope, intrigued by Henry Austen's 1818 reference to the poem, attempted (via the publisher Bentley) to persuade Austen-Leigh to include it in the *Memoir*, but with no success. Without having seen the poem, Stanhope supposed that it was evidence of 'the serenity of a conscience at peace, in the retrospect of a well-spent life, & in the anticipation of a joyful future – all tending to lightness & gaiety of spirit'. But Austen-Leigh's sister Caroline, his principal adviser in the matter, was set against making the poem public, since in 'the closing scene' of JA's life 'it would jar...a sad incongruity' (Le Faye, 1988, p. 90). These views prevailed and the poem's instatement had to await a later family biography, *Jane Austen's Sailor Brothers* (1906) by John and Edith Hubback, grandson and great-granddaughter of Francis Austen. They printed the poem for the first time, on the positive grounds that 'although of no great merit in themselves' these verses were evidence that 'her unselfish courage and cheerfulness never failed her' (p. 272).

What has not been taken into account in these and other discussions of the poem is that St Swithin became celebrated for miraculous cures. So the question arises: did JA intend this poem as an unspoken appeal for him to 'triumph in shewing' his 'powers' (l. 22) curatively in her direction too, since she was then staying at College Street, only a few hundred yards from the Cathedral? Or was it quite the other way round? – that someone at her bedside piously suggested a prayer of intercession to St Swithin and that JA rejected the idea out of hand with her very own retort, in robust verse, a palpable denial of invalidism, abundant in humour, high spirits and comic energy.

1.1 The Winchester races, held on a long oval track on Worthy Down, three miles north of the city, dated back to the 1640's. They usually took place over three successive days in July and in 1817 these were July 29th, 30th and 31st, dates set by the annual *Racing Calendar*. Details of the races were advertised locally in the *Hampshire Chronicle*.

ll.2-3: it was said that the founders of the races failed to pray for the consent of St Swithin (or Swithun), a Bishop of Winchester and Patron Saint of the City. When he died in 862, his wish was to be buried modestly outside the West Door of the Old Saxon Cathedral, that the 'sweet rain of heaven might fall upon his grave'. In 971 he was canonised and it was thought proper to honour the Saint with a grander burial place. So, on the day of the ceremony, 15 July, his body was brought within the Cathedral to be placed in a shrine worthy of a saint. One story has it that continuous rain for forty days delayed the ceremony; another, that a sudden storm blew up during the ceremony; both stories establishing the legend that the weather on St Swithin's Day sets the weather, wet or dry, for the next forty days, a belief versified in the vernacular: 'Saint Swithin's day, gif ye do rain,/ For forty days it will remain;/ Saint Swithin's day, an ye if be fair,/ For forty days 'twill rain na mair' (Michael Lapidge, *The Cult of St Swithun*, 2003, pp. 48-49).

l.4 William of Wykham: William of Wykeham (1324 -1404, Bishop of Winchester, 1367-1404), founder of Winchester College (1378), one of England's great schools, and of New College, Oxford (1379), and Lord Chancellor in the reigns of Edward III and Richard II. JA's mention of Wykeham could be a nod to the family since her brother Edward's six sons and a number of their cousins were educated at Winchester College.

l.7 satinn'd & ermin'd: JA's shorthand imagery for the race-goers' fine array, for since the seventeenth century the meeting had been an event which attracted the racing aristocracy and squirearchy of Hampshire and beyond as well as the ordinary citizens of Winchester.

l.11 Palace: Wolvesey Palace, the ruins of the twelfth-century Bishops' Palace a few hundred yards from the Cathedral.

l.13 subjects: the citizens could be so regarded in relation to their Patron Saint.

Venta: the Roman name for the camp and town on the site of Winchester was Venta Belgarum – the market town of the Belgae, as the Romans called the tribal inhabitants of Hampshire and Avon.

ll.14-15 When...immortal: in one of the manuscripts, these words are underlined, possibly by Cassandra as a tribute to her sister (Honan, p. 401).

l.17 revels...measures: as the races started late in the afternoon, the racegoers were able to indulge themselves at feast-like meals in the city; and 'so' (in the polite tones of a local historian) 'all went well primed for a full enjoyment of the afternoon's amusement' ('Winchester Races

Fifty Years Ago', *Hampshire Notes and Queries* (1883), vol. 1, p. 90).
Moreover, at the course itself were side-shows, entertainments and
sweepstakes; and , in the evening a race ball took place in the city.
1.18 neighbouring Plain: the racecourse was laid out on the level
ground between Worthy Down and the village of South Wonston.
1.23 Shift...race: over the years, the race-meeting had taken place at
various dates between Easter and October, but by this time July was the
established month. There was no fixed date for the event; sometimes it
came early in the month, sometimes late, depending on the particular
three days allocated in the annual *Racing Calendar*.

On the manuscript sheet, stanzas 1-4 occupy the recto, stanzas 5-6 are
on the verso. At right angles to stanzas 1-4 Cassandra wrote the copy of
an obituary notice headed:
'From the Courier (newspaper) 23ᵈ July 1817
Died at Winchester on the 18ᵗʰ Inᵗ: Miss Jane Austen / youngest Daughter
of the late Revᵈ: Geo: Austen / formerly Rector of Steventon in this
County – / Authoress of Emma, Mansfield Park, Pride and / Prejudice,
Sense and Sensibility – / Her manners were most gentle, her affections
/ ardent, her candor not to be surpassed & she / lived & died as became
an humble Christian.'
The *Courier* was a London newspaper and the notice was printed,
almost verbatim, in the issue for 22 July (not 23ʳᵈ, as Cassandra wrote)
1817, page 4 (the discrepancy in dates is explained by Southam in 'Jane
Austen', *Times Literary Supplement*, 30 November 1962, p. 944.)
Written across the page in a larger, unidentified, hand is 'Poetry by Miss
J.Austen'

*

APPENDIX

Two poems in Jane Austen's hand were judged by Chapman to be of her authorship, and included in the MW *Volume. Subsequently, they have been identified as the work of others:*

'On the Universities'
Manuscript   Berg Collection, New York Public Library.
This was included in MW (1954, p. 447). However, Chapman added a corrective note to the reprint of 1958, observing that 'On the Universities' was an anonymous work, first published in a schoolroom anthology, *Elegant Extracts, or useful and entertaining pieces of poetry* (1789), compiled by Vicesimus Knox.
See Gilson (1984, 1998), pp. 56, 59-60.

'On Capt. Foote's Marriage with Miss Patton'
Manuscript   Pierpont Morgan Library.
First published 1870 *Memoir*, where it is identified as the work of Mrs. Austen's brother, James Leigh Perrot (p. 55).
Chapman provides no explanation for attributing the poem to JA (MW, p. 452).
See Gilson (1984, 1998), p. 56.

The manuscripts of three further poems not of her authorship survive in Jane Austen's hand:

'Lines of Lord Byron, in the Character of Buonaparte'.
Manuscript   University of Southampton Library.
Jane Austen's transcription, with minor verbal changes, of Byron's poem now known as 'Napoleon's Farewell', first published, untitled and anonymous, in *The Examiner*, 30 July 1815. In the 1816 edition of Byron's collected *Poems*, it carries the title 'Farewell to France'.
First published, with facsimile, *Jane Austen Society Annual Report 2000* (Brian Southam, 'Was Jane Austen a Bonapartist?', pp. 29-37).
See Gilson (1984, 1998), p. 56.

'Charade by a Lady' by Catherine Maria Fanshawe.
Manuscript Warden and Fellows' Library, Winchester College.
First published under Fanshawe's name in her *Literary Remains* (1876),
pp. 61-62. In this volume are included two riddles, two charades and
other poems involving witty word-play very much to JA's taste. However,
there is no record that Jane Austen knew Fanshawe (1765-1834) in
person or through her writings which 'long remained in manuscript or in
private collections' (*DNB*); and how it was that she came to transcribe
the 'Charade' is unknown.
See Gilson (1984, 1998), pp. 57, 60.

'Kalendar of Flora'
Manuscript in the Austen family.
JA gave the poem its original title but did not name its author, Charlotte
Smith, *Minor Morals, Interspersed with Sketches of Natural History* (1798),
pp. 111-14 (see Le Faye, 'Jane Austen and the "Kalendar of Flora":
Verses Identified', *Notes and Queries* (December 1999), vol. 244, pp.
450-51).

Claimed to be in Jane Austen's hand and by her, but doubtful:

'Sigh Lady sigh'
Manuscript   Jane Austen Memorial Trust.
First published, Deirdre Le Faye, 'New Marginalia in Jane Austen's
Books', *The Book Collector* (2000), vol. 49, pp. 222-26. The quality of
the verse is so abysmal and tritely conventional that it is not possible to
attribute these line to JA.

Select Bibliography

(The titles listed here are for those works whose full details are not provided in the body of the Guide*)*

[anon], By a Genius, *Memoirs of the Bedford Coffee-House* (London: J.Single, sec edn 1763).

[anon], *New Bath Guide*, (Bath: J.Browne [1802]).

[anon], *East-Bourne and its Environs* (London: Hooper, 1787).

A Lady of Distinction, *The Mirror of the Graces...Female Accomplishments, Politeness, and Manners* (London: Crosby, 1811).

Adams, Samuel & Sarah, *The Complete Servant, being a practical guide to the peculiar duties and business of all descriptions of servants* (London: Knight, 1825).

Attwood, Thomas, *The Remedy, or, Thoughts on the Present Distress* (London: Wiltington, 1816, 2ⁿᵈ edn 1816).

Austen, Henry, 'Biographical Notice of the Author', *Northanger Abbey and Persuasion* (London: Murray, 1817).

Austen, James, *The Complete Poems of James Austen: Jane Austen's Eldest Brother*, ed David Selwyn (Chawton: Jane Austen Society, 2003).

Austen-Leigh, James Edward, *A Memoir of Jane Austen* (London: Richard Bentley, 1870, sec edn 1871).

Austen-Leigh, W. & R.A. *Jane Austen, Her Life and Letters: a family record*, (London: Smith, Elder, 1913).

Barrett, Eaton Stannard, *The Heroine, or Adventures of a Fair Romance Reader* (London: Colburn, 1813); re-titled for 2ⁿᵈ edn 1814, *The Heroine, or Adventures of Cherubina*; 3ʳᵈ edn 1815.

Bartell, Edmund, *Hints for Picturesque Improvement in Ornamental Cottages* (London: Taylor, 1804).

Blair, Hugh, *Lectures on Rhetoric and Belles Lettres* (1783, 13ᵗʰ edn, London: Cranwell, 1817).

Lectures on the English Poets (London: Taylor, 1818).

Boswell, James, *Life of Johnson*, ed G.B.Hill, rev L.F.Powell (Oxford: Clarendon Press, 1934).

Boyle, P., *The Fashionable Court Guide, or Town Visit Directory* (London: the Proprietor, 1793).

Brougham, Henry, *Speech of Henry Brougham, 9 April 1816, to the House of Commons, Upon the State of Agricultural Distress* (London: Longman, 1816).

Brunton, Mary, *Self-Control* (London: Longman, 1811).

Burke, Edmund, *Philosophical Enquiry into the Origin of our Ideas of the Sublime and Beautiful* (1757, 2nd edn, London: Dodsley, 1759).
Reflections on the Revolution in France (London: Dodsley, 1790).

Burney, Fanny, *Camilla, or, a Picture of Youth* (1796, edd Edward & Lillian Bloom, London: Oxford University Press, 1972).
The Wanderer (London: Longmans, 1814).

Burns, Robert, *Poems chiefly in the Scottish Dialect* (?Dumfries, 1789).
Poems (Edinburgh: Cadell, new edn 1800).
Poems (Edinburgh: Morison, 1811).
The Poetry and Songs of Robert Burns ed James Kinsley (Oxford: Clarendon Press, 1968).

Bussby, Frederick, *Jane Austen in Winchester* (Winchester: Friends of Winchester Cathedral, 1969).

Campbell, George, *The Philosophy of Rhetoric* (1776).

Campbell, Thomas, *Pleasures of Hope,* (Edinburgh: Mundell, 1799).

Capper, Benjamin Pitts, *A Topographical Dictionary of the United Kingdom* (London: Phillips, 1808).

Carlisle, Nicolas, *A Topographical Dictionary of England* (London: Longman, 1808).

Cary, John, *Cary's New Itinerary of the Great Roads* (London: Cary, 1798, 9th edn 1821).

Centlivre, Susannah, *The Wonder: A Woman Keeps a Secret* (London: Curll, 1714).

Chapman, R.W., *Jane Austen: A Critical Bibliography* (Oxford: Clarendon Press, 1953).

Chesterfield (Lord), *Letters to his Son Philip Stanhope* (London: Dodsley, 1774).

Chivers, G.M.S., *A Pocket Companion to the French and English Country Dancing* (London: Chivers, 1821).

Cowper, William, *Poems by William Cowper* (London: Johnson, 1814).

Cromek, R.H., *Reliques of Burns* (London: Cadell, 1808).

Cullen, William, *Lectures on Materia Medica* (London: Lowndes, 1773).

Dobree, ed Bonamy, *Letters of Philip Dormer Stanhope*, London: Eyre & Spottiswood, 1932.

Edgeworth, Maria, *Belinda* (London: Johnson, 1801).

Patronage (London: Johnson, 1814).

Encyclopaedia Britannica (Edinburgh: Constable, 1771, 5th edn 1817).

Evans, John, *A Picture of Worthing* (London: Arch, 1805, 2nd edn 1814).

Felton, William, *A Treatise on Carriages* (London: Debrett, 1794), *Supplement* (1796).

Gilpin, William, *Three Essays: On Picturesque Beauty; On Picturesque Travel; and on Sketching Landscape* (London: Blamire, 1792, 2nd edn 1794).

Gilson, David, *Jane Austen: Collected Articles and Introductions* (Privately Printed, 1998).

Hamilton, William Gerard, *The Life of Samuel Johnson L.L.D.* (London: Dilly, 1791).

Hazlitt, William, 'On Pedantry', *The Examiner*, (3 March 1816).

[Heatherly John], *A Description of East-Bourne and its Environs* (East-Bourne: Heatherly, 1819).

Hogarth, William, *The Analysis of Beauty*, 1753, ed Ronald Paulson (New Haven & London: Yale University Press, 1997).

Holland, John James Everett, *Memoirs of the Life and Writings of James Montgomery* (London: Longman, 1854).

Honan, Park, *Jane Austen: Her Life* (London: Weidenfield, 1988, 1996)

Hoyle, Edmond, *The Polite Gamester* (Dublin: Ewing, 1745)

Hume, David, *Essays Moral, Political and Literary* (1741-42, London: Oxford University Press, 1963).

Hunter, John, *The Natural History of the Human Teeth...A Practical Treatise on Diseases of the Teeth* (1771, London: Johnson, edn 1803).

Jeffrey, Francis, Review of *Reliques of Burns*, *Edinburgh Review*, (January, 1809).

Johnson, Samuel, *Dictionary of the English Language* (London: Johnson, 1755, 8th edn corrected and revised 1799).

Lives of the Most Eminent English Poets (London: Bathhurst, 1781).

Justice, George, '*Sanditon* and the Book', in edd Claudia Johnson & Clara Tuite, *Blackwell Companion to Jane Austen* (Oxford: Blackwell, 2007).

Knight, Fanny (Lady Knatchbull), ms Diaries, 1804-72 (Centre for Kentish Studies, Maidstone, Kent).

Knight, Richard Payne, *An Analytical Inquiry into the Principles of Taste*

(London: Payne, 1805, 4th edn 1808).

Koecker, Leonard, *Principles of Dental Surgery* (London: 1826).

Lefroy, John Henry, *Notes and Documents Relating to the Family of Laffroy* (Woolwich: for private ciculation, 1868), pp. 117-18.

Le Faye, Deirdre, 'Jane Austen's Verses and Lord Stanhope's Disappointment', *The Book Collector* (1988), vol. 37, pp. 86-91.

Locke, John, *Some Thoughts Concerning Education* (London: 1693).

Macaulay (Graham), Catherine, *Letters on Education* (London: Dilly, 1790).

Mackenzie, Henry, *The Man of Feeling* (London: Cadell, 1771).

Marcet, Jane, *Conversations on Chemistry; in which the Elements of that Science are familiarly Explained and Illustrated by Experiments* (London: Longman, 1806, 4th edn 1813).
Conversations on Political Economy; in which the Elements of that Science are familiarly Explained (London:Longman, 1816, 1817).

Montgomery, James, *The Abolition of the Slave Trade* (London: Montgomery, 1814).

More, Hannah, *Coelebs in Search of a Wife* (London: Cadell, 1809).
Sir Eldred of the Bower, and *The Bleeding Rock* (1776, 2nd edn 1778), 'The Bleeding Rock' in *Poems of Hannah More* (London: Cadell, 1816).
Moral Sketches of Prevailing Opinions and Manners (London: Cadell, 1819).

Motherby, George, *A New Medical Dictionary* (London: Johnson, 1775, 4th edn 1795).

Owenson, Sydney, *The Wild Irish Girl: A National Tale* (1806, London: Pickering, 2000).

Oxford Companion to English Literature ed H.P. Harvey (Oxford: Oxford University Press 1932, 2nd edn 1936).

Parry, J.D., *A Historical and Descriptive Account of the Coast of Sussex* (Brighton: Wright, 1833).

Pevsner, Nikolaus, 'Architectural Settings of Jane Austen', *Journal of the Warburg and Courtauld Institute* (1968, vol. 31, pp. 404-22).

Pevsner, Nikolaus & Ian Nairn, *The Buildings of England: Sussex* (Harmondsworth: Penguin Books 1965, 1977).

Reece, Richard, *A Practical Dictionary of Domestic Medicine* (London: 1808).
The Medical Guide, for the use of the Clergy, Heads of Families, and Practitioners in Medicine and Surgery (London: Longman, 12th edn

1817).

Richardson, Samuel, *Sir Charles Grandison* (London: Richardson, 1753-4).

Scott, Walter, *Marmion* (Edinburgh: Ballantyne, 1808).

Review of *Emma*, *Quarterly Review*, 14 (October 1815).

Review of *Reliques of Poetry*, *Quarterly Review*, 1 (January, 1809).

The Antiquary (Edinburgh: Ballantyne, 1816).

The Lady of the Lake (Edinburgh: Ballantyne, 1810).

Waverley (Edinburgh: Constable, 1814).

Selwyn, David, 'Poetry', *Jane Austen in Context*, ed. Janet Todd (Cambridge: Cambridge University Press, 2005).

Selwyn, David, ed *Jane Austen: Collected Poems and Verse of the Austen family* (Manchester: Carcanet & Jane Austen Society, 1996).

Selwyn, David, *Jane Austen and Leisure* (London: Hambledon,1999).

Shearsmith, John, *A Topographical Description of Worthing* (Worthing: Verrall, 1824).

Sheridan, Richard Brinsley, *The Critic* (London: 1781).

Sicklemore snr, R. *The History of Brighton* (Brighton: Sicklemore jnr, R. 1823)

Smith, Adam, *The Wealth of Nations* (London: Strahan, 1776).

Smollett, Tobias, *The Adventures of Peregrine Pickle* (London: 1751).

Southam, Brian, *Jane Austen:The Critical Heritage*, Volume 1, 1811-1870 (London: Routledge, 1968).

'Was Jane Austen a Bonapartist?', *Jane Austen Society Annual Report: 2000*, pp. 29-37).

Sterne, Laurence, *A Sentimental Journey* (London: Becket, 1768).

The Improved Bath Guide (Bath: Wood, 1809?).

Treitel, Guenter, *Jane Austen and the Law* (Great Malvern: Capella, 2006)

Trusler, John, *The Distinction between words esteemed Synonyms* (London: Parsons, 3rd edn, 1794).

Tuite, Clara, 'Decadent Austen, Entails, Forster, James, Firbank and the "Queer Taste" of *Sanditon*', in ed Deirdre Lynch, *Janeites: Austen's Disciples and Devotees* (Princeton: Princeton University Press, 2000), pp. 115-39.

Viveash, Chris, *James Stanier Clarke: A Biography*, privately printed, 2006.

Walton, John K., *The English Seaside Resort: A Social History 1750-1914* (Leicester: Leicester University Press, 1983).

West, Jane, *Letters to a Young Lady* (London: Longman, 2nd edn 1806).

White, E., *A Practical Treatise on the Game of Billiards* (London: T.M'Leary, new edn 1818).

William Buchan, *Domestic Medicine* (1769, London: Cadell, 21st edn, 1813).

Willich, A.F.M., *The Domestic Encyclopaedia* (London, 1802).

Wollstonecraft, Mary, *Thoughts on the Education of Daughters: with Reflections on Female Conduct, in the More Important Duties of Life* (1787), in *The Works of Mary Wollstonecraft*, Volume 4, edd Janet Todd & Marilyn Butler (London: Pickering & Chatto, 1989).

Thoughts on the Education of Daughters (London: Johnson, 1787).

Young, Arthur, *General View of the Agriculture of the County of Sussex* (London: Sherwood, 1813).

Index to the Annotation